INTELLIGENT COURAGE

Natural Resource Careers
That Make a Difference

INTELLIGENT COURAGE

Natural Resource Careers
That Make a Difference

Michael E. Fraidenburg

KRIEGER PUBLISHING COMPANY
Malabar, Florida
2007

Original Edition 2007

Printed and Published by
KRIEGER PUBLISHING COMPANY
KRIEGER DRIVE
MALABAR, FLORIDA 32950

Library of Congress Cataloging-in-Publication Data

Fraidenburg, Michael E., 1946-
　　Intelligent courage : natural resource careers that make a difference / by Michael E. Fraidenburg.
　　　　p. cm.
　　Includes bibliographical references and index.
　　ISBN-13: 978-1-57524-287-3 (alk. paper)
　　ISBN-10: 1-57524-287-7 (alk. paper)
　　1. Conservation of natural resources—United States—Interviews.
　　2. Conservationist—United States—Interviews. 3. Naturalists—United States—Interviews. I. Title.
　　S930.F687 2007
　　333.72092'2—dc22

　　　　　　　　　　　　　　　　　　　　　　　　2007010587

　　10　9　8　7　6　5　4　3　2

To my family for teaching the lesson, "to be of use."

To readers for searching for work that has significance.

To wild and natural things for calling us toward
useful meaning in our work.

To Linda for wisdom and imagination in this and
so many other shared experiences.

And a plea to readers—tell all the truth because,
"There is at least one thing more brutal than the truth, and that
is the consequence of saying less than the truth."
– Grace Atkinson

While remembering that,
"Every truth passes through three stages before it is recognized.
In the first it is ridiculed, in the second it is opposed, in the third it
is regarded as self-evident."
– Arthur Schopenhauer

Advance Reviews

Intelligent Courage is a fascinating, highly readable book devoted to Mike Fraidenburg's important theme; successful careers in natural resources, now more than ever, require conviction and strength to "do the right thing" ecologically for the American landscape and the American culture. Through fascinating interviews of successful leaders in resource management, Fraidenburg describes how their strength and use of people skills paid off, and how especially their use of "street smarts" helped them achieve their goals. I am highly recommending this great book to my friends and students!

> Estella B. Leopold
> Professor Emeritus, Department of Biology
> University of Washington

Most of our nation's natural resource managers are retiring in this decade taking with them the lessons they learned by working in their careers. A new generation of professionals must now step up to the plate and Fraidenburg's book is a user's guide for passing this accumulated wisdom on to the new leaders. Anyone wishing to improve as a natural resource professional will learn wise but practical ideas from the distinguished people interviewed in *Intelligent Courage*.

> Theodore Roosevelt IV
> The Governing Council, The Wilderness Society

Public resource managers are experiencing increased conflict as America hits its resource limits. Little has been done to prepare environmental students to deal with issues of conflict. By comparison, students of law or business management receive a broad foundation, through the use of the case study method, to effectively resolve conflicts in their work environment. *Intelligent Courage* provides a needed breakthrough with a selection of case studies of interesting and experienced resource professionals that will help solve this training problem and, in so doing, benefit natural resource stewardship in our nation.

> Huey Johnson
> Founder and President, Resource Renewal Institute,
> Former Secretary for Natural Resources, State of
> California
> Founder and former President, The Trust for
> Public Land

This book provides an insight into the reality of natural resource management. Through the stories of eight professionals in the field we learn of the joys and trials of working in natural resource management. This book will serve to inspire a new generation of biologists and provide them with a realistic appraisal of life after University.

> Ray Hilborn
> Professor, Aquatic and Fishery Sciences
> University of Washington

A fascinating, inspiring, and entertaining book for anyone who is interested in pursuing a career in natural resources management, who is already in that field, or who simply cares about the environment.

> Andrew W. Savitz
> Author of *The Triple Bottom Line: How the Best-Run*
> *Companies Are Achieving Economic, Social and*
> *Environmental Success–and How You Can Too*

An astonishingly straightforward and profound book. Mike Fraidenburg's interviews with eight conservation heroes are inspirational, instructional, and, ultimately, life changing. Composing a life of integrity is challenging enough; composing a life of integrity as natural resource professionals who honor their responsibilities not only to their employers but to the biosphere and future generations can seem overwhelming. Mike elicits insights from these people that show that it can be done with grace. These interviews reveal the common sense "street smarts" that will help smooth the way for anyone who chooses to follow in these footsteps. This book should be read by every student in ecology, conservation, and natural resource management, and every teacher should find a way to make sure that it happens, even if it means giving the book as a gift to every student.

Steve Trombulak
Professor of Biology and Environmental Studies
Middlebury College

In *Intelligent Courage*, Michael Fraidenburg has provided us wonderful career advice from some of America's top natural resource professionals. This book is filled with great anecdotes, important lessons, and a sense of what it takes to make a positive difference in natural resources conservation.

Scott A. Bonar, Ph.D.
Associate Professor and Leader, USGS Arizona
    Cooperative Fish and Wildlife Research Unit
Author of: *The Conservation Professional's Guide to
    Working With People*

We believe that this will be a very important book that will help young professionals prepare for and effectively navigate through their careers.

Western Division, American Fisheries Society

If you want to dedicate your life to making a difference in the world, read this book. While the environmental problems we face come into greater clarity, the challenge of solving them falls to those among us who choose to roll up their sleeves and get to work. This can be lonely, difficult and often unrecognized work; but it is critically important and can be deeply rewarding. As we embark on this path, we must learn from those who have come before us, not only to succeed, but also to simply survive. Fraidenburg's book helps us do that. He has compiled the collective wisdom of eight change agents who have chosen to challenge the status quo, defy the conventional wisdom, and upset the historic political interests. They have much to teach those who follow and this book can serve as a training manual for the next generation of change agents upon whom the future of our planet rests.

> Andrew J. Hoffman
> Holcim (US) Professor of Sustainable Enterprise
> University of Michigan

Young people are passionate about the natural world and the environment but they don't know where to begin. This book helps in this critical area through information, stories, and valuable insights from the pros. This is an important starting place for those interested in a natural resource career.

> Jeff Cook
> President and Founder, The Environmental Careers
> Organization

There are topics in this book that I wish I had the opportunity to discuss and debate while I was a student—topics involving natural resource professionals in real-life situations managing both people and natural resources in complex, real-life situations. This book would serve as an excellent supplement to an undergraduate course, a thought-provoking resource for a graduate student doing one-on-one work with his/her professor, or an interesting "lessons learned" read for a seasoned professional.

> Lisa DeBruyckere
> Oregon State Forests Program Director

The author blends compelling personal stories with insights that suggest both what it's like to be on the frontline of conservation today and how resource professionals, young and experienced alike, might navigate through the thicket of an ever widening array of controversies over how we use and abuse nature's bounty.

> Gordon Binder
> Senior Fellow, World Wildlife Fund

These are career stories that every undergraduate, natural resource student needs to read. These are people that every undergraduate, natural resource student needs to emulate. These are people who stand in stark contrast to everyone who asserts that good conservation work cannot be done from within the system. What is truly amazing and inspiring about the people featured in this book is that they are intellectually honest, they have vibrant minds, they are wise, they know how to set and solve problems, their moral compasses are pointed in the right direction, and they possess the humble tenacity to act on their moral commitments. Two things seem to bind all of these people together. First, they all acquired an ethical orientation that runs contrary to the dominant Western moral mindset; that is, they are all very ethically inclusive. And second, they are all people who chose to enact their moral commitments; that is, none of them suffers from what Aristotle called "Akrasia" or "weakness of the will."

Michael P. Nelson
Professor of Philosophy and Environmental Ethics,
University of Idaho
Co-author of *American Indian Environmental Ethics:
an Ojibwa Case Study*
Co-editor of *The Great New Wilderness Debate*

This book would seem appropriate for an upper-division seminar, in which the students would read portions of the book each week and then discuss the contents of their weekly readings.

Dr. Michael Hansen
University of Wisconsin, Stevens Point

Every natural resource professional spends his or her career searching for a compass to guide them—ideally so they can make a difference and blaze a trail for others to follow. Whether you're newly embarking on this journey or have been on this path-finding mission for 30 years like me, definitely read this book. It will help you find your personal compass and, thereby, recognize your ethical coordinates.

Richard Lincoln
Marine Stewardship Council, London

In 21st century America, public management of our scarce natural resources has come to be a career calling fraught with peril—from political ambushes to professional black holes. The pressures, choices, and crises facing conscientious land managers, scientists, and rangers are not taught in school. *Intelligent Courage* is an invaluable field guide to the potholes that may await those who dare to make our planet a better place.

Jeff Ruch
Executive Director
Public Employees for Environmental Responsibility

Contents

Foreword

Jeff DeBonis
Senior Associate, Training Resources for the Environmental Community
Founder, Association of Forest Service Employees for
Environmental Ethics
Founder, Public Employees for Environmental Responsibility

This is a must-read book for students aspiring to a career in public sector, natural resource management. It is the distillation of hundreds of years of experience in management mastery, a mastery that comes only from 'time on the ground,' searching yourself and your world for answers, experiencing the pain of failure and the satisfaction of success. This book has captured the essence of what it takes to create and maintain an ethical and socially responsible public service career in natural resource management.

The bad news in these pages is that such a career will not be easy. The pace of change in our society, the level of damage to our natural world, the growth of population, and resource demand worldwide will require even more strength, creativity, and skill from the next generation of resource managers than what was required by those chronicled here. And, as you read the stories told by these professionals, what you will see is one of the great paradoxes of our human existence. Through struggle and sometimes pain, by constantly questioning our viewpoint, challenging our current worldview, and then acting on our highest good, our highest values to both the biotic and human communities, you will find the deepest of satisfaction—even though this will be the hardest and, at times, most painful road to travel. It is in knowing in your heart that you are doing the right thing, the most environmentally responsible and ethical thing that you know how to do, that you will be most happy at the end of your career.

The road will not always be clear, but the steps outlined by those interviewed here will help guide you in times of turmoil. You will need to consciously seek your internal compass and ask for whom you are making decisions. Is it yourself, your family, the agency you work for, or the public good and the seventh generation of humans who will inherit this earth?

Obviously, not every decision will be of this magnitude. But I can assure you that there will be critical nodes along your path—moments of opportunity that by your choice will impact everything you do thereafter—for better or worse. The people in this book all experienced these moments, as I did. How we chose determined our next steps, the irreversible turn on our path, and ultimately, the successful building of an ethical career.

This book provides a roadmap, the ultimate checklist of what you will need, what you will encounter, the values and skills to survive and thrive. Go into your career with courage and humility, conviction and question, with a passion for learning and listening, energy and patience. Use your heart as much as your head and you will succeed. It is not an overstatement to say we need you to succeed as did the professionals in this book. Our planet is depending on you.

Acknowledgments

This book is a labor of love by me and a labor of patience for many people who listened to my ceaseless talk about the project, generously gave me good, practical advice, and waited a long time without complaining until the work was done. Like most things I have created in my career, the people around me deserve much of the credit for any success this work entails. A partial list of these valued colleagues and friends includes the Fisheries Management Section and the Western Division of the American Fisheries Society for grants supporting the early phases of the project (applause to them for this act that is an example of the risk-taking behavior our narrators talk about as important in a natural resource career); the narrators who gave me access in spite of busy schedules and 'hung in there' as we worked and reworked the interviews to articulate the lessons learned we thought most valuable for others to read; Lisa DeBruyckere for assistance preparing the book proposal that helped this work find a publisher; Apryl Jacques for transcribing the many hours of tape-recorded interviews; Susan Ellis, Don Oman, Steve McMullin, Paul Sekulich, Dan Zekor, Gary Skiba, Alfred 'Bubba' Cook, Linda Strever, Barry Troutman, and Dave Cannon for reviewing draft chapters; Jeff Boxrucker for encouragement and advice; the 130+ students who attended workshops I gave on the book and provided invaluable reactions and direct advice about the preliminary findings in this book; and my business partners in the Dynamic Solutions Group, LLC for encouragement and for sitting through a long, give-and-take discussion on a hot, humid day in the pine woods of New Jersey to give me feedback at a critical juncture of the project. Thanks to my editor at Krieger Publishing, Elaine Rudd, who wields an incisive but humane green pen that misses nothing in her environment of words, thoughts, and meanings. And most of all credit to Linda Fraidenburg—project confidant, unpaid consultant, sounding board, idea source, copy editor, and life partner.

If you find useful advice from these pages please pause to give these behind-the-scenes people credit for that success but reserve any criticism of the work's shortcomings for me.

1
Introduction - Mastery

This book is a study of artists engaged in the creative act all professionals face, shaping a career. All of the people we meet here either succeeded themselves or are observers of how others succeeded in shaping a natural resource career of meaning, purpose, and conservation achievement. The message is clear—successful natural resource professionals do this by intent but the process is one of improvisation—more like art than like engineering. As in art, materials, techniques, insight, and creativity are important. But art is not created without a willingness to commit ideas to canvas—to take action. The question is, how?

Gone is the traditional model of a natural resource career that begins with the study of a discipline like forestry, range management, wildlife biology, etc., followed by a real or implicit apprenticeship, usually as a junior grade biologist, forester, range manager, etc., followed by many relatively stable years of applying the tools of the trade to make fishing better, harvest trees, grow more cows on the range, or any number of other firm objectives. Over my 30 years of working in a state fish and wildlife agency, I saw radical change in the meaning of basic concepts like conservation, wise use, sustainability, professional expertise, and professional obligations. I've also seen society's generally accepted agreement about the 'right' way to manage natural resources break down as we struggle to move away from a utilitarian philosophy that treats resources as commodities to something broader. Careers today are less about managing natural resources for the material benefit of human communities and more about managing human communities to lessen impacts on natural resources. In the short span of my career there has been a profound shift from managing natural resource abundance to managing natural resource scarcity.

In my own career journey I've been an interested observer of colleagues who seemed to succeed more frequently than the rest of us. They approached their work as a creative act—a kind of improvisational art. These people had the education and apprenticeship foundation of a traditional natural resource career. But these professionals built from this foundation with an evolving exploration of new ideas needed to cope with a rapidly changing world. They were curious about their work environment and why it behaved the way it did. Career as improvisational art seemed an apt metaphor for understanding how these colleagues successfully mastered their profession. This book looks at natural resource careers as this kind of creative act; one that acknowledges the realities of the work environment but moves beyond the traditional tools of the trade to improvise something new.

A good share of the success I observed in the people I admired came from on-the-job learning; lessons learned by doing the work after their formal college educations were complete. When I asked my colleagues, "What makes a good fish biologist?" they said, "Good biologists pick up a lot of street smarts during their career." By using peer review and journal publications natural resource professions are good at passing along the technical facets of their disciplines. Despite plenty of random experimentation, however, professionals are poor at transferring street smarts. These survive only when successive generations of professionals learn through oral history, observation, and direct experience. The purpose of this book is to write down some of the street smarts learned by the eight people interviewed here who either mastered the art of being a natural resource professional or observed others who did.

This book started in conversations late in my career with people in my professional year class. We found ourselves talking about what we had learned from the events of our careers; trying to see if there were patterns that let us arrive at a better understanding of the whole. I decided to illuminate this whole by interviewing people who are good role models of adaptive career management. I asked these people to analyze their career experiences and, in so doing, provide valuable lessons learned for others to think about, modify, and use for their own careers. The premise for this book is that career biographies reveal principles behind a meaningful career while also giving a good bit of 'how-to' advice for managing specific events.

The process used to access these lessons learned is one of conversation and reflection. The interviews do not constitute a statistical sample, but they are an interesting one. Look upon the people we meet here as narrators who tell us stories from successful natural resource careers. This form of inquiry retains the richness and individuality of biography—something a survey could not provide. You will find that the narrators are different from each other but similar enough that their case histories reveal useful patterns for shaping or reshaping a life's work in natural resources. Success for me will be empowering the reader to create something new from the diversity of lessons these conversations reveal.

This is an exploratory study to examine what, how, and why common events happen in a natural resource career. The assumptions underlying this work are that (1) a natural resource career contains substantial on-the-job, trial-and-error learning; (2) many experiences encountered by professionals broadly recur across the spectrum of natural resource careers; and (3) sharing this experiential learning is a positive addition to a formal education in natural resource management. The unit of analysis is the individual career history and I use interviews to access this information. Conducting multiple interviews allows pattern matching of shared experiences and forms the basis for identifying broadly applicable lessons learned.

A good place to start exploring the ideas in this book is with the concept of personal mastery: *"Command or comprehensive knowledge of a subject, art, or process; pre-eminent skill in a particular sphere of activity"* (*Oxford English Dictionary*,1989). Despite this definition's first use in 1585 people are still trying to understand mastery and how to achieve it. Mastery translates into cultivating and refining a complex weave of skills, an ability to see the diverse elements of a working environment unified as a whole, and a great deal of self-knowledge. That pretty well sums up what you are about to read in the stories of the successful natural resource professionals presented here. In the end, the people appearing in these pages look on natural resource careers as a calling, not just a job. They are interested in career mastery as a way to achieve that larger purpose. These narrators spent substantial energy clarifying this sense of purpose for their life's work. Despite incentives to be passive these professionals used that personal sense of mission to punctuate their work lives with actions, not just thoughts.

Mastery for the narrators also means crossing personal boundaries. In their view careers are not bounded by a job description. Each career event gave these masters the insight needed to know what personal boundaries should be crossed so they could to do better with the next event in their career. Their road to mastery was about accessing full personal potential, seeing current reality clearly, and preserving the ability to act while others stood still—the act of showing intelligent courage.

Although our narrators' stories are about displaying intelligent courage, this book is not about heros. It does not define clichés for success. And it is not striving for a one-size-fits-all success checklist. I describe nine keystone issues observed by the narrators that other natural resource professionals will encounter. I report on the attributes our narrators think

were important in successfully managing these keystones. And I give a
list of premises important for a natural resource career that is not just a
job but is a conscious effort to achieve some larger purpose. View this book
as a set of field studies useful for formulating a beginning hypothesis of
career mastery in natural resources; a hypothesis that, no doubt, needs
more work.

Of necessity I use the word *success* to describe the careers of these
narrators. That word is ambiguous. Success with respect to what? Criteria
external to the person or success with respect to oneself? If external validation is what matters, whose opinion counts? If internal validation is what
matters, how do we ensure rigor? How can one talk about success in a book
like this? Here I used external evaluations of success to find people to
interview. When I found people recommended as achievers, I used that external evaluation as a signal that they might be worth talking to. When I
discovered a person who had willingly engaged in a high-profile issue in a
sustained way, regardless of the outcome, I used that as an external criterion of success. And when people were recommended to me as having gained
wisdom from their career, not just technical proficiency, I used that evaluation as a third criterion of success. So I used external criteria as a way to
discover candidates worth interviewing. Once in the interview, however, I
was silent about these external evaluations of reputation. Instead, I asked
the narrators to speak about success from their own perspective, not in
response to what others had to say about them. Thus, the definition of success used here contains a blend of extrinsic evaluations for narrator selection and the narrators' intrinsic evaluations for interview content.

My interview format was, in all but two cases, 1½ - 2 hour interviews on
three consecutive days. This schedule gave the narrator and me a chance
to talk in depth and to rethink what was said and then return to themes
needing further discussion. I used common questions with each narrator but
did not ask the questions in the same order or with the same wording. My
priority was to keep the interviews closely focused on the actual career
events each narrator encountered and what they had to say about these, not
centered on my preconceived ideas. I preferred an open-ended conversation
where the narrator acted as guide and mentor, not respondent. They picked
the defining moments in their careers that illustrate useful street smarts for
the next generation of professionals. Although the words were different, the
substance of the questioning was: What happened in your career or what did
you see happen to others? Why do you think it (an event) happened? Who
did what? Why do you think you/they behaved that way? What did you/they
do about it? What happened when you/they acted that way? What did you

learn? What would you do differently next time? What does it take to create change? And when you had to say no, how did you do it?

I approached the first interviews with considerable trepidation. Would I be able to keep three long conversations productive? No problem. Our narrators had already thought about my questions and only needed an invitation to begin talking—and talk they did! When I lacked insight to ask the right question they were smart enough to keep talking until I understood the "what happened" and the "whys" behind the events.

As a safety check on my ability to capture the meaning and intent of their stories the narrators reviewed their interviews as presented here. Except for final grammatical and organizational details you are reading their words, not an interpretation filtered through me. Think of their career stories as a series of field notes for you to analyze. Look for patterns defining recurring issues you are likely to encounter in your career. Look for strategies and tactics that will help you. Look for the personal attributes you feel are worth emulating in your career. Taken together, these patterns offer a way to improve your ability to diagnose career events and then formulate action strategies. In the last chapter I provide my synthesis of what I learned by interviewing the following, remarkable people.

Roger Contor broke from the mold of the typical National Park Service employee to innovate with controversial topics like fire management and redefining the purpose for a national park. As a Forest Service employee Gloria Flora took a profound journey inside herself to resolve conflicting pressures surrounding proposed oil and gas development along the Rocky Mountain Front Range and discovered deeper meaning and purpose for her career. Andrea Mead Lawrence applied the principles of an Olympic champion to her work in county government and activism for natural resources and changed land use in her community. As a professor of natural resource policy at Utah State University, Bern Shanks dug underneath the angry rhetoric of the sagebrush rebellion and found a diseased root system that caused him to speak truth to power while the people around him kept their heads covered. Tom Peterson prepared for multiple career options in natural resources. With that strategy he positioned himself to show substantial leadership helping states manage climate change. In a journey from fish biologist to Forest Service Chief, Mike Dombeck changed the purpose of the nation's largest land manager. When regional fish biologist Phil Pister reread *A Sand County Almanac* on a mid-career retreat, he emerged with a new internal compass to guide the rest of his life. And when Professor Max Bazerman started studying human decision-making behavior in business settings he began uncovering broadly applicable lessons that explain, in part, why human communities are doing a poor job of managing natural resources.

When I began compiling the tape-recorded interviews into written form hundreds of pages stood before me as raw material that I needed to cut down to book size. The choices were painful because the subject is deep, rewarding, and, unfortunately, largely undocumented in the natural resource professions. You are about to read a fraction of the rich material the narrators volunteered. The lessons learned by the narrators are valuable because they are complex and cannot be reduced to platitudes. Their stories are about the deep human potential and positive spirit that animates the natural resource professions and about how individuals can make a difference. And the collective story from these narrators is about combining hope with pragmatic ways to manage a career that is in harmony with a sense of purpose for a life's work. It is now time to open the field notes from the narrators' careers and analyze how to create a natural resource career of meaning, purpose, and conservation achievement—a career of intelligent courage.

2
Roger Contor - Intelligent Courage

Successful courage is intelligent courage.
– Roger Contor

Imagine this. You arrive in Washington State, alone. You have a pencil and a rental car. Now, go set up a new National Park. That was Roger Contor's challenge in 1968 when the National Park Service made him the first Superintendent of North Cascades National Park. Roger's job was to transform a law setting aside about 800 square miles of the Cascade Mountain Range into a national park and, in the process, create something different—a wilderness park. This emphasis on wilderness preservation was a significant innovation. New policies and different management approaches would be needed but these were sure to trouble visitors, local officials, and neighbors who held entrenched opinions about the "right" way to run a national park.

How would you go about setting up a program to implement the new park's mission? How would you manage the risks? These tasks fell to Contor.

Roger Contor grew up on an Idaho ranch near Yellowstone National Park. Yellowstone's calling first drew him into the Park for recreation and then into a 30-year-career that spanned a range of Park Service jobs from janitor to Regional Director. Along the way, Contor accomplished a few things, including consulting to the State of New South Wales in Australia helping to set up a new National Parks and Wildlife Service, serving as Secretary General of the Second World Conference on National Parks which focused on using parks as world heritage reserves, serving as Superintendent of Rocky Mountain National Park where they faced the challenge of reestablishing native cutthroat trout populations, serving as Superintendent of Olympic National Park where he ended 30 years of complacency and denial about non-native mountain goats damaging the Park, directing the Park Service's Washington, D.C. office on the Alaska National Interest Lands Classification Act which created 44 million acres of new parks—the largest park creation in world history, and working as the Regional Director of National Parks in Alaska responsible for 54 million acres of land, wildlife, natural heritage values, and Park relations with the broader Alaskan community.

Punctuating his stories with a Gilbert and Sullivan refrain, Roger reflects on changing land management in an agency comfortable with the status quo. Annie, Roger's German shorthair and dedicated hunting partner, joins us in the interview. Sitting on his feet with her head in Roger's lap, Annie reads his body language and alerts me with whimpering and sympathetic looks into his eyes each time Roger is especially stirred by a career story. I first notice this when Roger starts talking about the evolution of fire management in the Park Service.

A person's actions and decisions are usually predetermined by our conditioned value system. An example is our hatred for forest fires in the National Park Service. A student at Colorado State University told us one time, "You really shouldn't be putting out natural fires in National Parks." Our response was, "What the hell you mean, kid? We've always done it that way." He challenged our traditional thinking. But it finally came to the point where we looked at each other, and said, "He's right, now what do we do?"

The Smokey Bear mind set made it hard for us to change. When World War I was over the United States was a highly mobilized, highly activated society. Some psychologist decided that this highly energized public was a wonderful opportunity. We had hated the enemy and the thought occurred that we should turn this force into something good. Why not FIRE! It could be the moral equivalent of war.

That was the origin of the wonderful posters with flickering flames and charred trees. Most of the country's people, at that time, lived back east where we had wiped out the forests and wildlife. Feeling guilty about what we had done, the nation adopted an incredible, we-hate-fire mentality and did it so perfectly the public was brainwashed. The idea of striking a match in a forest became sinister, even sinful. Fueled by this anti-fire propaganda, government was quick to put money into fire control programs. Also, of course, in the '30s a little, scorched black bear cub was found who became Smokey Bear. Smokey got to be larger than life. The government started putting out all fires in national parks and we got good at it.

And so, in the early '60s that Colorado State student, probably not by himself, wrote to us at Rocky Mountain Park and said, "Putting out natural fires is against the basic purpose of a national park." At that time the purpose hadn't been defined as well as it is now. It was the dawn of realizing that a natural forest fire is important for sub-successional stages in plant communities and for maintaining many forms of wildlife that depend on fire-caused changes. The National Park Service still stubbornly said, "That won't work. The parks are too small. We can't let a fire get started and burn up the surrounding area." We were still preconditioned by the 40-year-old value system of, ". . . we must hate fire." It was an extremely successful public relations job and it was lucrative. Getting congressional money for fire fighting was especially easy with the patriotic overtones of campaigns like Keep Washington Green and Keep Oregon Green.

Also, in the 1960s, we got an unexpected boost from another crisis—the problem of too many elk in Yellowstone Park. When we shot a bunch of the elk to reduce over-browsing, the public said, "Wait a minute, you shouldn't be doing that." So, Secretary of the Interior Udall formed the Leopold Committee. He assembled the top scientists in the nation to make recommendations about wildlife management in national parks. The Leopold Committee's report (Leopold, et al., 1963) really set us straight—we should let natural fires burn wherever politically possible and logistically feasible. In short, they said, "Natural fires should be allowed to burn. If it is a man-caused fire, put it out since it is not a natural event." Eventually, most of us in the Park Service agreed that we should let natural fires burn, but nobody had the courage to do so.

Then along came the opportunity offered by North Cascades National Park. A brand new park. No history as a park. No built-in set of critics. No built-in industries. No built-in advocates for the status quo. After a park is in place for 20-30 years it is surrounded by critics, economic interests, and advocates who have pretty much made up their minds about how the park should be managed. That's a lot of inertia to overcome for a big policy change like let-it-burn.

I was the first superintendent of the North Cascades. Fortunately, I had a splendid director—John Rutter. He was way ahead of the pack. Nineteen seventy was a big fire year in Oregon and Washington. A lightening storm set 500 fires and everybody was very, very busy fighting fires. We were expected to put out fires and our guys in the Stehekin District near Lake Chelan, which is the southern half of North Cascades Park, put out all their fires in the first day or two. The Forest Service's Lake Chelan employees, who had more fire-fighting experience than even us, told their wives to get out the Sears Roebuck catalogs. It was time to pick out new furniture, freezers, and so on because there was going to be a lot of overtime pay. Then, after their fires grew large, they went to put them out. Guess what? Their fires got too big and grew to be multimillion-dollar fires. There was plenty of Forest Service overtime that year. Our guys had just screwed themselves out of overtime because they put out the fires right away.

In the north part of North Cascades Park the fires weren't so easy to put out. We brought in firefighters from the big center in Boise and were spending $100,000 a day but weren't making any real progress. The country is so steep and the fires so dangerous, rocks rolling and that kind of thing, that the firefighters couldn't get close enough to do any real good. The good news was that the fires weren't spreading very fast and it was late summer.

So I had a conversation with my fine Regional Director. We agreed that if we challenged the assumed emergency of these fires and viewed them as a natural event, we shouldn't be fighting them at all. I said, "It's September and it's going to rain. That's the only way they are going to go out anyway." John said, "Let me make a couple of calls." He called the director of the Park Service and asked if he was ready to let these natural fires burn. The director said, "I guess so, but check with Senator Jackson." John then called Senator Jackson and asked if he was ready to stand by us. The Senator thought it made good sense but thought we ought to talk to Scott Paper Company, the Park neighbor, so they would understand our thinking.

That evening I called in the fire bosses from our three big fires in the north part of the Park. I told them we were going to demobilize and just leave a crew to monitor the fires. Up to then the Park Service had never walked away from a burning forest fire in its history (not that we would admit anyway). We demobilized and saved taxpayers $100,000 a day over the next two weeks. That was a great risk. Everybody who fights fires is a hero and nobody ever asks how much it costs. Everyone acted on the assumption that fire is bad and the Park Service had always been well rewarded for aggressive firefighting. As we closed up our evening session and I headed back to my car, it started to rain. That was the same rain that not only put out our fires but also put out the Forest Service's fires.

The next day it hit the news that North Cascades Park was ignoring wildfires in keeping with the National Park Service's new let-it-burn philosophy. In came an immediate call from Keep Washington Green. They were very upset. Their director said, "Look, we've been showing that the average size of forest fires in Washington has been going down since 1920. Now you are going to let some fires run wild. Our statistics are going to be all screwed up." I said, "Here's a suggestion, just create two categories: one for fires that are suppressed and another for natural fires that are left to burn." He said, "Great idea!" They were totally happy and so was I. Next I called Scott Paper to talk about our decision to let certain fires burn. They laughingly said they wondered when we would get smart enough to do that.

You've got to be smart. At North Cascades, if it had been in June or July, we wouldn't have dared to let the fires burn. But the timing turned out to be right. We acted on our feeling that the fires weren't going anywhere. In the Pacific Northwest at that time of year there is a lot of dew at night and everything really cools down. And it was about to rain. Our fires grew to only about 200-300 acres. Timing our 'courageous' act was important.

That's the story. The origins track back to World War I and the conscious public relations effort of the Forest Service that created an industry—the forest fire suppression industry. There is a lot of money to be made by selling chemicals and fire-fighting equipment and through government programs like the Boise Interagency Fire Center. Wherever the government spends a lot of money you create entrenched industries to go after it—sometimes counterproductive industries.

Looking back, it is interesting to think about how our value system pre-determined our decisions. Before North Cascades we just went along with the given assumptions and were unable to change. It took 10 years after that Colorado State University student said we should stop putting out natural fires in National Parks before we finally tried it at North Cascades.

Mike: What makes the status quo so strong?

A lazy mind. We rationalized putting out fires as a good vs. evil issue, not a more complex question of land management. It was easy to buy into that mind-set and not think beyond those boundaries. Change as big as moving to a let-it-burn policy steps on peoples' economic toes. The path of least resistance is to keep the present situation intact. Expect people, even managers, to rationalize as we did in the Park Service. I have good friends in the public relations business and their persuasion approach is to simply say what they want the audience to believe and then keep repeating it. If you say it often enough it becomes truth. That is what we did about wild fires—to the point where everyone stopped questioning whether it was right or not. We had lazy minds.

Cowardice. Believe me, it took more than a little courage to let those North Cascades' fires burn. What if I was wrong? I'd have been transferred. A National Park Superintendent is very expendable. Make a big mistake and the easiest option for the Regional Manager is to replace the Superintendent. That makes all the critics happy. Leave the Superintendent in place and the critics are going to beat up on him and the Regional Director. A coward might have said we need to put out these fires and rationalize that they are not natural fires. It's always easy to come up with a rationalization. The status quo feels like a safe place.

Government employees basically avoid risk. I have no proof of this, but believe it is true. I was an insecure person. I wanted my mother and then the federal government to take care of me. I wanted to be able to retire from the Civil Service. I didn't want to have to worry about money so this was my personal route to security. That is one advantage that government jobs can offer. They are low-paying but usually satisfying and highly secure.

Let's talk about the courageous mistakes I've made. One time I didn't like my Regional Director. He had worked in only one national park in his life. Then he became the Regional Director over 40 parks. For years he gave extraordinary favors to the park he came from, ignoring responsibilities in the other parks. He was being unfair and it was wrong—by every standard of policy and principle. So, I told him so. After that I didn't get any offers for promotion. In those days you didn't apply for promotions. The regional offices looked around the various parks to see who might be ready for promotion and they would make you an offer. The Regional Director is a key player in making this judgment. I was put on a blacklist for a while.

I may have been courageous, but I was also stupid. Only pick a fight where you have some chance of succeeding and some chance of making a change. Don't walk into a bar fight if you don't have to. Go around it. I was reaccepted because most of the federal managers I worked with were courageous themselves. After that experience I was careful about when I was going to be courageous.

For example, a couple of times I went over the head of my supervisor to the Secretary of Interior pointing out that the Director of the Park Service was doing something that was wrong. But I knew that the Secretary didn't like the Director and that he liked me. We had a rapport. So it didn't take that much courage. It just looked like it. Smart courage means that once you take a courageous step have yourself a plan if you fail. The need to survive is an unfortunate part of working in a state or federal agency. Giving advice to new trainees is easy. It is easy to rabble-rouse and tell them to go out and be courageous. They love to hear this. But it's a little irresponsible because behind every successful manager is a sensible yellow stripe down his back.

My most gutsy act was taking the job of Regional Director in Alaska when James Watt was Secretary of Interior. Watt's agenda was to weaken the National Park Service and he succeeded to a large extent. Fairly early in the job I told his representatives to go to hell, saying things like, "No, that's wrong. I won't do it." Watt sent his local representative, who thought he supervised every Interior Department employee in Alaska, to confront me. I told him to go to hell. He went to Watt who then sent the Assistant Secretary to 'talk' to me. I told him the same thing.

Well, that sounds very courageous, doesn't it? At the time I met the requirements for early retirement and had earlier talked to my Director about exercising that option if things got bad enough. He agreed. I was really very safe. I also suspected that the leadership in Interior, including Watt, was in political trouble. Eventually the Assistant Secretary got fired. Then Watt got fired. And I stayed Regional Director. So I didn't have that much courage. The people who watched me just thought I did.

Mike: Talk more about change in a management agency.

In all western states the spoils system prevails in our governmental structure. In the federal government the shots are called by Congress, one way or another, and agencies get punished anytime they try to enforce an environmental law that steps on the toes of a farmer, miner, logger, or big industry. Why do I say, ". . . in the West?" When I worked in D.C., Morris Udall was Chair of the House Interior and Insular Affairs Committee. He would never schedule a vote on an environmental issue on Friday because D.C. was close enough that the eastern representatives go home on Friday, but the western representatives stay in town. Western legislators generally do not support conservation issues. They vote to exploit. So a vote on Friday was automatically a vote to exploit because the eastern representatives were at home, not in Washington, D.C.

In many ways the reward system in the National Park Service stifles change. It's always safe to duck a controversial issue and pass it on. Park Service employees are smart. They know what the incentives are, even if they are hidden. Gilbert and Sullivan got it right,

> Now landsmen all, whoever you may be,
> If you want to rise to the top of the tree,
> If your soul isn't fettered to an office stool,
> Be careful to be guided by this golden rule–
> Stick close to your desks and never go to sea,
> And you all may be rulers of the Queen's Navee!
> – H.M.S. Pinafore

'Don't rock the boat' is often a very successful career strategy, at least for conventional trappings like promotions. You've devoted yourself to doing good things for very little pay and if you are suddenly criticized for doing just that, it hurts. It's worse if your retirement is put at risk. Those are powerful incentives to be meek.

Sometimes you have to be changed from the top. Berkeley was an event that changed my life. When I was the superintendent of North

Cascades and a young, up-and-coming federal manager, they made me take an executive management course at Berkeley. My first thoughts, of course, were "What are they going to teach us? We're the professionals." Director Hartzog realized he had a bunch of ultraconservative managers. The world was changing and we weren't.

So the boss sent us to two weeks of training and some really good wine tours. That really loosened us up. One teacher showed up in sandals and a t-shirt. He looked at us and said, "If you think young people are dressed silly go out and look in the street. Who is dressed funny? Who is out of step? You guys are. You are the weirdos here." He made us confront our cultural rigidity. His teaching technique was much better than the way I'm telling it and I don't know if it affected everybody, but it certainly affected me. I realized you don't have to remain locked in an outdated framework. You actually have many choices but it is pretty easy to limit yourself by applying outdated norms without thinking.

Sometimes you have to stand up to the boss and change them. The first time I was stationed in D.C. my boss was a very strong director. We often disagreed. I was one of the few who would challenge him, but I always picked my battles. When I was Secretary General of the Second World Conference on National Parks, the director knew he was about to be fired so he was being careless and telling us to do things that were questionable. One time he told me to charter a 737 from one of the airlines because he wanted to fly sixty Congress members to the World Conference in Yellowstone. After checking around I confirmed that chartering a plane for that use wasn't legal. Who was going to risk the director's anger by telling him the bad news? That job fell to me. I told him, "You can't do that. It's illegal. Forget it." He looked at me and said, "Ok." He always trusted me. He knew that I wouldn't lie. But we never were good friends. I guess that taught me the importance of credibility. In creating change, credibility is the best asset you have to offer. That made it possible for us to disagree but for him to accept my advice.

From another perspective, good employees have good bosses. This was true for me. It's alright to be a *little* bit of an ass-kisser, a *little* bit of a glad-hander. That's alright as long as you don't abandon your principles. Don't lie. You have to be able to read your audience—your boss—and understand human nature. If a boss's evaluation of you is critical to your future, then a smart thing to do is to understand that person as well as possible. You don't want to talk much until you understand the terrain. Listen well and be very alert for feedback.

My regional director at North Cascades, John Rutter, would look for employees he could trust. He really didn't like phonies and he would throw out bait, saying a thing like, "I think we ought to do X," when he knew perfectly well that X was a stupid thing to do. He would invite anyone in the room to talk to him later about his idea. The flatterers would come rushing in and say, "X is a hell of a good idea." They were then written off. He never wanted their opinion after that. Another guy would come in and say, "I think you ought to think this thing over. X is really not a very good idea." Rutter would ask, "Why?" "Well, here's why . . . ," was the right response. The next time Rutter had a decision to make, he'd call in that person because he could trust his honesty. If you are too much of an ass-kisser and fawning over the boss, it's awful easy to see through it. There is a difference between respect and phoniness.

The one thing you must do is be honest with yourself. If you really screwed up, acknowledge it but don't be too quick to repent. People who change their loyalty and allegiance too often are very suspect. Good managers don't want somebody that gives up or buys into every new fad that flutters by. The other extreme is the chip-on-my-shoulder employee. These folks are so fearful of being the slightest bit of an ass-kisser that they go around insulting their bosses for no good reason.

Everything in life boils down to two things: freedom and restraint. The freedom to let the fires burn but the restraint to make sure that it is the right time to do it. Freedom to compliment your boss but restraint to make sure that it is sincere. It's just a simple matter of keeping the chip off your shoulder and being honest.

It's also tough being a director or boss of any organization because you can't tell your subordinates what pressures are on you. It's a code of honor. You don't tell them what some chairman of a congressional committee forced you to do. You are honor-bound to keep your mouth shut. It's tough when a seasonal ranger says to you that something is a good idea and you know it's true, but, for a whole lot of reasons, you can't let it happen and you can't tell him why.

It's also important to learn how to influence the system even if laws and regulations appear to bind your hands. I spent three years as an assistant director for Alaska, stationed in Washington, D.C. By law a federal employee cannot do anything to influence the action or decision of a member of Congress. But if they seek information you, as a federal employee, must provide it.

What you do is get acquainted with congressional staff who are interested in your issues. If you are working in Colorado you get acquainted with the staff of congressional members from there, especially any member who is the chair of a committee that influences your budget. I typically dealt with two senators and two representatives on any issue since many parks straddle the line between two congressional districts. Out of the four staff members I'd meet, at least two of them were glad to see me. They were busy people and appreciated my help. I developed a good working relationship with them. When I had a problem I could call the staffers and say something like, "Since you asked me this question, I have the answer for you now." They'd laugh and ask to be 'reminded' of what their question was. "Here's the question you asked me and here is the answer . . ." was what I'd say next.

You also must learn how important it is to meet with your enemy. The people who fought creation of North Cascades Park most were Scott Paper and the other timber companies. When I'd show up at their doorstep and ask how we could work with them they were caught off guard. That gesture opened their minds. It is a powerful strategy to look your potential enemy right in the eye and say, "Let's work out together what we can, so we can make things easier for all of us." Give them as many reasons as possible to like you and to cooperate with you. About a third of the time it works. When it does it is absolutely magic. When it doesn't work you at least have the basis for respectful disagreement and they can't criticize you for being aloof.

Learn how to weigh the odds. You need to know when you held out incorrectly and lost the issue. Maybe it's temporary, maybe it's permanent. But you've got to take risks if you are going to do any good. Risk is not always making changes. Sometimes it's keeping change from happening. In the Park Service that was our first priority—to preserve and, where necessary, reestablish natural ecosystem processes. Any decision has risks, even if you decide to do nothing. Risk is clearly there if you take bold action, like going against your boss or deciding to leak information. Expect that some of your risks are going to backfire. You have to be prepared for that. The worst event is personal discredit within your professional community and loss of peer approval and respect. There is always a slight risk of being fired, or at least being reassigned to an ignominious position. Once again—if you are going to change things, you have to take intelligent risks—those with a high probability of success and where you have a contingency plan if things go wrong. Sometimes the best thing to do is to wait and then be quick on your feet when opportunity arises.

You have to have a network. Maintain a close communication within your organization and field of interest. Maintain good communication with the people who really call the shots, like members of Congress, who can influence the whole organization. Maintain close personal communication with your peers so you can help them and you can rely upon them to help you.

Obviously, there is no set formula for risk management. You weigh all the consequences and have to decide how virtuous you want to be. How much of a risk are you willing to take? How many years left until your retirement? How interested are you in a career with another agency, in private business, or as a consultant? Have you checked those possibilities out? You can take more risks if you have alternatives. In my case I was a national park manager. Who else hires park managers? Almost nobody. Go back to the problem-solving process. What is the real problem? Make sure it's not just a perceived problem. What are your alternatives? Check them all out. Plan intelligently, not just with self-righteousness.

But, the flip side is that sometimes you can be too cautious. That's not uncommon. I worked for one director of the Park Service who compromised with so many people to become director that when he got into that position of real power, he was totally impotent. He couldn't say or do anything without fear of alienating someone to whom he owed a favor. He was essentially walking around saying, "What have I gotten myself into?" He turned to liquor and lost his job. Don't create a past that can catch up with you.

Careers are long-term processes. When disappointment comes your way consider how to achieve your dream in some other way or later in your career. I've always remembered Brock Adams's advice that ". . . conservation activism is constant pressure endlessly applied." My way of doing things is not to worry too much about the bad things that might happen. Spend your time working on progressive things that will work now and in the future and consider risk as an additional thing to manage. Above all, make a clear-cut decision to either do something or do nothing. Don't let decisions creep up on you by default. Being clear about when you are willing to show courage on an issue is half the battle you'll have with yourself. Then design some way to manage your courageous act. Don't just let it happen without forethought. Successful courage is intelligent courage.

3
Gloria Flora - Daring to Ask a Different Question

I'm glad I was criticized. It meant I was doing my job.
– Gloria Flora

How would you approach a billion-dollar decision to allow or not allow oil and natural gas development on public lands in the Rocky Mountains? What values would guide your decision making? Who would you listen to in making your decision? How would you set the stage for success in announcing your decision? Gloria Flora faced these questions in 1997 as the supervisor of the Lewis and Clark National Forest. She decided that maintaining the primitive grandeur of the landscape and protecting its wildlife had more value than the oil and gas the land might contain. She said no to new energy leases for at least 10 years on about 350,000 acres of the 1.8 million-acre national forest and she allowed only restricted exploration elsewhere in the forest. It was an unexpected act of bureaucratic assertiveness that made her friends and enemies.

When she decided oil and gas leasing was a bad idea the fallout included criticism, complaint, and a lawsuit from petroleum companies. The criticism was that she based her decision on emotion rather than science. The complaint was that she paid too much attention to the public. But the legal challenges, including an appeal to the U.S. Supreme Court, failed to reverse her ban on new energy leases.

Gloria began her 23-year-Forest-Service career with a landscape architecture degree and a desire to improve management of visual resources. She ended up running into some major conservation opportunities and facing some of the most intractable interests in the United States wanting to use public lands for private purposes. As the Forest Service's lumberjack culture was coming to an end she was one of the internal advocates for change to broader thinking about the meaning of natural landscapes. Flora made it her business to bust stereotypes about land management in the Rocky Mountains. In answering my questions she displays a comprehensive command of the region's history, science, and natural resources; draws on spiritual imagery to express her connection to nature and how sense of place is a legitimate reason to forego development; and uses reductionist, linear reasoning to tear apart the rhetoric of pro-development interests.

Her career achievements garnered awards from environmental groups, tribes, community organizations, the Forest Service, and *Sunset* magazine's award for Environmental Inspiration. 'Inspiring' is a good word to describe Gloria's career. As our interview progresses I notice that the logo on her sweatshirt says, "Trial by Fire." A gift from a colleague on the Lewis and Clark National Forest, 'Trial by Fire' is another good way to describe Gloria's career. We begin by considering the changes she saw during her time in the Forest Service.

Oh, huge. I got into the Forest Service in 1977. Later, a friend asked, "Were you discriminated against?" I was a woman, a landscape architect, young, fresh out of college, and from the East working in the West. So, yeah, there was discrimination. But I was never really sure which of these particular aspects angered which particular people. Previously, if you were a white, male forester you had every expectation that you would become a district ranger. Then you would go on to forest supervisor. Then, when you became one of the 'old greens,' you had a good shot at a leadership position in D.C. The people making promotion decisions selected people just like themselves. Sometimes it was malicious but most times promoting someone who was different just didn't feel right. That feeling was interpreted as meaning the candidate was not a good fit. At that time there were no women in line officer positions anywhere in the Forest Service.

The Service wasn't quite sure what landscape architects were supposed to do. They just knew they had to hire me. Even fewer people thought visual resource management was worth thinking about, let alone be used as a basis for making big decisions, like whether or not to cut trees. That left me wondering where I fit in. Looking around I didn't see other people like me. It was a very foreign environment yet it was absolutely fascinating watching the evolution of how social change outside the Forest Service affected the agency.

Imagine, you're 56 years old, got your 30 years in, and you worked hard to get into the good-old-boy club. As one of these old greens you're liked and respected by the people you work with. You hunt and fish with them. Your wives do girl-stuff together. Your kids are playmates and schoolmates. There is a good chance your kids will go on to college and become a forester just like you. You feel comfortable cutting a forest deal over the pew at church. It was not supposed to work that way, but it did. Everybody was comfortable. The change I saw in the Service was devastating to many individuals because they had such a secure picture of themselves and their future.

When I started in 1977, even though the National Environmental Policy Act (NEPA) had been around since 1969 and the National Forest Management Act since 1974, the Forest Service was still asking itself, "What do we do with these new environmental laws?" The laws were telling us to look beyond commodity production and start doing environmental planning. We had to acknowledge in our management the huge shift that was occurring in the evolving understanding of how natural systems work.

Along with these changes in agency life came the busting of the Great American Dream and the new reality of spouses working. No longer were Forest Service wives either housewives or in a portable profession like nursing or teaching. Wives became unwilling to uproot each time their forester husband got a new job. Until the mid-'80s Forest Service wives were experts in packing up and seamlessly moving the family to her husband's new job. In my era wives became unwilling to take on the traditional social jobs of the head ranger's wife such as organizing the cancer drive, hosting parties, and keeping peace in the Forest Service compound.

Now add to the mix new laws requiring public involvement. Suddenly, the Forest Service professionals—the white, male foresters who had been cranking out more boards every year—were being told, "Hey you guys, what you're doing is all wrong." The Forest Service went from being respected and liked to being questioned, cursed, and challenged. It took us 10 years to even acknowledge that public participation was a real part of NEPA. We were not comfortable with these requirements that meant giving up some power and making our decisions more visible.

The new laws dictated change, including the necessity of hiring a raft of young employees who were not foresters, who were wearing their hair in strange ways, and who didn't wear the uniform correctly—and didn't place much stock in doing so. Worse, these new employees were joining the new interdisciplinary teams you were forced to create and they start making preservation recommendations. Soon these become forest confrontation teams and now you've got to manage internal conflict over the very basic work you do.

It was absolutely amazing to watch the old guard, who had the rhythm of the old Forest Service down pat, turn into musk oxen. They backed up with their butts together and heads lowered to repel the threat of different thinking. After so many years of being the good guys they were being labeled as the bad guys and spending more time in conflict.

It was also a hard time in the Forest Service because we began reducing the power of our traditional stakeholders, like logging, mining, and ranching interests who'd long benefitted from the old order. These folks still had more influence and knew how to use local politics to react to this loss of privilege. So the system was still vulnerable. If you want a good case history just look at the whole saga of Don Oman.

Don was a district ranger in the Twin Falls Ranger District in Idaho who challenged several ranchers who were abusing their grazing allotment. For years they had gotten away with disregarding contract provisions and pretty much ran the place like they owned it. Well, Don wasn't that kind of manager. He would not let people trash Forest Service landscapes. He started requiring that ranchers reduce grazing. Some wouldn't do it and began to threaten Don. But Don insisted, essentially saying, "If you refuse to remove the cows, threaten me or my employees, or will not let us count the number of your cows that are on our land, then you're going to have to keep them home." That caused the ranchers to complain about Don. The initial reaction in the agency was to get rid of Don and not investigate contract violations or even go look at the ranchers' grazing practices on our land. Some in the Forest Service actually made comments in the press saying, "Well, obviously, Don is having some personal problems that are making it so he can't get along with people." The head of range management for the region even said, "Well, we're going to have to do something about Don; he's really overstepped his bounds." However, Don was well within his bounds which is why, by law, he had to do what he was doing. The agency couldn't fire Don because they violated a bunch of personnel procedures. Then someone looked at the land and said, "Oh my God. Don is right." Don got his job back but the agency had a new problem figuring out how to move him because he didn't get along with the local cattlemen. Well, it was not Don failing to get along with them. It was the ranchers violating contracts, absolutely trashing the land, and the agency turning a blind eye. This went on for several years and it was horrible for Don and his family. Eventually things settled down for Don but 'Don't cross a rancher in Idaho' was and probably still is an unwritten rule in the Forest Service.

Don's case history shows the importance of recognizing who in the agency can be trusted. A boss who publicly criticizes employees or tries to please a senator ahead of the law is not going to support you when things get dicey. Eventually, that thinking leads to poor land management. It also erodes trust, something the Forest Service has lost through their own actions in recent years.

The salvage rider is a classic example. In 1995, Mark Rey, who was then a congressional staffer but now is our Assistant Secretary of Agriculture in charge of the Forest Service, attached the salvage rider to an appropriations bill. He had quietly polled the agency about how much timber every forest could salvage absent environmental laws and no public involvement. Mark added these numbers together and attached it to the appropriations bill. The rider required that the Forest Service harvest all that salvageable timber and actually specified the amount, which was the simple sum of everything we forest supervisors gave to Mark.

Another section of the rider ordered the release of green timber, much of which was old growth, that had been prepared for sale but withdrawn because of environmental concerns. The rider also changed the definition of salvage to any dead tree, any tree that may die soon, and any green trees associated with these dead and dying trees that may be considered part of the same stand. Some forest supervisors went nuts thinking, "This is my chance to really shine. I am going to cut, cut, cut in the name of salvage."

At the time I was supervisor on the Lewis and Clark National Forest. We told the public we will not be building new roads, we will not salvage in roadless areas, we will do an environmental assessment even if it is not required, and we will do public involvement—including shooting videotapes of the areas that we're going to cut to show at an open house. We offered field trips if anybody wanted to take a look and discuss our plans. We followed the spirit of the former laws. Fortunately our forest submitted a small salvage number because I was suspicious of why someone would suddenly ask a question like, "What could you cut if environmental and public involvement laws were suspended?"

We cut what we said but it was a small amount, focusing on dead trees, more in line with ecosystem management concepts and applying fire safety precautions. Our public loved us. I know this because, coincidently, within weeks of our decision we had a public meeting to discuss the concept of merging the Lewis and Clark and the Helena National Forests. One hundred people turned out. They were clear, "Absolutely not. No way. We love you guys on the LC. We want to see those green trucks and your uniforms on the land."

Mike: What did you do or what circumstances allowed you to act in apparent conflict with the salvage rider law and survive in the agency?

Because I cut what I said I was going to cut. I had a correct hunch about the underlying intent of the legislation. At the same time the public didn't want us in roadless areas and I gave them that. They wanted us to listen to them and we continued to do so. And they wanted us to be environmental managers, not loggers, so we did environmental assessments anyway. The salvage rider did not change these underlying needs, it just ignored them. Our autonomy as Forest supervisors also helped. Mark Rey wasn't coming out to the Lewis and Clark to investigate the merits of the salvage number we submitted. The foresters who got in trouble were those who provided a high salvage figure and then realized that it would be really stupid or impossible to go get it. They not only had the problem of not being able to deliver on their objectives, they had to deal with a raft of complaints from critics watching their bad management.

That's exactly what happened recently in the Bitterroots. The Bitterroot National Forest had huge fires in 2000. The forest managers decided a moderate harvest of burned trees was warranted and in my opinion they were right. However, Forest Service headquarters decided to take it all with Mark Rey making the decision and signing the documents, including the environmental impact statement. That meant the decision could not be appealed because he is the highest level of appeal.

That decision went straight to court. The judge found the Forest Service in contempt and absolutely reamed the Service essentially saying, "I have never seen such a blatant attempt to rewrite law. Essentially, what you're doing is eliminating the appeal process because you want to dictate what happens. Guess what? That isn't happening. You, Mark Rey, are coming to Missoula and going into a room with the appellants and staying there until you come out with a different solution. This is your only choice or you're not cutting anything."

When everyone met, what do you think the agreement was? It was back to what the forest supervisor originally proposed! Start cutting in the front-country first, in areas that already have roads, and log in the winter with a gentle cut. Then evaluate this approach come summer to see how it looks. If things look good we'll go to phase two, but only if we do a good job in phase one. If we do a good job in phase two, we'll talk about phase three.

Now the Forest Service can't talk with environmentalists about forest health, timber salvage, or even forest restoration without them saying, "Bull. That's just a way to cut more trees." The Forest Service's management, thanks to the salvage rider, has now been labeled 'logging without laws.' I have recently talked to Forest supervisors who say they still haven't recovored from the salvage rider. The Department of Agriculture made this situation for itself. There is a tough lesson here. It is a lot easier to blow your trust than it is to get it back.

Mike: Tell me about the oil and natural gas issue on the Rocky Mountain Front Range.

The Rocky Mountain Front Range in Montana is a spectacular landscape where the Northern Rocky Mountains and Great Plains smash together. It takes only a glance at the Front Range to reveal a picture of world-class wild lands and top quality wildlife habitat. The fishing and the hunting are perhaps some of the world's finest. The Front also has the healthiest grizzly bear [*Ursus arctos horribilis*] population in the lower 48. The geologic history of the area is responsible for the area's striking appearance and wildlife values as well as its potential as an oil and gas reserve. In 1997, as supervisor on the Lewis and Clark National Forest, I decided to remove all national forest lands within the Rocky Mountain Front from further oil and gas leasing for at least 10 years. When I did it there was both overwhelming public support and challenges by the oil and gas industry. The detractors said it was an inappropriate decision improperly justified. I thank them for saying so. I also thank them for the criticism that I listened to the public too much.

Our first oil and gas leasing proposal was based on an array of fairly conservative alternatives. Very early it was clear that there was no way we could propose even a moderate level of development and have a decision survive without opposition. So we picked a range of truly feasible alternatives that the public might accept and that the land might tolerate. When we did our public scoping as well as the scientific analyses, we worked with industry to understand their requirements and their interests. Then we looked at the magnificent array of wildlife and plants along with the ecosystem functioning of the landscape. From this we came up with criteria—needed distances from calving areas, timing to avoid winter range, and so forth—to guide how development projects could be distributed on the landscape. The draft decision proposed leasing a very small percentage of land right along the fringe stipulating no surface occupancy. The proposed decision was a response to the way the royalty laws are written. The federal government is owed royalties for oil and gas extraction from under its land only if the federal land is considered leasable. Otherwise, someone drilling on private land but drawing resources from under public land does not pay federal royalties. So, I thought we'd try the fringe leasing approach and see if it worked.

The response to this draft plan was overwhelmingly negative. More than 80 percent of the people responded firmly against any leasing. Ten percent seemed okay with the proposal. And another 10 percent, primarily from industries, wanted far more leasing. But the overwhelming feedback was, "You aren't listening." That sent us back for a year of gathering and analyzing more scientific data because, among other concerns, people pointed out more potential grizzly bear and westslope cutthroat trout [*Oncorhynchus clarki lewisi*] impacts. We ended up with a huge amount of scientific information indicating there was very little land available for leasing without the significant compromise of a natural system or sensitive species.

One time I took some industry people from Texas on a field trip into the potential lease area. Individuals would drift back on the trail to talk with me. Once alone they'd say, for example, "My wife would give her right arm to see this place, just once. We don't need to be here. We're going to mess this up if we come in." So there were people within industry that didn't feel drilling in the Front was that critical. Of course, they could never break ranks and say that in public. Their next best alternative was to whisper in my ear. Still, it was refreshing to know that their human side, their 'nonbusiness' side could find voice when they saw that landscape.

We had the option of developing mitigation measures and stipulations. However, when I thought deeper about what people were saying, there was another very important message. They weren't just expressing a concern for bears or fish. They were saying, "I love this place." "It has deep meaning to me." "I first came here with my grandfather." "My family has vacationed here for years." The things people were saying about why they didn't want development only dealt in part with the physical and biological attributes. The other part was the human dimension—the significance of the landscape—the sense of place, of connection between generations, of connection with your spiritual beliefs about creation. Those were the kinds of values that people told me were really important.

When I looked at this noneconomic message compared to our traditional justifications for decisions I thought, "How can I make a decision that avoids mentioning sense of place even though some people say the concept is too touchy-feely?" I started to fall into the trap that because you can't put a dollar value on it, it shouldn't be mentioned. Then it hit me, that was all the more reason to talk about it. So we ended up with a decision based on a two-fold justification. On the one hand was the important biological and physical attributes of the land—the traditional technical measurement of impacts. On the other hand was open acknowledgment that the meaning a landscape gives people is also a legitimate basis for decision making.

Needless to say, industry felt the decision was arbitrary, capricious, and unfounded. They carried that thinking into their lawsuit. None of these criticisms were upheld. The court told them they lacked standing and even if they did, they'd lose on the merits. Industry then appealed to the Ninth Circuit Court. That court declared the plaintiffs' appeal out of bounds because they brought up different issues in their appeal than they did in the original lawsuit. That court saw the appeal as a fishing expedition. Industry even implied that because I was female I was too easily swayed and too emotional. The judges said it is not outside the

scope of NEPA to consider psychological impacts on people. So I'm pleased
to be accused of using these other values. Just because we can't put a
price tag on something does not mean it has no value.

In the Rocky Mountain Front decision I simply admitted that landscapes affect us in meaningful ways beyond extracting oil or gas. I was
willing to question the assumption that making a decision about landscape is only about extraction values. Admitting landscape values into
the decision-making process upset some people. I eventually figured out
that we didn't have to disprove their criticism before taking action. I
was willing to consider people's relationship with landscapes as a legitimate social phenomenon and relevant to making choices about how we
use the public's land.

When you base a decision on nontraditional values, don't expect
your traditional management organization to rise up in forceful support—at least at first. When I made the oil and gas decision, my chain of
command tended to distance themselves. Many of these folks didn't want
to wear any of the decision if it went south. Before the public announcement I talked my decision through the Forest Service; then the Department of Agriculture; then the Bureau of Land Management; and then
the Department of Interior. I had to tell each successively bigger boss
what I was doing and why. Any one of them could have busted my chops
and tried to change the decision. However, none did because it made
sense. They couldn't find an argument to counter what I was proposing.

In the month between my signing the final decision and printing it
for the public announcement at least 60 to 70 people in the various
federal agencies knew about it. Nobody leaked it, which was phenom-
enal. That meant people were concerned that potential backlash might
splash on them. You can feel very isolated in those moments. Curiously,
I felt completely at peace. The anguish before I made the decision was
intense until I sat down on a river bank and had a long talk with myself
about me and my future. It became abundantly clear that this decision
wasn't about me. It didn't matter if I got fired or exiled to some remote
Forest Service outpost. When I realized the decision was bigger than
me it simplified my choice and eased my mind. That realization liber-
ated me to move forward understanding it was the right decision. After
my river-bank conversation I had no doubt there should be no drilling.
As I explained my decision my colleagues would say, "You can't do that.
You've got to give them something." It just did not occur to them that
we could say no.

When we released the decision you would have thought I'd been canonized. The response was tremendous. Immediately, 400 letters and phone calls of support came in. I had people send me flowers. I had people send me pictures of their grandchildren and say, "This is who you made the decision for." One fellow called me saying, "I'm in a traffic jam in L.A., but I just heard on National Public Radio what you did and I wanted to call and say, thank you." Famous writers like Ivan Doig and Annie Dillard sent me personal letters. Even better, people within the Forest Service wrote me e-mails saying, "Today, for the first time in years, I was proud to put on my uniform." "You made a great decision." "You listened to the public." "You recognized that this is a special place." "You didn't buckle to industry pressure." "Thank you for modeling what I thought I was getting in the Forest Service to do." When the Montana Senate's minority leader called me he asked me to hold on while he put the phone down. I could hear him go bump, bump. When he got back on the phone he said, "I just kept my promise to do a back flip if you did what you just did!"

Don't make any mistake, there was push back. I had three appeals. One was bogus. We couldn't even understand what that person was trying to say. Two were from industry. In contrast, the last time there was a leasing action on the Front in 1982 there were 52 appeals. The two credible appeals to my decision were subsequently combined and led to the Rocky Mountain Oil and Gas Association deciding to sue. Over the next nine months, as they were preparing the case, their organization folded for lack of interest and lack of members' financial support.

Then the Independent Petroleum Producers Association felt compelled to step in and take over the lawsuit. I think the guy that heads it up hates me personally. You can still find quotations from him on the Internet about what an idiot I am. They gave the suit to the only lawyers who would take it, the pro-industry Mountain State's Legal Foundation. They botched it but still tried to appeal all the way to the Supreme Court; even after being turned down in two lower courts. The Supreme Court refused to hear their appeal.

In public land management, industry—and I use that term very broadly—assumes that they get half to start with and then government negotiates from there. Surprisingly, agencies often behave like they are right! I love it when industry comes to the table saying, "Well, okay, we'll give up this public resource over here as long as we get this other public resource over there." I always enjoyed reminding them that neither of these public resources was theirs in the first place. If you think about it, it's like somebody walking into my house, taking my possessions, and then saying "Okay. If you give me your TV system, I'll give back your stereo system." It is surprising how much trouble agencies make for themselves by automatically assuming that industry gets a piece. However, future generations own it all and I'm their negotiator, their trustee. My ground rule is, "What can industry have without shafting future generations? The negotiation starts from zero. It's all about the interests of future generations—we'll talk from there."

The usual response I got from colleagues was that, "We're a multiple-use agency. That means we must give them something if we possibly can." I liked to break that unwritten rule. It's not necessary to give every requester something. On every forest I was in I would mentally divide our acreage by the population we were serving. That meant when an individual came to me insisting that an ATV trail be opened to help him get his elk out of the back country because his knee hurts, I could say, "Okay, let's look at this in context. You pay your taxes and that entitles you to management of one square foot of land. So you're going to have to get a lot more people together whose land your going to be using to convince me that this is for the greater good." Of course you don't talk to constituents that way but I say it that way here to make my point. What you try to do is put it in perspective that this is a multiple use agency but that doesn't mean that we have to spread all uses across all landscapes. We're looking at the whole 191 million acres of land managed by the Forest Service and responsibility to a whole lot of people, some unborn, not just those who want to pursue a particular activity today. Thus spatially, temporally, and demographically the agency's duty is much bigger than a single human life span and the narrow set of people who want you to fix their problem now. I think 100 years, 191 million acres, millions of stakeholders, and future generations. They're thinking next year, five acres, and my needs. It's very seductive for agency people to give them what they want because they don't want to deal with citizen complaints and because it is easy to rationalize that it is only a small piece of the forest. Uh-uh. That's not good enough. It's got to fit into a broader picture of responsibility.

If I had any important insight in the oil and gas decision it was to ask a different question, "Well, where on earth would you *not* put such a development if you're willing to put it on the Rocky Mountain Front Range—one of the most spectacular and richest ecological, cultural, historical, and beautiful landscapes in the entire Forest Service system?" That was a breakthrough. Then it became clear, "Well sure. Of all places in the United States, the Rocky Mountain Front is the last place you would drill." Then, all the confusing noise like, "How do we give them something?" "Will they complain?" "Are there mitigation measures?" and "What will happen to my career?" went away. But, to choose no development was a leap after being well trained in the agency to always look for the compromise, always presume mitigation, always look for the "can-do" accomplishment.

I was also tempted by the costs we'd already sunk into decision making. That is just another false justification that implies you must take action. There was an unstated assumption that all the time and money we spent to study the proposal meant we had to do something. The rationale is that you need to make that investment worthwhile or, worse, that you're doing the assessment work to support designing project implementation, not a true yes-versus-no decision. In other words, the environmental assessment work gets co-opted as part of the development work. It's just another version of you-gotta-give-them-something thinking.

Of course, I had to examine what could happen to me. As much as we try to be altruistic, one part of our brain is always asking that question. I thought, "Well, that's a question I dang-well better answer." I realized I needed to get congruent with my values and that's what happened. I got into the mind-set of not caring what happened to me because I was not important enough in this drama. Many times people are stopped by fear of a potential outcome rather than the true risk. Often, I see managers stewing over a long line of What-if? questions and it's all made up stuff. It depends on how active and vivid your imagination is and how risk averse you are. Now I'm not an aggressive risk taker. I like to protect myself. But it was truly freeing when I realized it wasn't going to kill me to make this decision. There was great release in making the shift from 'if' to 'how' we were going to make something positive happen. Arriving at that state builds self-confidence. When I was making the rounds to pre-alert the agencies about the oil and gas leasing decision I felt very good and very confident.

Once I made that decision my personal mission became clear—accomplish this goal and see that the decision goes forward. I was not going to sit in the back room, be beat up, or be forced to modify my decision and then put my name on it. I did have What-if? fears. My solution was to let objectors take me to the woodshed publicly and not pretend that I think a different decision is a better decision.

The manager's temptation is to downplay the consequences of a decision by saying, "Oh, that loss is a drop in the bucket. It was just a bad experiment. We won't do that again." I can trivialize a management decision that removes 200 acres from productivity by allowing an activity like unsustainable grazing. But, the multiplication of similar decisions over the thousands of land managers in the nation and over the 30 or so years that we're all working adds up to a lot of resource loss for future generations.

I'm not responsible just for providing products and recreation for visitors. I'm also supposed to look seven generations out—literally at the needs of the unborn. So, my role as a public land steward is not just to run around and tidy up after the exploiters are done. To make sure that wildlife is more-or-less happy. To make sure that we're not trashing streams too much. No. My job is to think in much broader, deeper terms about why I'm really doing my work and the consequences of doing my job poorly.

You can expect to encounter two responses when you make a decision like I did. One is trying to chase the decision maker back into the science box. Fortunately, more and more universities are including exposure to broader management perspectives so the present-day manager can turn around and say, "You must have missed that class. These are legitimate justifications for a decision and here are the reasons why." The other response is to attack the manager. First, they'll criticize your behavior and try to corral you back into what they think is your job description. If that doesn't work expect personal attacks; the notion that you're bad, sick, stupid, or crazy, including questioning your integrity. They'll do that by saying something seemingly objective like, "Well, that's so touchy-feely" or "Beauty is in the eye of the beholder."

There are reams, just reams, of scientific studies about what people find attractive in the natural landscape and there are ways of addressing aesthetics through management. You look at contrast, line, form, color, texture. There are very credible approaches to evaluating and assessing the aesthetic quality of a landscape. This form of science just was not admitted into the decision-making arena. It's been 20 years now and finally people accept that aesthetics are important. We've made progress. I now see the argument shifting to criticisms of sustainability as, "Oh, it's soft, it's mushy." Not true. But traditional decision-making is still not ready to admit sustainability into the club.

I am delighted to be accused of using nonmarket values and nonscientific reasons for a decision because that tells me I'm doing my job. My job is not running a business. My job is leaving a legacy for the future. The natural resource agencies are not just producing goods and services; it's goods, services, experiences, and a legacy. If you ask somebody at the end of their life what they remember about public lands they're not going to say, "Well, I think some of the wood in my front porch came from a national forest and I think, let's see, 5 percent of the meat that's produced in the United States is raised on public land, so I guess maybe 5 percent of my hamburgers came from public land." No. They're going to say, "I remember going up to Sun River with my dad and that is where he showed me how to fish. Now I take my grandkids up there and we fish in the same place." That is the way people express the priceless legacy of the public's wild lands. These memories and experiences are so much more poignant than the fact that some wood in their house came from a national forest.

Now, that puts a different spin on the criticism that I used nontraditional values and that I listened to the public. It's not that I'm just speaking for the land or representing the American public. I'm representing future generations. What a huge responsibility. It's almost impossible to anticipate what these people might need, but just by virtue of being human you know they will need clean air, clean water, and the opportunity to find beauty and meaning in nature. And those are going to be in highest demand and in least supply as our population increases. Those are incredibly meaningful values. I'm glad I was criticized. It meant I was doing my job.

Mike: Why, in an agency, is making the shift to a new way of doing business difficult?

Most people within an organization, private or public, would rather not take a risk which may negatively impact their career, their income, their family, or their standing within the organization. That is not meant as a criticism, even though it may sound that way. People think about these things when there is a risk. I certainly went through that thought process. It helped me that my life style is to not be in debt. I could afford some self-confidence that I would survive if things turned out badly. If you're financially vulnerable, you can suddenly find there is pressure to accept things that your value system would suggest you not accept. That's a big source of inner conflict for many resource managers I've met. That dynamic changes people's willingness to take a risk. And this is not about government employees being more risk averse than private sector employees. The same conflicting incentives exist for them as well.

Things are also slow to change because of the rewards and the culture in an organization. The behaviors rewarded in the Forest Service were making people happy, keeping things calm, keeping people from writing senators about us, not letting complaints reach the Forest Supervisor, and not getting us bashed in the local newspaper. Rocking the boat, even legitimately, even completely within the law, even completely within your responsibility as a land manger is not welcome. It makes life uncomfortable for the chain of command.

For ourselves we wanted to sustain our image of the agency culture—the ideal of a popular, can-do organization. There is a lot of stock placed in that self-image and it has, in many ways, served the Forest Service very well. It really became evident after World War II when the thousands of returning GIs needed houses for their new families. The agency was caught up in the national ethic of helping servicemen who had sacrificed for a free world. In addition, Americans who stayed home were still struggling out of the Depression and had made their own sacrifices for the war effort. The focus was how we, as the Forest Service, could help. Well, we could provide cheap building materials. So we started cutting more because real people who'd made real sacrifices needed it. Fulfilling that need became a national ethic and the agency felt good about doing its part.

To make this happen the Forest Service augmented its mission. Providing cheap wood became defined as the important work of the Service. Well, it was actually a shift because the real mission never said anything about cutting the huge quantity of trees needed to fuel that kind of development. Gifford Pinchot talked a lot about the greatest good for the greatest number in the long run but the long run was playing second fiddle. The idea that we were dealing with finite resources and providing for the needs of far distant generations got lost.

Another obstacle to change was the culture in the Forest Service that we were a 'family.' It's very important to remember that, from the very early days, the Forest Service prided itself on being a family. Some of that was bred in by living in remote stations where you really did form a community with your co-workers and their families. That attitude, with all its advantages, was everywhere in the agency, even as I moved between forests in the '80s and '90s. To act outside the family norms was frowned upon. We took a human core value and gave it to an agency and, thereby, gave the agency the power and rights of a family. Conferring those rights meant loyalty to the agency was and is highly prized, just as is loyalty to one's own family. This was a shock for the new generation of employees in my era who didn't feel like they were being treated like family, who didn't really want to be a member of the Forest Service family, and who felt a much stronger allegiance to their own family and their own values. This split in loyalties caused a great deal of personal strife among employees and it caused a great deal of instability in the agency. That was a sure recipe for a culture clash.

Mike: I've read about the very controversial issue you encountered on the Jarbidge River. Tell me about it and what you learned.

There is a dirt track road in Nevada, on the Humboldt-Toiyabe National Forest, that runs up the Jarbidge River. It dead-ends at a wilderness area. The Jarbidge issue began when a rain-on-snow flood washed out the last mile and a half of the road. I hesitate to call the Jarbidge a river; it is more like a big creek. But it lies in a very deep, narrow canyon about four miles outside of the town of Jarbidge, which has a population of about 26 and is 100 miles of gravel and dirt road from the nearest Nevada community of any size. When the Jarbidge road blew out in 1995 the Forest Service decided to rebuild it. But the river happens to have a bull trout [*Salvelinus confluentus*] population. To grab hold of flood repair money while it was available the Forest Service decided very rapidly to rebuild the road. That decision was appealed by Trout Unlimited because there was no consideration of impacts on bull trout.

The appeal was bumped up two levels to the Intermountain Regional Office. They agreed with Trout Unlimited and directed the district to go back and assess the potential effects on bull trout. Unfortunately, even at the first look it became obvious there were problems. This was the southernmost population of bull trout in the United States. Bull trout in the Jarbidge River were not yet listed because Nevada is a very difficult state for ESA (Endangered Species Act) issues but bull trout were listed in many other places. It was pretty easy to document damage to these fish from previous road maintenance and other management activities along the lower stretches of the river. So the District Ranger reevaluates and says, "Whoa, this road blows out continually. Usually not this bad, but it's a bad place to put a road. There's always sediment dumping into the river. It's probably not so smart to rebuild. The only place the road goes is to the wilderness trail head and a couple of picnic tables. We could move the wilderness trail head or we could just construct a good trail up to the old trail head."

While this may not sound like a big deal, it had taken several years to get to this point.

The District Ranger announced that the Forest Service would probably replace that road with a trail. He tried to contact the Elko County commissioners but he didn't talk to them directly. One reason was because in January 1998 the Commission passed a resolution that commissioners were forbidden to meet directly with Forest Service and BLM (Bureau of Land Management) employees because we were considered the enemy. So the District Ranger tried to go through the County's Public Land-Use Advisory Committee, which represented the Commission in dealing with public land. In fact, these Committee members were appointed by the commissioners and all of the Committee members had a troubled history with government land managers.

Before the District Ranger actually made the preliminary decision, the County Commission directed their road department to bulldoze a new road over the landslide. They ended up channelizing 900 feet of river into what looked like an irrigation ditch, tearing out a significant amount of riparian vegetation, and laying 50 or 60 feet of new road below the level of the channelized river. I didn't realize it but these turned out to be the good old days. That was the start of the chain of events leading to my leaving the Forest Service in protest. The federal Attorney General and members of Congress were ineffective and unsupportive. By their inaction they pretty much joined the rest of Nevada who thought it great sport to watch the Elko County Commission intimidate local Forest Service employees and their families.

The barrier put between the District Ranger and the County Commission and the inability of federal land managers to engage higher levels of help as things heated up was the foundation of a really ugly series of events. The County's bulldozers gouged out the new road the day after I arrived on the Forest as the new Forest Supervisor. The campaign against government employees became very personal with slogans like, "Elko County against Gloria." "Freedom Fighters against Gloria." "The Shovel Brigade against Gloria." I became a target because I challenged them in a public way. I suggested that what they were doing was inappropriate, incorrect, illegal and that they were going to have to return to the taxpayers the $400,000 it cost to undo the damage they had done.

Jarbidge also shows the importance of media. The owner of the local newspaper in that corner of Nevada was a right-wing zealot. My husband, Marc, e-mailed the publisher asking him to stop vilifying me. Marc said he had no problem with him expressing his views, denigrating the federal government or whatever, but personally attacking his wife made him very uncomfortable for my safety and it's inappropriate. He said, "I'm asking you as another human being to please stop the personal attacks. This is a way to foment violence." The editor responded saying, "No. Violence is coming and it will start when a Forest Service employee says the wrong thing to the wrong person. Then the revolution will begin and people will pick up arms."

One option was for me to ask the U.S. Attorney in Nevada to investigate and provide legal coverage but I was not hopeful. I could not even get her to investigate less controversial issues like cattle trespass. We'd given the U.S. Attorney 53 misdemeanors and 26 felony cases and she refused to act. Of course, when the local public picked up on this lack of support they felt free to do whatever they wanted. They even bombed a Forest Service office and an employee's home. The previous district ranger in the area had quit before I arrived because there was a threat to burn her house. With that track record my pessimism about the U.S. Attorney helping us on the Jarbidge issue was, unfortunately, right. Even before I got to the Humboldt-Toiyabe Forest the policy was, generally, "Do not wear your uniform in the field, do not go alone in the field, and do not drive a Forest Service vehicle." We used unmarked General Service Administration vehicles rather than the distinctive green Forest Service rigs. In response to our pleading for intervention during a planned and publicized act of civil disobedience, the second in command in Janet Reno's Department of Justice told us, "You will not have any employee within 100 miles of the Jarbidge site." All we could do was watch as Forest Service land was damaged.

So our hands were tied. We lacked direct access to the county officials before they started acting out. The land-use advisory committee we were forced to go through was a biased gatekeeper. The media were similarly biased and antagonistic. Threats made it difficult for Forest Service employees to do their job. And the safety net of the legal system was withheld. There were no options.

By the time I got there the situation was already out of control and burst open the day after I arrived. In natural resources work you need to build allies, which I attempted to do, but discovered that the elected officials in Nevada did not want to openly support the federal government. The normal things a person would do to work through a conflict, and I and my colleagues working on that forest were pretty good at doing them, were simply not accessible. An absence of a sizeable conservation community in Nevada did not help. Any conservationists living in rural Nevada are very quiet about their activities and their memberships. Members of the public would come to us privately to tell us of their support but did not want their names to be known because their businesses would be boycotted, or their tires slashed, or their spouses abused, and so forth. Consequently, at the outset any allies had been scared underground.

We were also working against an ideology embedded in an outdated law. RS 2477 is a statute attached to an 1865 mining law giving counties the right-of-way on roads that existed in their county prior to designation of a national forest. Under the law a county can claim ownership of that road. In the Jarbidge case Elko County made a claim even though there was no documentation showing that the road predated creation of the forest. The County reasoned they owned the right-of-way because a trail may have been there before the road. Even though the County insisted they owned the road they expected the federal government to pay the maintenance bills—the same federal government they hated and wanted kicked out of their county.

At the County's and Senator Harry Reid's request we went through a collaborative problem-solving process. Despite all this bad history we, that is, all the involved federal agencies, nongovernment organizations, and other government authorities including Elko County Commission representatives, succeeded in arriving at a consensus about how to best handle the Jarbidge road situation. The core agreements were to have the Forest Service build an ATV trail higher up on the side of the hill instead of a road, give the county a leadership role, have the Service do bull trout habitat enhancement, and we agreed not to denigrate each other in the press. The negotiation seemed to include all the right players; two members of the County Commission, the future leader of the Jarbidge Rebellion, an assemblyman from Nevada, lawyers from Trout Unlimited, staffers of a Senator and a Congressman, and the decision makers from the affected government agencies. It looked to me like the consensus we hammered out could work.

The consensus lasted 36 hours! The representatives from the County went back to the rest of the county commissioners and voted five to zero rejecting the findings and the agreement. Then they ripped me a new one in the press. All this happened after months of consensus building and, supposedly, good faith negotiation. Senator Harry Reid would not even mention that we had gone through the consensus process. This was the senior senator who encouraged us to use a consensus process in the first place. Despite working out a solution with all the key players the County torpedoed the process and no one was willing to hold them accountable. Jarbidge was not your average situation where normal problem-solving skills and techniques were successful. To understand something like Jarbidge you have to get down to the ideology behind the behavior; Jarbidge was about antifederal sentiments and county supremacy not about people driving along a road to picnic, sight see, or whatever.

One of the revealing things I learned from Jarbidge is an understanding of the importance of having effective attorneys at your back. It took us three months and four significant reports—and I'm talking inches thick—to justify why the U.S. Attorney should sue these people for channelizing 900 feet of river on public lands. The EPA said it was an egregious violation of the Clean Water Act. The U.S. Fish and Wildlife Service did an emergency listing of bull trout as endangered in the Jarbidge River because of what the county had done to the habitat. Yet, the U.S. Attorney would not even put forth a cease and desist pleading. One of her assistant attorneys told a group of us federal agency leaders from Nevada and California, "You probably shouldn't bring us a case if the violator is a native Nevadan, over 65, or a rancher. And if they're all three, forget it. Don't even bother calling us." He said it as a joke, but it was clear that it wasn't really a joke. That meant there was an unofficial hands-off policy in rural Nevada because of the antigovernment sentiment. A smart manager makes sure the will to act is behind them before an issue like Jarbidge breaks out. We made that mistake.

Mike: Reflect on the question of a public manager's role *vis-à-vis* advocacy?

We need to speak for the unborn. That is the unique trust given to agencies. We're simply passing something on as our primary mission, not making a profit in this life time. Unlike a corporation that can best represent its shareholders by liquidating one portfolio to acquire a new one, the public resource manager can't cut and run. Their shareholders are stuck with a static portfolio and their interests are best served by sustainability.

Not every public employee is comfortable being out in front on these kinds of decisions. These more reserved folks still have value to the agency, even if advocacy terms like "sustainability," "thinking long-term," and "future generations" somehow feel odd, too esoteric, too uncomfortable. That's okay. Let's talk about it in a different language. Their ability to analyze the consequences of different actions against a standard like sustainability is just fine. That's an important role. It's not going to be a decision-making role in my organization, but it's still an important role.

I don't expect everyone to run around saying, "I'm here for future generations. Don't make me do anything that's not sustainable." You need to be very practical about it. God knows, I've made hundreds of decisions that were not sustainable. I tried to move them more toward sustainability. What I say when I'm discussing my current organization [Sustainable Obtainable Solutions], whose mission is all about sustainability, is that we aim for sustainability. If we get one step closer that is a huge improvement.

It is impossible to be human and not be an advocate. Let me qualify that. Tempered, respectful advocacy is appropriate. I expect us to have opinions and I prefer strong opinions and I prefer deep thought about why you and I have our opinions. I define inappropriate advocacy as when a public manager uses a particular worldview to influence their scientific study and their communication of the technical aspects of management. It's imperative for a public manager to maintain an open mind when approaching a project analysis. A scientist who enters into an experiment or an analysis with a foregone conclusion usually finds the 'data' to prove that conclusion.

I've seen the full range of advocacy within the Forest Service, from complete absence, where you'd like to slap the person in the face to see if they're still awake, to people that were a pain in the butt and you wish they'd go to sleep. The zealots are usually less effective. They usually become troubled and unhappy in the bureaucracy because their temperament is not suited for that work environment.

When I get the chance, I like talking about when we've just given it our all and a decision didn't turn out the way we wanted. I try to turn people's attention away from, "Oh God, I failed," to "I tried as hard as I could. What could I do differently or better next time?" and to, "Let me find my friends who understand so we can go have a beer and talk about it." Celebrate your hard work regardless of outcome, learn from the experiences, then come Monday, go back to work. What I encourage people to do is think about how important it is to sustain the spirit because there's always another opportunity coming up. Each work experience is a learning opportunity and a right of passage to fight another day with greater effectiveness.

I absolutely love the mission of the Forest Service, "Caring for the land, serving people." There were a lot of jokes when that came out 10 or 12 years ago, but I thought it was pretty clever because it is what we do. The Forest Service likes to put itself forward as the best conservation leader in the world and, really, if you look at it, it is. And that can be scary because some might think, "Oh my God, is that the best we can do?" But the Service has so much capability. That's the beauty of working in the agency. Even though we focus on the things that look grim, you have a heck of a lot more resources available than other people. With a career in an agency like the Forest Service you've also got a longevity, the time to learn how to do it right. Another strength is the many intelligent and dedicated people. If they're not at the office working, they're often working at home. It's a passion, not just a job.

I like to think back on Forest Service people I've known who asked some important questions like, "What am I contributing?" "What is my legacy?" "Is my being here on earth doing anything?" They can answer these questions. It is not the same if you are in a business just to make a buck. My Forest Service colleagues and friends are doing something really important. The idea of being able to work with large landscapes and to effect change to help communities and help people enjoy and appreciate the natural world. My God, what a calling. What service.

So, I absolutely love public land management agencies and I love the Forest Service. They have the capability and power to do good things. You just don't get it any other place. As a landscape architect, did I want to go around and make yards pretty? No! Did I want to clean up an industrial zone and make it more user friendly? No! Did I want the privilege to work with six and a half million acres and make decisions that affect future generations? Yes! That's something you can dedicate yourself to. There's something about the legacy value of our work that sets it apart. It's fulfilling a promise, a desire I have to be a good ancestor. Someone once said, "In the spiral of time when the eyes of the future gaze back into ours, pray we see no tears because we failed to act." That's why the work we do is important. Let the spirit inspire action. This work is my way of taking action.

4
Andrea Mead Lawrence - Extension

. . . your journey into risk is to explore boundaries
and free yourself to extend, not just win.
– Andrea Mead Lawrence

Three-time Olympian and environmental activist Andrea Mead Lawrence has won many awards. When she invited me into her home for this interview, I was surprised to see no symbols of her many honors. When I ask her why there are no winning photographs on the wall, no Olympic Gold Medals on display, or no framed certificates hung among her nature art she just says, "A person's most important achievement is the next one."

At the Oslo 1952 Winter Olympics, Andrea became the first U.S. alpine skier and first woman in the world to win two Gold Medals in a single Winter Olympics. Her Olympic victories, and her U.S. championship titles in the downhill, slalom, and alpine in 1950, 1952, and 1955 and the giant slalom in

1953 earned her a place in the International Women's Sports Hall of Fame. Sports filmmaker Bud Greenspan calls her the greatest winter Olympian of all time. She has been on the cover of *Time* magazine. And she is included in *The Columbia World of Quotations* for,

> Competition can be a very intense experience and a very reward-ing one, or it can be enormously destructive. External pressure, whether it's exerted by a coach, a school, a ski club, or a country, is what can make it a negative thing. When they use you to satisfy their need to succeed, when they impose their value system on you, then competition isn't personally rewarding anymore. . . . You're either a winner or a loser. . . . There's no way in my mind that you can divide humanity into those two categories.

Since the end of her racing career, Andrea has focused on protecting the environment, primarily in the Eastern Sierra Nevada Mountains around her home in Mammoth Lakes, California. Lawrence helped found the Friends of Mammoth, served on the Mono County Board of Supervisors (the county commission) for 16 years where she made environmental protection a part of their decision making, and has been a longtime advocate for Mono Lake protection. In 1993 she helped form the Sierra Nevada Alliance, an organization that represents more than 43 grass-roots community groups bound together to help protect the environment and economy of communi-ties in the region. Andrea's board memberships include Board of Directors for the Eastern Sierra Land Trust, The Mono Lake Committee, The Sequoia Fund, and the Coalition for Unified Recreation in the Eastern Sierra. Andrea also served as Project Director for the Sierra Nevada Regional Initiative, a novel process to assure the sustainability of the Sierras by helping the busi-ness community understand the link between environmental quality and a successful economy.

She won the 2001 Havoline Star Award in recognition of her many contri-butions to the environment. Andrea is a recipient of the Sierra Business Council's Vision 20/20 Lifetime Achievement Award for her efforts to secure the economic and environmental health of the Sierra Nevada. And the Ameri-can Planning Association honored Andrea with its Distinguished Leadership Award as a citizen planner.

From her environmental activism and experience as a County Supervi-sor Andrea has something to say about the role of natural resource profes-sionals in our democratic political processes. As an Olympic ski champion she also has important advice about achieving personal excellence.

When I moved to Mammoth Lakes in 1968, the first thing I got involved with was land use planning. I've lived in mountains all my life. A deep core of me just loves the mountain environment. This environment compels me to stand up and take a position on certain things. It started in Aspen back in the '60s. I was on its planning commission. I also engaged because I am an old Vermonter. As a youngster I just absorbed the ethic that you are supposed to get involved in politics; it's part of being a New England Yankee. So, it was pretty natural that I just get involved.

Mono County had never been zoned. All that the county's planning director had done to qualify for his job was hammer a few nails in some houses; those were his credentials. He went down to the growing megacities in Southern California, picked up the idea of their flat-land planning grid and just started slapping it on our mountains. When I was speaking up at the public hearings, NEPA [National Environmental Policy Act] had just passed. Then, on the heels of that, the California Environmental Quality Act passed. My comments were easy to legitimize using these laws. I expressed what little I knew about planning, based on my Aspen experiences, and what I thought was just common sense. From the technical aspects of planning, which is just zoning, it was pretty straightforward. You don't put your high density next to your low density and you don't put commercial next to low density. So, I kept talking about those kinds of principles and about being mindful of things like the quality of the environment.

Eventually a grid was approved but it didn't stick. There was pressure to re-zone parts of Mammoth Lakes for more intensive use. Several of us who were following the planning felt, "That's too bizarre. Why would anybody want a down zone where they want it?" Well, commercial developers building some high-rises didn't want the expense of building underground parking. That meant there would be no place to put the cars other than sprawl. That's how we got into the lawsuit. One night the phone rang and this person I know in town said, "Do you want to head up a new organization to stop the high rise?" I said, "Sure." I never even thought about it. That's how Friends of Mammoth was born.

All of a sudden we were in the middle of the politics over land use that, up to that time, was driven by the network of who knows whom and pressures to promote commercial interests versus other visions for the town. The county officials didn't even try a public process of establishing what the town should look like. Instead, they just went ahead and approved the special zoning changes that the handful of developers wanted. All this was happening while an exchange deal was being worked out with the Forest Service. The first areas developed in town were, actually, the result of Forest Service land swaps. That history of land swaps to support development in Mammoth carries forward into what is the current controversy between ski area development and other land uses. As somebody used to say, "This land belongs as much to a taxi driver in New York City as it does to any of us who live here." But the reality is that local people and the agencies get to be, well, kind of too close.

The Forest Service is political, maybe not as political as the State Fish and Game, but very politicized from its headquarters in D.C. As a nation we're outgrowing our natural resources and that has huge implications for agencies like the Forest Service. We don't yet know what the new pattern or the new models will be for our agencies. Whatever the solution, it is time to revisit all possibilities for managing natural resources that span from grazing, to mining, to timber, to water, to recreation. But, currently, agencies are controlled by special interests. The 1872 Mining Act is a classic example. If the current agencies are not performing, we need to ask, why is that? Well, in part it is because they are too close to the special interests who benefit from public land or too close to the local communities who are their neighbors. It's gotten muddled. Who do the large federal land agencies work for? A taxi driver in New York? A ski developer in Mammoth? Who?

As much as I like Forest Service people as individuals, it is basically a dysfunctional organization. They are certainly vulnerable. The Forest Service people I know feel threatened. When you feel threatened you go into a bunker mentality. You avoid a clear decision. And, of course, from my value system there comes a time when you have to make a clear decision on the side of the land. That's our legacy. Once we lose a forest we'll never get it back.

It is easy to understand how the Forest Service people got to this point. They're the taffy in the middle of a giant taffy pull. They're assaulted by the private property rights people. They're assaulted by the environmentalists. They're assaulted by cattlemen. They're assaulted by oil people. They're assaulted by all kinds of issues driving society today. In that context, they're under the gun.

I use the county supremacy movement as an example. Take this crazy guy over in Nevada, Dick whatever his name was, who decided to take a bulldozer onto Forest Service land and redo a road. Just imagine being the poor Forest Service guy who went out to stop the bulldozer? They took a gun after him and kept on dozing. All the Forest Service guy could do was get out of the way. These kinds of events trickle down. Eventually, employees get the message—be fearful of making a decision. Be fearful of taking a forthright stand. Try to be everybody's friend. The reality, of course, is that you can't be a friend to everybody when you are speaking on behalf of the resources. You have to make the tough decisions.

When subject to criticism from all sides, to being battered and bashed about, a normal response is to crawl inside yourself. You become more passive. Then it begins to turn toward accommodating. Then to trying to silence the squeaky wheels with favorable decisions. You gotta admit, it's a pretty loud squeak when a developer gets his senator to write or call the local forest supervisor to complain about you and your management. So there is a subtle shift in the goals —from management actions designed to support stewardship to management actions designed to silence squeaky wheels. In that kind of situation it is pretty easy for the agency person to say, "The hell with it. Why should I bother?" So there is a lot more at stake than what happens to one piece of land. We're also damaging the managers we depend upon to show the stewardship leadership we need. Damage the managers and you can't help but damage stewardship.

One thing I learned as a county supervisor is that nothing is concrete in this government that we have. It can change any minute. I found that in politics we always make short-term decisions. There is constant pressure for instant gratification. It's inherent in our political system. First of all, you are subject to whether or not you get voted into office. Once you get voted in, people really put the push on for what they want. If they don't get it, they're not going to vote for you again and may even mount a campaign against you. There are a few laws that help shield politicians from some of this—conflict of interest laws and so forth. But, there still is pressure for the short-term fix. Then there is the power of money in a community. A ski developer here in Mammoth is a good example. When he came to town and just casually let it be known he was going to drop $500 million into our community it just sucked the oxygen right out of town. So, of course, the community pressure builds on elected officials to say to big money, "Yes, what do you want?" That's when they start modifying the zoning plan to funnel new money into town. My take is that you should be able to say, "Well, you're more than welcome to come into our town, but here are the rules of the game. Just play by the rules. Don't expect us to change the rules just for you." It seemed to work for me, but, it's not a sure way to get reelected. This is just one of the many examples of economics trumping democracy.

Mike: What attributes of a natural resource professional do you admire?

Well, first is a professional standard of education. Second is thoroughly understanding your ethical core. Know what stressors you may run into and what might push you to say, "That's not a decision I'm going to make to accommodate your need," assuming you're being asked to do the wrong thing. It comes down to personal insight into what constitutes the public interest coupled with an awareness of your own standards. And third, a professional should know about human behavior. Resource management is about collective action and you don't get that by studying only the animals or only the land or only the trees, despite the obvious importance of these.

There also is a certain expectation for leadership. To me the first leadership responsibility is to tell it as it is. Leadership also is the ability to convey your knowledge—the ability to take your issue and present it in a way that is lucid, intelligent, makes sense, and explains consequences of actions and, importantly, the consequence of inaction. And I see this need for leadership coming from people like the forester, the biologist, or whomever is responsible for everyday work, not just the boss. It begins with these people giving absolutely the best knowledge and the very best opinions they've got.

Some might ask, "When I get my first job, why can't I just do what the boss tells me and that means I've met my professional responsibility?" Well, of course, the answer is, you can. If that's your choice that's what you should do. But there are other options, depending on how you feel about yourself, how you feel about your profession, what standards you've set for yourself, how far you want to go, and depending on how content you are with just doing your job and doing what you're told. It always comes down to that kind of a personal choice.

There is a recent example, in my own back yard, with a little meadow here in Mammoth. It's a snow creek meadow and absolutely wonderful. I called the state Fish and Game Department because somebody was cutting down willows in the stream. They were doing it out of ignorance, but, there are rules and regulations to protect the meadow as a public place. When I called Fish and Game I got one of the new people who was a bit timid. She didn't want to write a strong letter to the people who were doing the illegal cutting. She was new and there was a self-confidence issue. She didn't know the area, didn't know the politics, didn't know the personalities, and didn't know how far she could go. So her response was to write a nonletter. She just didn't say much of anything. Then I asked another woman I know in the Department to come out and take a look. She was very clear in the strength of her convictions about protecting wildlife and habitat. She also knew how you go about things like confronting people. This time, under her leadership, the Department took a much stronger stand. She knew how to take the lead. The younger employee had yet to learn that skill. It is a complicated question about why some professionals hold back—don't show that second kind of leadership.

Perhaps the deepest trouble is when professionals are asked to approve something they think is wrong. Assuming their intelligence and training has given them the insight to know that a project is bad, we go right back to personal ethics and principles. For me, it begins by knowing that nobody has a right to ask them to compromise their principles. It comes to a very personal choice. There are different ways to act on your conscience at that point. One way is to say, quietly as you exit, "I'm sorry, I see this as a bad project and I cannot support it." If the agency, with full knowledge of the consequences, still wants to proceed, that's its decision to make. But, it's not necessarily your decision to go along with. There is another choice, though. The most controversial stance is going outside the organization with your concerns and opinions. There is a certain instinct that this is an unethical thing to do. On one side are strategic leaks from Washington. They get to be kind of a joke. These are sanctioned, but not admitted by authorities and the media. Fortunately, the media do not react to these with as much credibility as an individual professional leaking the truth. Given how often agencies have acted unethically, or even illegally, and then tried to hide it, going outside has been, at times, a valuable public service. That is a difficult choice for the individual because the agency can strike back at the truth teller. It is also oversimplified for someone like me to say there is a one-size-fits-all answer. But, unauthorized leaking has certainly brought the nation around very strongly on some issues. So, I can't tell anyone how to act. It's a deeply personal choice.

Mike: In your book (Lawrence and Burnaby 1980) you have a chapter titled 'Danger and Daring.' What did you learn about risk taking as an athlete that parallels the natural resource professional's challenge of managing a career?

Our limits are set by our perceptions. Growing up I never knew that dreams and acts are separate for some. In my childhood it was just a given—they were the same. I have a lot of mixed feelings about the way we teach children to compete, which in too many cases destroys spirit. Yet, the spirit is the most essential thing they have. It has to be nurtured, inspired, moved and, sometimes given a kick in the pants. Because—and this is key to everything—you can't expect people to achieve if their spirit is not sustained. In my experience with resource professionals part of that spark has been put out.

My sense of risk taking is that you have to calculate what's out there and understand that dealing with risk is a very inner process. Then you have to realize where your boundaries are and how far you can push yourself. I'm talking about my experience in skiing but it is the same thing in my environmental work. You have to understand that the mind drives the body and all our behavior, no matter what you're doing. You have to know yourself and your field of endeavor well enough so, at the point of launching yourself into the face of a risk, you understand what you are doing. Through understanding you give yourself permission to take the risk, acknowledging that success is in the doing, not in winning.

While you are taking a risk, it's not foolhardy, not reckless. It's a very deliberate putting together of the patterns, the steps, the incidents, and the bits and the pieces of the puzzle. And then, when these come together, you sense your limits. I don't mean this in a constrained sense. At some point you feel free to just turn yourself over to it and engage with full commitment. So, you end up feeling that your journey into risk is to explore boundaries and free yourself to extend, not just win. It is a connection between your mind, your spirit, and your body. It doesn't mean you don't make mistakes. You do. But, at some point spirit sets you free to extend. It is a very personal journey.

An example is one of my races as a youngster, when I was 11 or 12. I'd entered the Kate Smith Trophy Race at Lake Placid, New York. At that time we did not have the chance to test run a course before the race. Our only chance to scope out a strategy was by looking at the course as we climbed to the starting gate. As I was climbing I realized there was one point on the run where I would have to ski over a hill without being able to see what was coming next. I knew my nature would be, as would anybody's, to pull back a bit so I could peek over just to be sure I was safe and positioned exactly where I wanted to be. I knew I couldn't do that and win. I realized I had to be absolutely committed to skiing through that visual barrier no matter how fearful. So I made myself do it; just absolutely made myself do it. When I got to that part of the run I went over without hesitation and was exactly where I wanted to be. I was euphoric. I was yodeling and whooping and hollering. Then, as I approached the finish line, I hooked a ski tip and cartwheeled. I just went, tk-tk-tk-tk-tk, head-over-heels and came up with a broken ski; which is the first and only time I did that. So, I got up and hobbled across the finish line having no idea of my time or the race results. But I did have a vivid idea of what I accomplished for myself. I had extended and created a new boundary. I was a success in that event even though I didn't win. In my skiing I made extensions like that and, as a result, I created a series of learning moments.

Once experienced, extension is a moment that is very potent and it's a quality you can reaccess when you need new strengths. When you practice extension, when you put 150% of yourself into what you do, when you begin to have some success, you build confidence. That's a very inner quality. It's not cocky. Then, when you're a little off the mark you just know it and reengage at your maximum level having learned a little bit from your mistake.

I've been asked a lot about my mistake in the slalom at the 1952 Olympics. I caught a ski tip on a gate in the first run. I spun around and slid backwards down the hill. I managed to climb back up to the gate, get back on the course, and finish fourth in the first run. People always ask, "How did you know how much it would take to overcome your mistake to beat the competition in the second run?" My answer: "I didn't do any calculations." It never even occurred to me to do any. That question is not my answer. My answer, and it is all metaphor, is that I was in this very deep, dark still area inside myself. I'd moved into that area when I got on the airplane in Zurich. It doesn't mean I wasn't interacting normally with people, but, for my competitive side I was somewhere very, very deep inside myself. It is a very nice, steady place. It's a constant kind of beat. It's a humming going on inside. Outwardly you are very calm and very quiet. You just go deep down inside to a wonderful place where things are strongly held and where you feel strong.

When I got into the starting gate for the second run, I felt I was in this deep, still pool of black water. Now, that's a very powerful image because black is all color and the deep, still pool is the gathering of all energy. Then, when the count came down—three, two, one, go—I was released. For me that meant I was able to win the second run with a margin of two seconds over the other racers and create the best combined time to win the Gold Medal. If I hadn't spent the previous year in Europe racing and practicing extension with each new experience, I don't know what I would have done to recover from my mistake in the first run. Everybody can experience extension in their own way. But, without nurturing spirit it does not occur.

The same applies to the excellent people I've met who work with natural resources. If you have a calling for something, that tells me that you've got a deeper part of yourself engaged in it. You just didn't go through college and say, "Well, I could do this or I could do that or I'll flip a coin to decide what kind of job to take." A calling is much more serious. It takes courage and courage is such a big word. I want to see courage from a good professional as much as I do from a good athlete. I expect them to be able to make tough calls and be able to say "You should be doing it this way, not the other way." Then be able to offer explanations for that decision. How do you get courage? Well, you have to believe in something. Your belief system brings conviction and conviction is the entry point for courage. Then you have to nurture the spirit and practice extension.

Only rarely do you have a moment in time when what you say and what you do truly makes an abrupt change. An example of how things often move slowly is Fish and Game here in California. Even though they're a group of people I'm very fond of, they're a many-headed hydra. First of all, they're laboring in an outdated system. Agency support comes from selling fishing and hunting licenses. That means every time they impose a new limit on the amount of hunting or fishing they lower their income by reducing license sales. They also risk angering their constituents who will then get their legislators, who control the agency budget, to intervene. So, that's a built-in conflict from day one.

Then you've got the governor making totally political appointments to the Fish and Game Commission—people like cattlemen, hunters, environmentalists, and the like who are supposed to represent their own group on the Commission. That is a recipe for constant conflict. It is not very practical to think they'll act much like a team or a board of directors pulling for the same objective. For Fish and Game that constant conflict can make the system schizophrenic. Fish and Game staff can be looking at a deer herd and know, inside themselves, that they should be saying, "This is not a year that we should be letting anybody go out and hunt." But, they also know they're not going to get that because there is pressure to keep selling the licenses that support the agency. They also know that is not a message the hunting faction on the Commission wants to hear. As a staff person a pretty natural response is to make a recommendation that you think is the best you can hope for, not what is needed to address the real need. The incentives are all screwed up.

And in some issues staff are trapped by mistakes of the past. I'm thinking about the native frogs we have here in the Sierras [mountain yellow-legged frogs, (*Rana muscosa*)]. Fish and Game has stocked lakes in the high country for years because the packers—they are a real driver here—want fish in the back country for their clients to catch. There never were fish in these lakes before stocking. As it turned out the stocked fish will eat the tadpoles. If Fish and Game stops stocking, the people who want fish will cause no end of grief. If they keep stocking, people who care about frogs will kick up a fuss and the agency's endangered species problems will get worse. Fish and Game is trapped. Making things worse for Fish and Game staff are the independent scientists doing the research and writing that is defining the link between frog declines and the Department's actions. These independent scientists are now a significant source of competition with the Department's expertise who undermine the credibility of the Department's science. There's the dilemma for an employee in Fish and Game who wants to make things better. They're being challenged on both the merit of and the technical justification for their decisions.

As a citizen who cares about keeping natural things natural, there is an upside to the frog story despite the problems it's created for my friends in Fish and Game. It reveals how just making something visible can cause the system to begin changing. Until someone made the link between frogs and fish stocking apparent, no one even thought about it. Now we are starting to have the right debate. Now we have a choice. Awareness has been the key. Unfortunately, for current Department employees, they are now managing a dilemma made by the Department's own past. They are trapped by their own history.

Sometimes you experience a defeat to build toward a long-term success. As a county supervisor I went down to defeat in a lot of four to one votes. The interesting thing about many of my lone votes is that they stood the test of time. It's a combination of your own personal values but also there's strategy. When you lose on these votes like I did, you've also raised the issue to a greater level of awareness. Then, when it comes up again, you can raise it another notch, even with another losing vote. Eventually there is general acceptance that you've got a real issue here. Then you can start making a change. But it can be slow. That's one frustration. There is a difference between losing a single vote and winning over the long haul.

It's like when they started talking about ecosystem management in the Forest Service. They didn't have a clue what it meant and there was active resistance. Then, as they talked about it more, both understanding and acceptance grew. Then talking started changing to action on the ground. Now there is no question that ecosystem management will be a part of what the Forest Service does but how far it will go is still uncertain. At some point it will just become commonplace—just an every day kind of function. But, like most things, there was initial resistance.

That is where activists come in. An activist, in many cases, is why things start moving. Usually there is a trigger. A problem or injustice makes a group of people madder than hell. That starts getting other people's attention. Eventually, after enough people engage, a change happens. Think back to an issue such as women's right to vote. When Elizabeth Stanton and Susan B. Anthony started agitating for women's rights they were considered strident, but they could articulate the simple injustice of not being equal to men who were making all the decisions. Initially, the men would just pat them on the head and say, "Listen, little woman, go home." So, a next logical step was for them to get more active, which for them meant marching in the streets. So, that's a role for the activist—making people with power aware of the abuses of that power; puncturing the comfort of the present situation.

Activists really have a very important role to play in natural resource management. They are thorns in your side but they can also be a voice of conscience. A smart manager realizes a couple of things when an activist confronts them. First is to accept that your first, natural response is to resist the activist—usually by denying the legitimacy of the claims. A manager should just expect that reaction in yourself and in your employees. The second thing is that there may be useful information buried behind an activist's behavior. The people who denied women the vote did so for what they saw as a bunch of good excuses and could not see, or did not want to see, a pretty basic issue—injustice. So the existence of activists can be symptom of underlying problems.

Today, a good manager is willing to accept that not everybody in the world thinks the same way. The many different people who care about natural resources have different values. They want different things. How do you bring that together so people feel they have been heard, they feel they have been treated fairly, and they feel their issues are being taken care of? The world is not out there to have the same point of view. In the final analysis it is the resource manager's job to work with these differences. But, therein also lies the opportunity–getting the diversity of people who care about natural resources to work together when you can. When you can't, it is getting past those moments of fear that set up barriers inside ourselves, remaining true to your ethical core, and showing the courage to take the bold action needed.

It is interesting the way one lives their life by personal belief where, in kinds and degrees, danger and daring appear as true measurements of the mastery of any practice. In my competitive skiing I had to understand fear as a process through which I could extend the practice of my own daring. Fear was an opening of possibility, desire, reward, and faith. It was one thing to gather the instruments of my competitive skiing and another to dare to use them. There is much to be discovered by going through the slot toward mastery. You find that slot through the practice of extending yourself.

5
Bern Shanks - Always Advocating

... professionals are advocates, even when they remain silent.
– Bern Shanks

Bern Shanks has gotten around more than most conservationists. In addition to a Ph.D. in natural resources development from Michigan State University, Shanks has worked for two governors, four universities, and federal, state, and municipal governments. He has been a gubernatorial advisor, a university professor, and the chief executive officer of local and state government agencies. He has held jobs in eight of the western states and several national parks. His responsibilities have included land, water, fish, wildlife, and environmental management. Shanks has authored three books and over 50 articles on environmental policy and natural resource management. His honors include Trout Unlimited's 1997 Conservationist of the Year award. He has held board appointments for The Wilderness Society and Defenders of Wildlife. When interviewed Bern was working for the U.S. Geological Survey, Biological Resource Division, Arlington, VA.

Reflecting on 30+ years experience as both professor and practitioner, Shanks describes advocacy as inherent in the work of natural resource professionals. In his various academic and executive jobs Shanks not only experienced first hand the advisor's challenge, he also supervised staff with high-profile advisory responsibilities. Shanks took on the 'sagebrush rebellion,' a story he tells in his own book, *This Land Is Your Land* (Shanks 1984). He began speaking out against the rebellion when he was a professor of Natural Resources at Utah State University—a position he was encouraged to vacate after sagebrush rebels made their displeasure of his activism known to University administrators. Shanks had gone public with a sweeping critique of the rebels' broad agenda to take control of public lands in the West. His critique pointed out that the real meaning of the rebellion was a massive transfer of broad public land values and material wealth to private interests—not a popular message in Utah. Shanks drew into sharp focus this gifting of public resources to the rebels by using pointed rhetoric. As a lightening-rod critic of the sagebrush rebellion Shanks attracted predictable lightening strikes. In his book (Shanks 1984), Bern said, "The sagebrush rebellion pointed out a fundamental weakness in how the public lands had been protected. . . . The sagebrush rebels repeated the lie of 'returning' federal lands to the states and were not refuted by the agencies, challenged by the media, or corrected by the academics." He begins by telling what happened and why.

The sagebrush rebellion was an organized resistance, mostly in the West, to federal policies on the public's land. It came to a head as a movement to give federal lands back to the states during Ronald Reagan's presidency. The Utah legislature actually passed a bill laying claim to all the federal lands in Utah. Reagan supported the rebellion through James Watt, his Secretary of the Interior. When the sagebrush rebellion erupted in the 1970s, I was on the faculty of Utah State University teaching federal land policy. I went around for months grousing about how stupid the whole idea of the rebellion was and how their underlying premises were totally wrong. A colleague said, "Well, you should give a seminar." So I did.

The rebellion was unique because it was concentrated in the West. At the time people in the East didn't know what the rebellion was. It was really centered on states with a lot of federal land such as Utah, Nevada, and Arizona. Because agencies like the Bureau of Land Management were responsible for much of this land they became a target. The sagebrush rebels were even threatening BLM employees.

A powerful rebel in Utah was a guy named Calvin Black. He'd been in the Legislature and had been a very influential county commissioner. Black was making statements that BLM employees should travel in groups because it wasn't safe to travel alone. The rebels labeled BLM employees as jack-booted thugs. Then western political leaders, like Senator Hatch [Utah], started using the same tactic calling federal employees dictators who were out-of-touch federal bureaucrats trying to, ". . . tell us what to do." And it worked. Many BLM people, especially in rural areas, feared for their well-being because the talk was so venomous. In my seminar I laid out the history that the public domain was not something that happened by accident in American history. The Continental Congress debated for a year about what to do with those lands. They made a conscious decision that there would be significant federal land ownership. In the next two hundred years there were thousands of laws passed that carried out that decision. So there was a very rich history that established the legitimacy and purpose for federal land ownership.

I was also up on the rebels' arguments and their rhetoric, partly because they used canned phrases, like, "You should give the lands back to the states." I simply posed some obvious questions back. "Give federal lands back to the states? Maybe we should give it back to Mexico. The U.S. federal government seized these lands from Mexico, they didn't seize it from the state of Utah or the Utah territory. Maybe the issue is we should give the lands back to the Indians. Who are the rightful owners of these lands? Certainly not the states. It was the U.S. Marine Corps in Mexico City that gave us California and Nevada and Utah and Arizona and New Mexico and part of Colorado. It wasn't the Utah National Guard."

One of the ironies I pointed out in my seminar was that the College of Natural Resources at Utah State had more alumni who were BLM employees than any other university. Our product, as the College of Natural Resources, was our alumni. These federal employees were applying the skills we taught them. They were not jack-booted thugs running wild over the range. The University entering into the public debate about their performance seemed like the responsible thing to do. Remaining silent was condoning the dishonest criticisms being heaped on our alumni by the rebels. I thought the University had that kind of responsibility but the University and my colleagues did not act. Years later some of these same colleagues talked about how terrible were the things that happened in the sagebrush rebellion. But at the time they sat on their hands.

Attending the seminar was a stringer for the *New York Times*. He met with me after my talk and said, "You know, you've really got some good stuff. If you package it a little different your message will really get out. Here's what the newspapers will pick up on . . ." I took his advice and really worked at making my message vivid. That's when I started talking about the sagebrush rebellion being like the Four Horsemen of the Apocalypse riding around the West. But this time the Four Horsemen are named Dishonesty, Slander, Hysteria, and Greed—these are the real forces behind the rebellion. The press is compelled to give both sides of a story, so, as the only one speaking out against the rebellion, I soon became the source reporters would interview for that opposing view. I started getting quoted in newspaper stories which spawned more invitations to speak, mostly from environmental groups. Eventually these groups organized a rally on the steps of the Idaho state capital and I was the featured speaker; this time in front of network television cameras. In the course of a few months I gave this talk 25 or 30 times around the western states. It was my first experience with a little notoriety.

When the sagebrush rebellion broke out of the rural west and began to be picked up by urban newspapers like those in Denver and Salt Lake City and by the national papers in the East, what got reported? Reporters sought out the weather-burned rancher running a thousand head of cattle on a BLM lease, who was complaining about having to take some of them off the range. Out would come these gripping human-interest stories of the hard-working cowboy losing his life style. There was no reporting that this colorful stereotype had, in reality, been overgrazing public land, not private land, for years and in the process damaging the public's natural resources like wildlife, soil, and riparian environments. What sold was a mythical image—like the photograph on the cover of *Newsweek* showing the Nevada cowboy, rifle in hand, sitting tall on his horse, against the faceless, unfeeling bureaucrats. In my writing and speaking I would say this image was bullshit and that the sagebrush rebels were really on a system of welfare; essentially stealing the public's natural resources. I became more and more identified as the Utah State professor who was a dissenting voice. Before that the sagebrush rebellion got up a head of steam because no one refuted them. No one. Here was me, a Utah State University professor, lambasting the rebellion as bunk. Mine was not a popular message. Local Utah politicians got very upset. Cal Black organized a complaint letter about me signed by the Utah Wool Growers Association, the Cattlemen's Association, and the Farm Bureau. They told my dean that as long as I was on the faculty the University was not going to get a new building for the College of Natural Resources, which was the dean's fondest hope. The president of the University wrote back saying they were taking care of the problem—which was me. I didn't know about these letters until several years later.

As my activities became more public many of my University colleagues were very offended. I can remember one old forestry professor saying, "You've just screwed us for years." The silent and not-so-silent criticism from colleagues was painful and very ironic because universities pride themselves on academic freedom. I watched my university colleagues wax eloquent in a faculty meeting about academic freedom and how no one should interfere with what they said in the classroom. Then the next day criticize me for speaking in front of five hundred environmentalists and the media on something as politically volatile as the sagebrush rebellion. I could talk to 25 scientists in some obscure meeting where there was no press coverage and say anything I wanted. That would be fine. Saying the same thing in public was a different matter. It's context. My university colleagues breathed a sigh of relief when I left. I guess I learned that organizations, even universities, do not like freedom of thought if there are embarrassing consequences.

A fact of work life these days is that politicians can always take cheap shots at public agencies. That is the safest, most successful way to put yourself in the media. They know that criticizing public managers makes them look good to their constituents, like they're crusaders. But the reality is that agency leaders will never respond. Well, never is probably too strong. But they will respond only to the most outrageous charges. When leaders of the sagebrush rebellion, people like Orrin Hatch, would talk about the jack-booted thugs in the BLM and Forest Service, he knew perfectly well that agency leaders would not confront him. After all, the forest supervisor of the Dixie National Forest in Southern Utah is not going to take on a U.S. Senator. Despite state universities in the West being public icons for the notion of resource stewardship, they are inside this same system of unwritten rules. In my case state legislators were also key leaders of the sagebrush rebellion. The

University was not about to take on the people who controlled their budget, despite the rebel's philosophy being at odds with the University's teaching and the rebels attacking our alumni. My university's behavior to not take a stand made sense as a response to these outside pressures, even if it was at odds with our stated principles.

The dean, who was a professor of range management and a son of Texas ranching, had given talks expressing sympathy with the rebels. He also had a hope that one of his legacies would be a new building for the College of Natural Resources. The rebels' letter saying that, ". . . as long as Shanks is there, you're not going to get a new building," stood to end this hope. Organizations are first concerned about their own survival and they measure this on an annual basis, usually with the budget. That's the reality that administrators face. That's how they get those marginal increases to create new programs or, in this case, a new building. That is how an administrator's success is measured and how symbols of their lasting contribution are created. Something that gets in the way is defined as a problem.

I'm sure part of it was that I was too extreme and too blunt in my criticisms. Each time the rebels criticized federal managers I responded by ridiculing the critics, saying that they were motivated by greed and selfishness. But for my dean I'm sure I was a problem. I brought undue attention to the University. I was acting outside the norm, even though my academic job was to teach about these larger political and economic forces that influence public land management. In most western universities there is one faculty position designated as their resource policy position. I had that job at Utah State. It wasn't like I was speaking out on technical issues of forestry or range or wildlife. My job description meant I was supposed to comment on the public policy aspects of land management. They just didn't like my message or my going public with it. I met Bruce Babbitt during that time. He was the one western governor [Arizona] who decided to take on the rebellion. His staff stayed in touch with me and Babbitt started using a lot of my stock phrases.

After several months of activism I had a performance evaluation. For the first time in my academic career I was rated unsatisfactory. Later I counted up that I had more pages of published articles that year than the rest of the twelve faculty in the Department of Forestry combined. I also had better student evaluations than the other faculty. But the University said I was not making adequate progress toward tenure. It was part of a decision, I think made at the University president's level, to show me the door.

When I left to go to work in California, the rebel leaders bragged that they got me fired. Well, I didn't get fired but life was uncomfortable and I wasn't going to get any salary increases and I wasn't going to be welcome at the University. This was just an example of solving the problem by getting rid of those who point out the problem.

One of the ironies was that my choice to speak out landed me a speaking engagement on a panel with the Secretary of Resources from California, Huey Johnson. He prides himself on being a flamboyant, radical environmentalist. This was the first time somebody on a panel was more radical than he was. Huey came up to me afterwards and said, "I've got a master's degree from Utah State. I can't believe that any professor from that place is saying these things." I said, "They're trying to fire me." And he said, "Well, you should come to work for me." And that's eventually what happened. So another irony arising from the University pressuring me that turned into a personal success was that it moved me into the political process. I went from this obscure, associate professor at Utah State to being one of the senior advisors to California's Secretary of Resources, an agency with fourteen thousand employees. The first night I worked in California I ended up going to a party in Sacramento. Huey introduced me to Governor Jerry Brown and had me brief him on the sagebrush rebellion. I was like a kid in a candy store in terms of an opportunity to influence natural resource policy.

During the ascent of the sagebrush rebellion several free market economists weighed in. A couple I knew formed an institute at Montana State funded by grants from various cattlemen's associations and conservative think tanks like the Heritage Foundation and the Manhattan Institute. They wrote and spoke on how the best conservation was by a free market system, which gave a certain intellectual legitimacy to the rebels' rhetoric. One of the things they did very, very effectively was challenge the basic premise behind public lands.

Their impact was ironic because Marion Clawson, the second director of the BLM, wrote a few dozen books on the history of public lands that you can find in any library. One of his conclusions was that the argument over disposing of public lands was over. Americans now accepted the map of the United States with its public lands permanently in place. The free market economists and conservative think tanks challenged this premise of public land ownership. They did this by articulating an economic theory that the private sector was a better conservationist than the public sector. Environmentalists, at that time, were simply unable to refute that argument. Any time you have a one-sided, intellectual rationale in the public debate, that single argument takes on a legitimacy. And no matter what the question about a public resource, the free marketers had one answer—privatization. No one refuted that claim.

To me those arguments were dishonest but the media picked up on the portrayal of the rancher as not only a rebel but also as a better conservationist than some faceless bureaucrat. They'd reference higher value of private land and attribute that difference to better conservation. The reality was just the opposite. Private ranch land in the West was in worse shape, not in better shape, than public lands. If you dug deeper, the simple fact was that the best quality lands in the West were long ago creamed off to private ownership.

In that environment it was difficult to articulate the public's values and easy to articulate private values as being equivalent to the public interest. The rebels' objective was very simple—self-interest. They wrapped this real objective inside the compelling myth of the hard-working cowboy who became the poster child for the sagebrush rebellion. Then there was systematic and relentless criticism of public managers. Then there was a one-sided debate about free markets being the best conservation approach. Bringing these factors together eroded the long-standing purposes for public land stewardship. But at its core, the rebels were out to make a buck and they didn't want anybody to say they couldn't do so; totally at the expense of the public's resources and broader public values. I don't think I've ever been as fearful in my life as then. It was incomprehensible that America's rich history of public land stewardship, a thing that I valued so much, would potentially be reversed in my lifetime or my son's lifetime.

To explain why it was hard to articulate the value of preserving public land you have to track back to the first and second generations of conservationists in this country. They were broadly educated and had a sense of history, philosophy, and ethics about public land stewardship that was an inseparable part of our democracy. They knew the details about the early history of conservation thinking that led to creating public lands. The explosion of higher education after World War II brought specialized management programs—forestry, range, wildlife, fisheries, watershed management, and the like. Then the environmental movement in the late sixties created an explosion of environmental jobs that further took conservation into a series of specialties. We've developed a generation of managers who were specialists about technical details but lost the ability to advocate for broader public values in management. In my experience with the sagebrush rebellion these new conservationists were invariably bright, knowledgeable, and very capable people. They had more expertise and more skills than earlier generations of professionals. But they did not have the breadth or the sense of history to deal with the challenge to the fundamental premises of public land ownership mounted by the rebels and their intellectual hired guns. They rightly regarded the rebels' arguments as superfluous and crazy and extreme, but they couldn't refute them. If free market economists had to confront Teddy Roosevelt he would have pounded the table for an hour articulating in very compelling, democratic, inspirational words why they were full of shit. We didn't have anybody who could or would do that during the sagebrush rebellion.

On the one side were values that were easy to measure—acres of land, number of cows, loss of income, and so forth. These were easy for the press to report and sell to their readers. Conversely, the values of public lands were not easy to measure and the press had a hard time articulating these because they are more abstract. As a result readers had difficulty identifying with these values. The average American reader has trouble visualizing the meaning of lost top soil or trashed riparian areas but has an immediate, personal, and visceral understanding of what it means to lose a job. So you had a calculus problem where you could easily show tangible losses to the hard-working, new American rebel but on the other side of the ledger things were fuzzy.

Also in play was an asymmetry—concentration of the benefits versus diffusion of impacts. The rebels' cause benefitted a few people. Their chance to gain big created an incentive to get involved and spend money on the rebellion. On the other side the costs of transferring public land values to the rebels were widely diffused among a broad array of taxpayers who never felt any real pain. You are always disadvantaged when there is concentration of benefits but a diffusion of the costs, especially when these are abstract and hidden from view.

Eventually, the sagebrush rebellion lost credibility and it became safe to join in the criticism. When James Watt, who was a leader in the rebellion, became Secretary of Interior there was about three years of controversy over his management. By the end of Watt's tenure he was considered a joke and there was a general sense that the rebels were right-wing extremists and a tool of the industries profiting from the public's resources. The rebel reign actually reinforced environmental organizations who capitalized on the rebellion to spur a tremendous increase in membership and budgets. Somewhere I have a book of nothing but Watt cartoons where every cartoonist in the country was laughing at him. His downfall certainly was an example of how that pendulum swung back to a different point. At that point it became safe to criticize the rebels and only then did my Utah State colleagues start to engage. Unfortunately, by then a great deal of damage was done.

Most of the people in leadership, rather than say anything about the sagebrush rebellion, simply did nothing. The dean was one of the few people who did speak. He would go to the annual meeting of the Cattlemen's Association and express sympathy for their concerns. He wouldn't endorse the sagebrush rebels, but it would be messages like, "I understand what you're going through and it's terrible what you're being subjected to." But for most of the University people in a position to speak knowledgeably, their response was just silence.

One of the things I learned from this experience was that we should be very clear and very explicit about why resources like public lands are important and why public ownership makes sense. Because there was that kind of vacuum, the rebels' ideas became accepted as the more American principle for managing public lands. In reality, they just worshiped greed. If you work for a public land management agency, you should be able to clearly and concisely articulate why public lands are important to this generation and the next generation. Very, very clear and very, very compelling. A lot of public managers in responsible positions still cannot do that. If you don't do it or if the agencies won't do it, then the public's lands are always vulnerable to some crazy movement like the sagebrush rebellion. In contrast, think about people like Teddy Roosevelt and Gifford Pinchot. Teddy and Gifford would tell the story of good versus evil. They had simple, understandable, democratic reasons for the value of public land stewardship. We didn't and the rebels gained ground.

Mike: You obviously had to confront the question of staff speaking out in public. You did it during the sagebrush rebellion but in your other jobs you've also supervised professionals who did it. What is your take on the role of professionals and advocacy?

When I was a young faculty person, I argued with my colleagues about advocacy versus science. My experience is that the traditional natural resource disciplines, particularly range management, forestry, and I think to a lesser extent wildlife management, have built-in advocacy principles. A lot of my academic colleagues were, through their technical discipline, really advocates for the traditional use of resources—maximum sustained yield in forestry, the idea that we should improve rangeland to grow more cows—that sort of thing. They cloaked their arguments in science but really, they had a very traditional, utilitarian worldview.

I've seen a kind of evolution toward viewing scientific advice as important but not the dominant statement of values guiding management of the public's natural resources. Now there is more emphasis on broader ecosystem ideas, like the ideas of Leopold. The example I am thinking about is fishery managers' historic faith that we could improve things with hatcheries, of course with an eye to producing only desirable fish. Now we see there are lot of pitfalls in that thinking.

It seems like most of my career has straddled the period where the traditional resource professions—forestry, range, wildlife, and fisheries are struggling because of the implicit advocacy inherent in the narrow focus of their discipline. There's been a lot of progress with students now coming out of universities with a much broader and more integrated recognition that other objectives, like diversity and ecological integrity, should be appreciated as values in themselves. Managers still very much focus on commodity production, but things seem to be changing.

A lot of people in natural resources don't recognize that professionals are advocates, even when they remain silent. Consequently, whether you choose to speak out or remain silent, it is important to understand the basic assumptions behind your advocacy. Forestry courses used to talk about multiple use. Now they also talk about sustainability. There are value assumptions behind both of those management objectives. We could say sustainability is a biological principle, but, in what context, what sort of time frame, for whose benefit, etc.? In most cases we're talking about public resources and for me that embodies certain philosophical and ethical principles that are very different than if you're working for Ford or General Motors or Weyerhaeuser Timber Company.

One thing distinguishing public managers is the visibility of our management. There is an expectation that professionals ought to use the best science. Most people coming out of universities are pretty good at this part of their job. They've had training in statistics, know how to set up an experiment, and how to get a credible scientific result. That is the descriptive side of management. The difficult part is with topics that are prescriptive, like giving recommendations that are in the greater public interest. Do you manage for commercial fisherman? sport anglers? tribes?

ranchers? farmers? the resource itself? or do you have an ethical obligation to assure that the next generation has the same resource opportunity we have today? Most managers are not comfortable talking openly about their management obligation to future generations and most political discussions avoid this question.

Part of this problem is a time-frame issue. We see this with Northwest salmon. There you're managing species with conservation needs that are longer than the planning horizon of elected officials or government budgeting—which are two-, four-, or six-year cycles. Compared to election and budget cycles is the reality of a life cycle like that of chinook salmon. It takes a decade or more to recover that species. The mismatch is much worse for something like old-growth forests. Those planning horizons are hundreds of years. It is tough to maintain political resolve with that disconnect. Decisions get skewed toward the present.

Another issue holding back conservation is the sense of isolation felt by advocates who are more assertive. If you're a strong advocate, the people you work with every day can make you feel like an outcast. It may not be overt. There are lots of little, subtle things that tell you you're not fitting in. It is, of course, most problematic in a small, rural town where friends and neighbors can also create social pressure on not only you but also on your family. I am thinking about towns like Elko, Nevada; Miles City, Montana; or Yuma, Arizona. Many government managers decide that life in these communities and working in beautiful environments like Yellowstone and the Arizona desert are more important than a traditionally successful career which will usually take you to an urban center. In small, rural communities, taking an aggressive, visible conservation stand can cause you and your family to pay a price. That is a strong incentive to be meek. My first solution to this dilemma was to leave the Park Service and go to graduate school and then get a job at a university. My hope was to achieve independence and be able to influence public land management in a new way. But when the sagebrush rebellion came along I had the same experience in the university as I did as an agency employee. It is a part of any institution and I guess it is good to recognize that going in.

I think there are many strategies for those who advocate. It depends on a person's personality, skills, and commitment. It also depends on your employer. Some are more tolerant than others. A lot of times it depends on how the person presents his or her dissent. A few of the scientists I work with here at USGS are advocates through a lifetime of focusing on a particular species and being able to articulate the biological bottlenecks for the success with that species. They're quite open about it. They do a lot of outside educational work through reporters, popular magazines, public speaking—that sort of thing. There are boundaries but as long as they don't go beyond their science and data and they don't speculate too much, they are generally left alone to speak their mind. Others are more out front. These are the people who more publicly voice strong opinions about right and wrong public policy. Agencies have a mixed tolerance for these advocates. Then there are people who are confrontational. Tolerance tends to be thin for these people. They make their conservation principles clear and persuasive. Their goal is to bring along their team members and their organization when they can. In the end, though, they're willing to leave others behind as they speak their mind. Often these more overt people become one of the legends of an organization. One strategy, that wasn't available when you and I were starting, is to work for an environmental advocacy organization. There is an array of these from the more conservative Nature Conservancy to the more assertive like Greenpeace with plenty of very respectable alternatives in between.

The advocates who most excite reprisals are the covert advocates inside a traditional management organization. These people often pay a price, both emotional and careerwise. There's a whole array of tactics if you adopt that strategy. The most notorious is leaking information. Another, often unacknowledged tactic, is simply resisting change that you disagree with. A more formal version of this is a legal approach, like using formal whistleblower laws.

Whatever your advocacy approach, speaking out means testing the boundary lines. A lot of times something you do is too visible and you elicit jealousy from one of your bosses or it's defined as activity that is beyond your job description. For example, it might be okay for your boss to be quoted in a newspaper but as an apprentice biologist that is not acceptable. The boundaries may be invisible but they are real. To a large extent the institution defines what is and is not appropriate even if they do this by their behavior instead of by telling you. There is an expectation, even if it is implicit, about you not being too public, too much out in front. Here at USGS the Biological Resources Division is primarily a research agency. No one is supposed to advocate anything, just provide scientific information. But we have one biologist, David Mattson, who is a grizzly bear expert. He believes that the bear population is not growing as fast as other researchers think and he is vocal about it. Mattson has created a grievous sin in this institution by talking to Todd Wilkinson who wrote *Science Under Siege*, a book that looks at government agencies stifling scientific findings [Wilkinson 1998]. It is difficult to know if the rub is about Mattson speaking in public or about the technical merits of his argument. But the revealing part of his story is that the advocacy question is part of the corporate culture of every conservation organization. You have to make some effort to understand and know the boundaries and then reconcile yourself with choosing whether or not to cross them.

   Mike: How do professionals recognize an opportunity for real change?

   The agents of big change in the conservation movement and, later, the environmental movement, were individuals that had real broad, classical educations. They weren't specialists. A hero of mine is George Perkins Marsh. He was President Zachary Taylor's ambassador to Arabia. Later, Abraham Lincoln made him the first U.S. minister to the new kingdom of Italy. He was a scholar who spoke something like a dozen languages. He could read another eight or ten. He was just an incredible cosmographer with an insatiable curiosity. He knew that Cleopatra built her navy with cedar from the mountains of Lebanon. He'd ride up there on a mule and there were no trees and no history of reforestation and make the connection to Egypt losing its sea power. He'd read ancient Greek texts on how they had watershed protection programs, including the death penalty for grazing sheep and goats in a watershed. He'd look at the contemporary Grecian watersheds and see sheep and goats and rocks—no soil, no grass, no brush, no trees–just rocks, and make the connection to contemporary water problems in Greece. In Vermont, where he was from, when the Industrial Revolution got underway he observed all manner of junk being dumped into the rivers. Well, he'd get some salmon, put them in a barrel and then dump in this stuff coming out of the factories and guess what? The salmon would go belly up. Again, he would make a cause and effect connection. Because he read so many languages, was broadly educated, and was such a curious person, he could put all this information, historical as well as his personal observations, into context. He wrote *Man and Nature* [later, *The Earth as Modified by Human Action,* Marsh 1885]. A lot of people credit that book as the real start of science-based conservation. Gifford Pinchot, John Muir, Teddy Roosevelt—that whole bunch of first-generation conservationists were dramatically influenced by Marsh's book. Only somebody with his incredible breadth could have put it together. The

people who followed Marsh, like Pinchot and Muir as well as the generation of conservation leaders after them that I knew, like the Murie family and Bob Marshall, were still people who were very broadly educated,
who had a very strong knowledge of history, and had a very strong sense
of ethics and philosophy.

With a very broad perspective like that you can recognize where we
are in time and the historical evolution of conservation. Today, because
we're trained narrowly and as specialists, we access only a small piece of
the conservation picture. If you're not reading widely and studying a
larger context, you just do not have the knowledge base to diagnose the
existence of a change opportunity.

Change is most possible during a crisis of some sort. That's when
you need a vision. Some leaders will even try to manufacture a crisis to
move change along. The crisis can be about any number of things—
budget woes, resource collapse, social stress— but a perception of crisis
often is an opportunity in disguise. When there is a panic over the hole
in the side of your ship, the person with an idea of how to plug it is given
leadership.

Change can be precipitated at other times when the scientific theory
or the tenet of faith driving management gets out on a cul-de-sac and
then collapses. Clear-cutting as a dominant land management style in
the West is an example. The hatchery production model for salmon in
the Northwest is another example. Lichatowich [1999] has probably told
that story better than anybody. Dams are entering that critique now.
We're just beginning to make a major change in how we think about
large reservoirs and dams. When the technical underpinnings of management are kicked out, people start looking for something to replace
them—another opportunity for the person with a vision to cause change
in the direction they think is important.

Sometimes a critical mass of information is forming around an issue
and represents a change opportunity. A symptom is a problem that remains unrecognized or there is denial that a problem even exists. In
this case progress results from raising awareness or busting through
the denial. Perhaps the best example is Rachel Carson exposing the
impact of DDT and other hard pesticides in Silent Spring [Carson 1962].
Few things in our lifetime have been more dramatic. Here is this little
old lady who loved birds and had a solid grasp of science but was not
considered a real researcher. She comes to the issue as a bit of an outsider able to see what insiders can't or won't look at. She has the skill to
put the critical mass of information together and it spells out a stinging

blow to accepted management belief. Of course, it helped that she had the gift of being able to write so well. This is an example of the established management community denying the meaning of scientific information until an outsider makes the problem visible in a way that could no longer be ignored.

I've always found the S-shaped curve a useful way to look at change. The horizontal axis is time and the vertical axis is the percentage of people who accept the belief that we have a serious issue needing attention. At the lower end of the curve are early adopters. These people are first to recognize the problem. But awareness or acceptance grows slowly at first. After that there is a period of a rapidly increasing acceptance. Then the curve tapers off at the top with those people, the conservative extreme, who refuse to admit there is problem. The timing of the curve can be compressed in some cases or can be spread out over decades, but that sort of evolving awareness seems to exist. To create positive change it is helpful to have a sense of where you are on that curve.

Another way something becomes an issue is when there is a perception of scarcity. The extreme is a perception of imminent loss. It also helps if there is some drama. With DDT a critical mass of scientific information was coming together but the drama was that bald eagles and peregrine falcons—these spectacular, charismatic critters—were very scarce and that was combined with graphic images of eggs breaking in the nest. That drama helped capture the public's imagination and in so doing quickly moved the issue up the S-shaped curve to greater awareness and acceptance. Historically, we've experienced this with the magnificent bison herds of the Great Plains. Their collapse to near extinction was so dramatic that it stimulated a lot of the early conservation efforts. The loss of passenger pigeons did the same thing but we were too late. More recently we're seeing this same phenomenon with amphibians. What has helped is not so much the data on the demise of amphibians but the images of six-legged frogs, particularly when school children are making these discoveries. It certainly helps to have images of appealing players making dramatic discoveries.

A critical question is how people are moved to acceptance. Down at the lower end of the curve the early adopters have the ability to perceive there's a problem. These people can be technical specialists and scientists, but, often they are perceptive citizens whose concern comes out when they say things like, "Hey, we can't continue this." The first real challenge is getting to the people in the middle of the curve. In our modern world the media are critical in moving an issue up to the middle of the curve. When *Silent Spring* came out Americans didn't accept that there was a downside to pesticides. We were way down the acceptance curve. When the media picked up the drama of the story we were high up the curve in a matter of months. A variety of things can trigger the media. In the case of *Silent Spring*, Stewart Udall was Secretary of Interior and he knew Rachel Carson and her work. There were also a lot of environmental leaders who respected her and seized onto her work. Recruiting these prominent people who regularly talked to the media helped. Acceptance is sometimes triggered by a media-frenzy event like the *Exxon Valdez* oil spill or the Santa Barbara blowout in the sixties. Other times it can be an event like the first Earth Day. In this case the scale of the event was the drama and the media responded with hundreds of newspaper, magazine, and television stories. In our modern world the media are an important force.

Getting to the point of 100 percent acceptance is always tough because the top of the curve is where the entrenched opposition lives. They're either unable to understand or have such an economic or psychological stake that they feel grave risk. They're the tobacco companies on lung cancer. They're the chemical companies on DDT. They're the fishing companies and Atlantic cod. Unfortunately, you really don't get into serious discussions about solutions until you're well up near the top of the curve, where the most opposed people reside. At some point there's overwhelming awareness of the problem and support for a solution. Only at that point does it become safe for the political process in America to act. Until then the narrow interests in the opposition have more power in the political process.

A professional's biggest opportunity probably lies in the section of the curve where there is growing awareness as an issue moves out of a narrow technical definition and the public first starts learning about the issue. That's the most obvious place for the technical person because people who know the details and who are considered credible are in demand as information sources. The audiences may vary; it might be school kids and their teachers, it might be a science reporter for a newspaper, or it might be key political leaders, but, once there is eagerness to learn, professionals with information can really move things up the curve.

A professional's role also changes over time depending on where we are on the curve. What is appropriate to say and do when an issue is new may not be appropriate in the middle or towards the end of the acceptance curve. It also depends on the kind of job you have. If you're a manager or if you're involved in the policy end of things then you're probably going to get involved at the top of the curve as pressure mounts to sort out the choices that will work to fix things. If you're a researcher or scientist, you're probably going to be more involved near the beginning.

It is clear to me that to be successful as change agents the next generation of resource professionals will need more breadth. Less focus on preparing for a narrow technical career as a wildlife manager, fisheries biologist, forester, range manager and greater ability to work across different discipline lines and with this whole phenomenon of social change. In terms of management skills government has hitched its wagon to the management revolution driven by corporate America. A lot of those management skills are going to be useful for the resource professional. Skills like good communications, the ability to assimilate information and knowledge from diverse fields, and strategic thinking in an uncertain world.

One thing that will be different is that government decision making will continue to become more fragmented. It will involve more people and organizations who are growing further apart in their world views about the 'right' way to manage natural resources. The proliferation of information available to far more people will create a work environment where information will shift as a source of power from the resource manager to more of a source of empowerment for stakeholders. Successful resource managers are going to be less the technical expert and become more of a process coordinator who can mediate inside this divided work environment. And all of this is occurring inside a work environment where trust in government and trust in corporations to do the right thing has significantly eroded.

Although I get discouraged at times, I have been surprised in my life how quickly we can move from the bottom to the top of the acceptance curve. We've done it on dams in the last few years. It is just remarkable. Here, in my office, there tends to be mostly researchers who are down low on the curve on all kinds of issues, including dams. They are saying, "Yeah, we're going to be tearing down hundreds of dams. How do we get ready? How do we get research money now because when we get there the job is going to be a complex geological, hydrological, and biological problem?" That issue is now moving up the curve and recruiting acceptance beyond these technical professionals. It's been absolutely stunning to me that there is serious discussion about tearing down several big dams in the Snake River. That has surprised me as much as banning DDT astonished me when I was a young student. Back then I had a bumper sticker on my car that said, "Ban DDT." I knew it wasn't going to happen in my lifetime but, you know, it did. My bumper sticker must have worked!

6
Tom Peterson - Self-Determination and Creating Change

Success emerged by shifting to leadership by service,
not by command.
– Tom Peterson

Tom Peterson founded the Center for Climate Strategies to help governments do a better job managing climate change. In a journey from a Christian fellowship club at college to this world-scale issue Peterson has used
the principle of stakeholder self-determination as an effective way to create
change. Tom's professional experience includes a current post as Senior
Research Associate at Penn State University where he teaches Climate
Law and Policy and past positions as Director of Domestic Policy at the
Center for Clean Air Policy; economist with the Environmental Protection
Agency; advisor to the White House Climate Change Task Force; Brookings
Legislative Fellow to U.S. Senator Joe Lieberman; Vice President of Market-

ing for DSL Capital Corporation in Washington, D.C.; Marketing Specialist for the law firm of Brown Maroney and Oaks Hartline in Austin, Texas; Chief of Information and Education for the Arkansas Game and Fish Commission; and Assistant Director of the Arkansas Nature Conservancy.

Having that string of jobs has also been a career management strategy. He made this diversity of jobs accessible by getting three degrees: a BS in Biology from the College of William and Mary, a Master of Environmental Management from Duke University, and an MBA from the University of Texas at Austin. The EPA gave Tom two Gold Medals for his contributions to Pacific Northwest forest and Northern spotted owl management; he won a Bronze Medal from the International Film and Television Festival of New York for co-producing the wildlife documentary series *Natural, Wild and Free*; and he was selected as Conservationist of the Year by the Arkansas Wildlife Federation. Tom's approach to career management features diversity of personal preparation as a way to maximize diversity of job opportunities and as a way to maximize his chance to create change—a skill he has been honing since college.

One of my early experiences with the power of self-determination as a way to create change was in college. I joined a campus Christian fellowship group that was caught up in the intolerance of the Charismatic Movement. Their inability to deal with alternate viewpoints caused the group to dwindle and almost disband. Basically, some members of the group ran off anybody who was not just like them. As a fellow member I asked for the opposite—a group that was an open forum for examining different thinking. That was a case of not being careful what I asked for. I found myself elected their next president! It became my job to create a new way. We shifted to a model featuring self-determination built on respect for different viewpoints and the notion that nobody has the corner on the truth. The group itself decided what it wanted to talk about and how participants would relate to one another. After we changed, membership built back up. That experience was formative because it dealt with the phenomenon of very passionate viewpoints being used to exclude others and reject open inquiry. What I discovered was that people need just the opposite if there is to be any chance of building community.

That lesson came with me when I entered the wildlife profession a few years later. In Arkansas we were trying to develop a new approach to youth environmental education. The most helpful program was Project Wild. As a result of my college experience our spin on Project Wild became teaching kids how to think, not what to think. That has become a recurrent theme in the things I've tried to do in environmental management—giving people an opportunity to think on their own but empowering them to learn how to think, not telling them the correct answer—which is a mistake we made more than once while I was at the Arkansas Game and Fish Commission.

Deer hunting is an important social and economic activity in Arkansas, probably as valuable as the state's soybean crop. When I moved there the big issue was getting deer densities under control and balancing the sex ratio of the herd. Doing that required reforming the regulatory framework. But setting a season to harvest female deer was not acceptable to hunters. A big enforcement problem also existed in south Arkansas where it was tradition to hunt illegally.

In response my agency declared doe hunting seasons in key areas of the state. No attempt to work with the folks affected by the decision. We just announced it and it was resisted strongly. The dyed-in-the-wool hunters in south Arkansas were particularly upset. Steve Wilson, the director of the Game and Fish Commission, told me, "I think we need to do a meeting down there. I'm hearing just awful things about their reaction to our decision." So I put together a public meeting at the Bradley County Courthouse, in the heart of south Arkansas deer-hunting country where many hunters did not accept our management ideas. The local game wardens recommended I not come down because the last public meeting, held 15+ years before, ended with some sort of scuffle involving agency employees.

I'll never forget being terribly sick with the flu the day of the meeting. When I got to the Courthouse, things looked a lot worse than my illness. Several hundred people were waiting—all very upset and all hostile. I started our meeting by saying, "There's just two things I want to tell you tonight. First, I have the flu and I'm not feeling very well. That means I'm really not in the mood to put up with too much aggravation. And second, we haven't come down here to tell you what we're going to do or what we think you ought to do. We're going to tell you what we think we know about the deer situation and options we have for dealing with it. Then I want to hear what you think we ought to do to deal with the problems facing us."

I then laid out basic numbers on deer population status, the expected results from different management approaches, and the conclusion that all this information suggested the agency ought to change regulations. Then I turned to the audience and said, "Let's hear from you." What ensued was several hours of these guys spilling their guts. Ultimately they reached a fair degree of convergence toward our ideas. As the meeting was wrapping up a huge, old guy in bib overalls, who I later learned was a millionaire and owned many thousands of acres down there, stood up and said, "I'm not sure I agree with what you guys think. But the more I hear everybody talking, I think you're probably right. The one thing you government guys need to understand is that this is the first time in my life anybody from your agency came down here and asked us how we felt about anything." We must have struck a chord with him because after the meeting I kept getting Thanksgiving dinner invitations from him! Today the state has instituted sweeping regulatory reform for deer management by working collaboratively with stakeholders.

Another example I encountered where a lack of self-determination was a factor was a really bad land deal the Arkansas Game and Fish Commission got itself into. The wildlife management director was a bit of a traditionalist in his management style. His division felt they didn't need to ask permission from the public or even enter into a dialogue with them before making decisions justified by resource management needs. A timber company owned several hundred thousand acres of land between Little Rock and Pine Bluff, not too far out of the major population center of the state. The area was, effectively, open range. It had been overused and, frankly, abused by the public—excessive and illegal hunting, abusive all terrain vehicle use, and the like. That resource abuse became accepted as part of the culture of the community. The timber company had been pretty gracious about not restricting access but it also didn't want to get the woods burned down; the agency enforcement crew was not able to keep up with the flagrant regulation violations; and deer populations were being overexploited.

The deal cut by the wildlife management division and the timber company was to turn the land into a wildlife management area—the Lost Creek Wildlife Area. That would transfer management of hunting access to the Game and Fish Commission giving it more control to straighten out the problems with deer management. By us taking over access management the timber company's people problem would go away. And the timber company would get visible credit for making their land available to the public even though, realistically, it was already open.

Our wildlife management director at the time discussed the deal privately with the agency director without using our normal procedure for internal review. The decision was to immediately shut down for two years all public access to the several hundred thousand acres of land in the new Lost Creek Wildlife Area. The wildlife division also did not hold a single meeting or do any outreach to the affected stakeholders. Again, the decision was just announced. We kicked everybody off the land with no warning! Needless to say, the many, many thousands of people who used this land as their personal playground were upset—well, they were quite a bit more emotional than that. As head of the agency's public information program I found out when the phones started ringing off the wall.

There was a huge backlash. The legislature convened a public hearing where hundreds of people just screamed bloody murder. "What's going on here?" "Isn't this a democracy?" "We live in the United States." "The Game and Fish Commission just decided to kick us out of here." "Where's our voice?" "Aren't you a public agency?" "Aren't you using our money?" "Don't you work for us?" The agency made things worse by having no response. I went to the hearing as the lone agency representative but only as an observer. The next morning a couple bills showed up in the legislature to eliminate the agency. They were bogus bills. They never were going anywhere. But the point was made. People were upset.

I got the chance to explain to the director that our management of this event was, in my estimation, a fairly serious error. Fortunately, he could understand that we needed to extricate ourselves and start over. He authorized me to withdraw the agency from our commitment to the timber company. When I called the timber company vice-president he said, "Look. We never intended anything like this to happen." So we agreed I would put out an announcement that we were ending the agreement, going back to the drawing board to look at alternatives, and that there would be public consultations.

We typically don't think of hunting as a big social issue. But when I held a press conference the following day to make the announcement, every single radio and television station in Arkansas, it seemed, was there. I talked through the case history of what had happened and some of the errors the agency made in not conferring with the public, issued an apology, announced that the timber company and we were withdrawing from the agreement, and that we were starting over. We then kept our promise to implement a more open process. Ultimately that land was turned into a wildlife management area and the managers and public found a solution that included a mix of restricting access and improving public behavior. Today this land is protected and well managed.

Bradley County Courthouse and Lost Creek were crash and burn experiences. They contained the lesson that public resource managers who think they have the right to do things any way they want risk getting their management plans kicked back in their face. These experiences taught me that people need a chance to see, feel, and come to believe all the information that relates to their issue. To come to their own new understanding, not just be told to accept our understanding. In these two cases most people in the agency thought the issue was about deer. The real issue was about self-determination. When these Arkansas deer hunters participated in an open, fact-based discussion, the light bulbs start coming on in their minds. They came into the issue with one mind set but reached new conclusions. Lasting solutions emerged from the agency and these hunters, kind of, remeshing their gears so separate perspectives started evolving together. Fortunately, we had a director who was sensitive to this lesson and was willing to experiment with a new 'business model' of how we made these kinds of decisions.

Mike: Given what you know now, what principles were violated in the Bradley County Courthouse and Lost Creek case histories?

Transparency, inclusion, respect for others' viewpoints, respect for the basic principles of democracy, commitment to shared decision making, and, I think, fear. Fear by the managers to let others share in the control of wildlife assets. The fear that, somehow, these other people couldn't be trusted to do the right thing. I think it boils down to a matter of respect for others and a faith that, given good information, coaching, and a pathway to put it all into some sensible context, people will make decisions that are in the best public interest.

The agency also had a militaristic culture; very much a command and control chain of command. When I got into the agency I heard an awful lot of management philosophy that came from World War II—a vertical hierarchy that used a closed decision-making approach. "You're the boss. Here are the mechanics of how wildlife management works. You get to make the decisions because you're the keeper of the tools. Just go put them in place." The focus was on execution and not consultation. One of the first things you learn in business school is that's how you go bankrupt. Wildlife management in Arkansas is what motivated me to study marketing research, product development, and corporate strategy when I went to business school. These topics are about all the ways you make things work right with customers.

I think our ability to turn things around after the Bradley County Courthouse and Lost Creek failures came, in good measure, by using a lot of patience. This is the business concept of a conceptual sales cycle—how long it takes to get somebody to change their mind and buy your product. In the 1960s IBM was a pioneer using this concept. In selling office equipment they figured it took eighteen months, on average, to go through the cycle of understanding customer needs and persuasion—for customers to understand the value of a new system of office equipment and then take action. IBM had the patience to do a lot of listening to what customers wanted and needed, a lot of relationship building, and a lot of educating their customers. After about eighteen months customers were ready to actually buy something.

Another business school concept that helps explain the problems we got into with the Bradley County Courthouse and Lost Creek controversies is the psychology of personal commitment. In marketing there are low involvement goods, like buying a ballpoint pen. You don't sweat too much over that level of decision. It is different for high involvement goods, like buying a house. The support people need to make decisions about high involvement goods is dramatically different. Many times in natural resource conservation and environmental management we're asking people to make life style changes. That's a high involvement decision. It may take a while—our version of a conceptual sales cycle and it may take support—our version of selling high involvement goods. You can't get frustrated too quickly.

When the Arkansas Game and Fish Commission started doing some things right with our customers, it paid off. Ultimately the agency got public support for a wildlife sales tax. A good share of that success came from learning how to work with the public. Success emerged by shifting to leadership by service, not by command. It was gratifying to start being recognized as public servants with a very, very important mission that people supported instead of being criticized as managers who just went off and did what they wanted without talking to anyone. To be fair, there is a legitimate way to gather and translate public input into action and you have to be cautious in structuring those mechanisms so they are not manipulative. And there still is an important mission the agency holds as its responsibility. So it is important to make the work you do with stakeholders support the mission, not compromise the mission to

curry favor from customers. Where the purpose and systems were right
I've seen good things happen when stakeholders are made part of the
solution.

What I do now at the Center for Climate Strategies is work on climate change using democratic processes. We go into states and, by working with diverse groups of people who have very different views and
don't get along well together, attempt to build a new response—find a
new way to deal with this very big issue. Environmental management
today is more than ever about getting communities to change. A resource manager who can build community around their issue is more
likely to succeed than one who does not.

**Mike: Any advice about how an individual manager creates the kind of
community change you are thinking about?**

Find opportunities by meshing a natural resource need with people
who can accept that the present situation won't work in the future and
who are ready to accept that they need help—which is you. You become
the 'go-to' person by positioning—being in the right place doing the right
thing that makes you a valuable resource.

One of my teaching partners at Penn State tells the fascinating history of national environmental laws. The states tend to take action long
before the federal government. It's amazing that very few people in
policy making understand that precursor state policy is a major deter-
minant of national environmental policy. Hopefully, the states will do a
lot of good things that role-model a wise national policy on managing
climate change for Congress and the federal agencies. At CCS we feel
that states are sensing the need, that they are willing to accept our
help, and that they are more comfortable exerting a measure of self-
determination rather than waiting to have solutions imposed by the
federal government. With those three things in alignment we believe
there is opportunity to raise the bar of climate management by states.

CCS helps states develop climate-change management plans. Craft-
ing such a plan requires considerable change. The change process we
use is a hybrid of corporate planning, collaborative decision making, and
alternative dispute resolution. What we do is multiparty, multi-issue,
science-intensive mediation. While we adjust our process to fit the par-
ticulars of different clients, we use some guiding principles.

The first principle is to decouple people from their own history. One
major barrier to change is people just accepting hand-me-down beliefs

without much examination. Only a relatively small percentage of folks are insightful about science issues in general and natural science in particular. As a result, most of our change processes need to begin with fact finding. While we begin with that, we simultaneously recognize that our diverse stakeholders come to the table with different views. We try from the outset to broaden their horizons, helping them understand that the problems and solutions are potentially far greater than their first impression. We design processes that keep people from acting unilaterally, which is an enormous barrier. And we want the group to adopt the ground rule that points of view be stated as objectively as possible followed by an explanation, in some factual form, why that view is more accurate. If you think something's too expensive, is that based on a study? If so, what study? Why is this a better way to look at the question in front of us?

Providing a degree of self-determination is a big safety net for the people we work with. It's often very difficult to get the process started. People are afraid that they may have to change. I think an origin of this fear stems from what academicians call rearranging the power dynamic. Democracy does that. It says if you've got a little fiefdom and you join a democratic group that fiefdom could disappear. You may no longer be the big fish in the little pond. That is why self-determination works for us. People are more willing to rearrange the power dynamic when the choices are voluntary. We take on, instead of avoiding, the hard issues but the participants get to decide what they do with these. It's not a situation where the problem is stuck out there and everybody gets to shoot at us. So, our second principle is to confer both responsibilities—problem definition and solution finding—together in a process where people can decide for themselves.

Getting diverse people to a new, shared place is where real change happens. For us it is more than compromise. It is finding a new way, or a constructive alternative that the participants think is better than leaving things alone or splitting the difference. You have to assess whether or not people are willing and able to move beyond their current positions. You've got to be wise enough to know when somebody is saying they want collaboration when, in reality, they are just faking it. In the end, though, creating a good faith process is our third guiding principle.

Then we build their confidence that there is a way to move forward. CCS is, essentially, a group of about 20 consultants who can help participants deal with all the technical details of managing climate change. It helps when I can turn to a new group and say, basically, "I know this seems very daunting but others have done this and so can you." Psychologically, if people hear there's a problem but they don't hear there are solutions, they tune you out. In our climate change work, the message about global warming and the science behind it is frightening. People say, "Great. You just laid a really big bummer on us. Now we feel there is nothing we can do. So fine. Go away. We give up." It is a different conversation when we follow the problem statement with, "Oh, by the way, here are about 250 different things you can do about it—based on the actions already in place." We use this as a starting place to get people together to figure out what makes sense for their particular circumstance. So our fourth principle is to anticipate that perceptions or ploys about insufficient information will emerge as a reason to not deal with tough issues. It is our job to be there with the information laying out problem, solution, and process in the same breath. Doing that increases your chance of success. Managers who do not build that kind of technical support capacity risk failure.

Our fifth principle is leadership. Convening our kind of process requires somebody in a position of great authority to say, "Managing climate change in our state is an important issue. I'm not satisfied with where it stands right now. I want to get folks around a table to help me make the right decision." That kind of commitment tells everybody that business as usual is no longer an alternative; things are going to change no matter what; and hugging old turf is no longer the best available alternative. These days I go looking for someone in a leadership position who can champion our work.

With all of the above in place the best available alternative now becomes figuring out how to work effectively with the new crowd. Of course, the first thing participants want to do is steer the process in their own direction. We just expect this behavior at the beginning when participants don't really want to deal with others as equals. I've had problems with clients and funders that tried to manipulate the process. And, of course, the participants try to manipulate each other at some point. When it comes right down to it, people want special treatment. That is our sixth principle—be prepared for steering behaviors. I know it sounds trite, but a strong sense of justice and a faith in democracy is critical. One of the things we do in response to steering behavior, and it's typical in processes like these, is establish some criteria for how we are going to make decisions. For our climate change work this typically involves costs and benefits. That amplifies the importance of being able to do expert technical analysis. It also helps a lot to separate out all the different issues that are wrapped together. Having staff support that can do this work for the group in a fairly clear, crisp, and organized way helps diagnose the specific points of concern. Getting specific is the key to finding potential solutions. We are constantly dissecting general criticisms or concerns to find the specific cause of the heartburn. Only then can we intervene effectively. Of course, evaluation is complex in the world of environmental management because a lot of what we deal with is not purely monetary. So there's quite a thicket to get through in doing value-based analysis of environmental options. Many of our disagreements end up being over values. Nevertheless, negotiating decision criteria up front and making people be very specific about their concerns are pretty successful counters to steering behaviors.

And our seventh principle is to maintain full transparency and full inclusion so everybody's voice gets heard and everything is up for consideration. We're pretty careful to protect this credibility of our process. There are no secret decisions. If you violate that principle the discussion explodes. I've gone to the wall with one client who tried to manipulate our process and create private side conversations to cut deals. We get a written agreement on this point to serve much like a contract. In this case the party wanting private meetings got caught, it exploded in their face, and they got dragged back into the process by their governor and my funders. Fortunately, that rarely happens.

Mike: My guess is that in your work with the states on climate change you've experienced the need to manage difficult news. Talk about the dynamics of bad news.

I've had some interesting experiences with organizations I worked for—one handled bad news well and two did not. The unsuccessful organizations were a small investment bank and a small nonprofit agency.

In the investment bank they hired a consultant who specialized in group and individual psychology to help them figure out why their business was in decline. In his assessment one really, really big thing stood out. Unilateralism was the real organizational model despite all the talk about collaboration. This resulted from the power structure among the owners. They used pressure tactics to force one another to do things that didn't make sense for the organization as a whole. Rather than accepting the need for change, as indicated by a variety of data from customers and staff, the firm's owners and managers resisted shared decision making and pressed even harder in the same unilateral direction. The bank responded to the consultant's finding by rejecting it, refusing to pay his fees, and firing some staff. In the end the venture-capital funder of the firm fired the president and seized the firm's assets. It closed shortly thereafter.

In the small nonprofit the consultant was an organizational psychologist. She was brought in because there was concern about enormous staff turnover. She diagnosed that, again, there was tremendous unilateralism, this time coming from the director. He'd founded the organization and wanted everything to be done his way, regardless of input from others. He was the type of person who was able to put a best face forward for a first impression. But this best face was not consistent with the director's actual behavior which included chronic dishonesty, abuse, and a denial of information counter to his existing views. The consultant had the courage to bring these findings to the director's attention. In the end the psychologist was fired, her recommendations shelved, the dysfunctional director remained, several senior managers were fired, several top staff people left, the organization shrunk in overall size, and it lost its major line of business as well as much of its revenue stream. This was another classic case of shooting the messenger to the detriment of everyone's interests.

In contrast was the experience I had with a Texas law firm of about 100 attorneys. They asked me to do some business performance evaluations. The firm had done very well in the Texas real estate boom, through the mid-'80s. Then real estate went bust and they were rapidly losing clients. Their other practice areas were a combination of losers and winners—with no real strong options to fall back upon when their highest revenue market segment failed. One high-volume practice area was insurance defense. When I dug into the numbers it was, in reality, a net loss area with relatively low pay rates and high expenses, despite the high volume. Pay among the partners was calculated on gross rather than net receipts. So the insurance lawyers, some of whom were making $500,000 a year, were soaking the rest of the firm for their compensation because they were racking up lots of hours on low-profitability insurance cases. When we put together the information on net revenue and cost performance the law firm looked at the net cost numbers and said, "I get it. This is bad news. This requires change. Now, what are we going to do about it?" By making all sorts of changes to their lines of business—keeping the winners and getting rid of or reforming the losers—the firm grew into a very, very strong law practice. A success because they didn't deny the bad news and, I'm happy to say, they didn't fire the consultant—who was me!

In these experiences all three organizations faced the same test, what to do about bad news? In the investment bank the answer was to shove people around and cheat. In the nonprofit it was to get rid of people so the bad news didn't get out. In the law firm it was to tackle it head on and act. That took guts.

To translate these experiences into what I do now, tomorrow morning I'm heading to North Carolina to launch a climate change advisory group. It's going to be the first southern state to pull together a state climate plan. We will begin with an inventory—looking backwards at the origins of greenhouse gas emissions across all economic sectors in the state. Then we'll forecast for the next 15 years so. There is a lot of numbers work yet to do but it's going to show they're on a very steep climb in emissions. Knowing that this conclusion will not be well received means we will be working from the outset at building a consensus around the facts. We don't want anybody running away from the facts saying, "Oh gosh, I don't believe it." Our ground rule will be some version of, "If you don't believe it, say why. Is it the data sources, the methods, the assumptions? Now give us your proposal for how we can fix your concern so you can believe the information." We want a process where objectors don't get off easy. It is powerful to make objectors answer the question, "What will it take for you to agree?" We also will make our discussions nonbinding. Our suggestions will go out for further consideration by a governor and a legislature. That takes at least a year and a half. That gives people time to think and time for us to work through their issues, and, hopefully, jointly find ways forward. Again, it's our version of a conceptual sales cycle to make a high involvement decision.

Mike: I am aware of your work on Northern spotted owls (*Strix occidentalis*). What did that experience teach you?

Sometimes, when there is pressure to ignore or deny bad news, saying no to the powers that be is appropriate. That's the owl story. It was a classic case where the facts weren't there to support the administration's position—this is the George H. W. Bush administration—but they tried to either manipulate or suppress data and force agency people either to say things that just weren't so or to keep quiet. I think I articulated many of these incidents in *The God Squad* [Hart 2001].

The Pacific Northwest is an enormous rain forest. Historic timber removals altered the overall ecosystem. One indicator was the decline of the spotted owl. They are dependent on old growth forests. But the owl was just an indicator of other ecosystem dimensions that were being lost—salmon for example. The issue also involved value conflicts—how much are different components of the ecosystem worth and where do you draw the line for preservation—those sorts of discussions.

The Endangered Species Act says that a species in decline must be protected and it prescribes a set of rules for decision making. In the parlance of public policy, it was a settled issue; one where the American people came together, debated all sides, and decided there are some standards we want to live by. The Act envisioned there would be circumstances where not maintaining the normal standards of protection could be justified if some very strict criteria were met. That decision rested with a group of officials appointed to a review committee that came to be known as the God Squad. At the time I worked at the Environmental Protection Agency and our Administrator, Bill Reilly, was on the God Squad Committee. If the majority of committee members said so there could be an exemption from the Endangered Species Act.

The start of the God Squad story was a Bureau of Land Management plan to allow 44 timber sales in Oregon's remaining old growth forest. But the U.S. Fish and Wildlife Service's ESA review determined that these sales were likely to further jeopardize spotted owls. The BLM then asked for and received a God Squad review to decide whether or not an exemption should be granted from the provisions of the ESA.

There were two of us at the Environmental Protection Agency monitoring the God Squad proceedings and both of us reached the same conclusion—recommend that the EPA vote no to the exemption request. The EPA's acting general counsel went to an interagency meeting at the White House where the spotted owl issue came up. At the meeting the administration gave its position that an exemption should be given and they directed the agencies to make that happen. When our general counsel brought that message back to EPA it stepped down the chain of command into our office. It arrived as a directive that our recommendation to the EPA Administrator, Bill Reilly, should say an exemption was scientifically warranted.

When I interviewed for my job at EPA I asked my future boss, Rob Wolcott, "What do you do here when people ask you to do things that you believe are not right?" There was no equivocation whatsoever in Rob's response, "We don't do it. We either say no or we find a way not to do it. You're not going to be asked by me to do anything you don't believe is right." That was one of the reasons I went to work for him. That understanding became very important throughout our whole time working on owls because we were repeatedly asked to do things that were not right. Rob was extremely skilled at saying no and saying it in ways that didn't cost more than was needed. He kept his word. When the request came trickling down from the White House, we said no.

That generated a very angry note from the EPA deputy assistant administrator for policy saying, essentially, "What are you guys doing? Why aren't you doing what we want? Get it straight and do it now." Then the general counsel and one of his attorneys weighed in pressuring us to give Bill Reilly a memo containing a bunch of conclusions we knew were not correct. The general counsel wanted no difference of opinion in the EPA chain of command presented to Administrator Reilly. When the general counsel came to me through Rob asking that I change my recommendation so it fit the party line I said, "Sorry, can't do it." Then he went to my EPA colleague sharing duty with me in the owl proceedings and did the same thing. What finally came tumbling out of his mouth to her was, "I know this sounds like I'm asking you to be a whore, but, I guess that's what I'm asking you to do. Can you just change the answer to yes?" Something to that effect. She was shell-shocked and did not immediately respond because she was so infuriated. After she collected her thoughts, she said no. Before we were done, the general counsel became personally abusive and went above our heads to the policy administrator to create pressure on us.

Then came an effort to cut off our access to Administrator Reilly. That is a severe problem I've seen in Washington, D.C. politics—efforts to gate keep—shutting down access to decision makers so they don't have access to full information, especially information that is in conflict with the party line. On the upside the gatekeepers in EPA didn't know— or I guess fully appreciate—that Reilly is a very shrewd guy. He had no intention of not having full information. While Bill asked his general counsel to advise him on owls he also asked that Rob Wolcott and I directly advise him. We ended up briefing Reilly's chief of staff 22 times. That is a sign of a good manager. He sought out multiple viewpoints. Reilly and his chief would hear the party line from the general counsel—a direct pipeline from the White House. Then they'd call me and ask, "What are you hearing from the trial? What are you hearing from staff at the other agencies?" And then, "What are the facts?" If it hadn't been for Bill and his deputy being honorable and smart enough to break ranks, dissenting information would have been short-stopped. These leaders' aggressive pursuit of all the information was one contribution to the eventual win on the owl issue.

It took considerable courage by Reilly to buck the party line. Despite White House gatekeepers trying to cut off his access, Reilly ended up talking directly with the president. As Reilly related to me, during a lunch with the president and his gatekeepers he turned to the president and said, "You wouldn't believe the crazy thing we're being asked to do over this God Squad hearing. All the evidence says an exemption is something we shouldn't even be talking about. It does not meet the conditions of the law. I certainly think this is a terrible thing for you to be a part of; terrible for your reputation and it won't do any good for the country. There's a better way to deal with all of this so I would appreciate your support in letting me advise you on this decision and vote my conscience when the time comes." Bush was, kind of, astounded. He just sat there because the Secretary of the Interior, the Secretary of Agriculture, and the White House Chief of Staff were at the table—all of whom were pushing for the exemption. Here was Reilly saying something totally different. Bush looked at Reilly and said, "Of course, you should vote your conscience."

When Reilly went on the offense the presidential gatekeepers were stunned. Bill told me he would not have been able to stay on very long if Bush had been reelected. The gatekeepers would have let him name his date but he would be gone. Reilly also heard later, through other channels, that the Republican Party would never again have an environmental professional at EPA. He'd been too independent.

The God Squad's decision ended up being a poison pill for the BLM. It came down to a one vote decision of Administrator Knauss, from the National Oceanic and Atmospheric Administration. Because of pressure from the White House he decided to vote in favor of the exemption for just a few of the 44 proposed sales even though he did not believe it was justified. In doing that he requested and got an amendment to the exemption that required additional BLM consultation with the Fish and Wildlife Service on all future sales. That turned out to be a knock-out blow to BLM. Through political arm twisting the BLM, in some sense, got the decision they wanted but the way they got it obligated them to do consultations perpetually into the future. When they realized they had swallowed that poison pill, they backed out of all the timber sales.

The spotted owl issue was set up, like so many are, as a series of warring headlines. "Jobs Versus Owls" was the one created by forest industry public relations firms. But it was not a jobs-versus-owls issue. It was really an issue of ecosystem decline, a lot of tradeoffs, and where the lines should be drawn. It was also about the Pacific Northwest timber industry and the timber-dependent communities already being in economic decline from market forces that had no relationship to owls.

Initially, as an economist in the EPA, I didn't think the incremental reduction in the spotted owl population was enough justification to forego the proposed BLM timber harvest. The cost to timber workers, firms, and families was just too great. Coming from a wood-products family, both my mom's dad and her brother ran sawmills, and the extensive study I did in college of forest economics told me how much value was in that timber and what it meant to real peoples' lives. I also have a good enough background in wildlife biology to know that the proposed cut was not going to affect much of the owl population. I felt there had to be something a heck of a lot bigger going on for this controversy to be really worth making a big fuss about. My entry point was thinking that the BLM sales really weren't that big a deal.

Part of my transformation came from accessing information. Coming in I had just a small set of facts. These made the issue appear one way. Then getting into a much broader and deeper set of facts made the issue look very different. One thing I learned in business school is the importance of gathering facts and then going deeper with more facts to the next level of detail to see if conclusions change. The process is to keep going deeper and deeper until you're satisfied that additional detail and depth of factual information is not going to change the direction of decision making.

I came to conclude there was a lot more at stake than the 44 timber sales. First there was a precedent of what a God Squad exemption would do to the Endangered Species Act. Then there were all of the biodiversity implications resulting from further degradation of that ecosystem. I concluded the God Squad process was a fake drill. The rhetoric was about protecting the timber communities in the Pacific Northwest, which I think was a very serious issue. But continuing unsustainable timber management could not help. The economic support system for the Pacific Northwest was at risk but the real cause was modernization of the timber industry displacing workers. We were being faked out by a debate over owls which had no hope of fixing this economic problem. We were experiencing the same process the nation went through with farmers but trying to deny that it was happening with Pacific Northwest timber.

Mike: Think back on the process you used in the spotted owl story and talk about how to say no in the most effective way?

I wish I could say that I've done this entirely effectively in my entire career, but I haven't. One solution goes back to being able to explain your reasoning so there's a transparency about how you arrived at your decision. Be able to clearly and directly say, "These were the things I considered and here's why my decision is appropriate." Deliver a rational decision, not one that is perceived as arbitrary or capricious. And a decision is stronger when you can say that a logical, credible group of people conferred and, ultimately, the decision was based on the wisdom of that group of reasonable people.

It helps if you can get somebody else to conclude on their own that no is the right answer. But there is the huge caveat to not be manipulative, like withholding or slanting information to force your answer. That is just the basic ethics of a professional. It is more like showing what you know, what you think are the different options, the decision criteria that are in place and, because of all of that, the logical answer is no. Then asking what they think. If they think differently from you, be prepared to respectfully argue with them a bit. Reserve your ability to say you heard and understand their concerns but you still have to recommend no. I think a harder version of this challenge is dealing with somebody who's decided they don't want to deal with your recommendation because they either don't respect you or they want to manipulate the decision. Then you've got a relationship problem in addition to a disagreement over the facts.

One of my role models is my former boss at EPA, Rob Wolcott. He is a capable manger who's been more successful than most when he had to say no. He had the ability to be strong and straight yet courteous as he delivered unpleasant news. His good standing in the management community was another asset. It is more difficult getting rid of somebody who has a very, very strong positive reputation and strong relationships with a lot of people. He had a reputation for giving a straight answer and people knew that going into their dealings with him. He insisted on openness in decision making. He also was pretty assertive in setting boundaries for a decision. More than once I saw him begin meetings with new people by talking about how the decision was going to be made.

He'd say something like, "Here's how I propose to handle this. I need your agreement on that approach and that our decision will be based on . . ." then he would describe the standards he felt should guide our work. Getting that kind of up-front agreement and holding people to it was a pretty successful tactic.

One of the mistakes I've made is, sort of, feeling like it was up to me to prove myself. That's only half the issue. The other half is the other side proving to you that they're worth your commitment to them. It is a two-way street. If the other side doesn't fully appreciate and treat you as a whole partner you need to keep shopping for somewhere else to use your professional talents. It is important to find that kind of healthy work environment.

It's good to think about the pluses and minuses of the way we've chosen to manage natural resources. The way institutions work is a sort of stair step. You'll make progress and then it will plateau. If you can institutionalize that progress so it's permanent, you've done well. Having a management organization on a continuous path of improvement is very difficult. There are windows of opportunity for constructive change. You make the most you possibly can of those times. But those windows eventually close. My personal decision at that point is to not get stuck on the plateau. I tend to move on to other opportunities to raise the bar again.

My career has not been linear where you start doing one thing, stick with it, and then progress up the ladder. I moved into opportunities that fit and enabled me to do what I thought was making the best use of my abilities at the time. Then, when those opportunities were expiring or led to something better, I moved on. That required a lot of gear-shifting but having some educational diversification has given me that kind of flexibility. That strategy also seems to make sense because we work in a world that's changing fast. Everything in environmental employment is less predictable than in the past. But the work that environmental managers do is more important than ever because we live in a broken world. Managers have some responsibility to mend it. If we can't mend it, at least strive to leave it in better shape than we found it. And if we can't do that, at the very least learn from our mistakes and not repeat them. To know there's something you can do and do nothing, or having a gift that can help and not using it, bothers me. It is important to not turn your back when you can make a difference.

Being able to manage your own choices about career steps provides

more opportunity than signing up with an employer and patiently waiting for them to provide opportunities. That was a big motivation behind
my return to business school for an MBA. I wanted more than one career choice so I could more easily move toward opportunities. One of my
professors at William and Mary—Mitchell Bird, Dr. Bird, the ornitholo-
gist—advised me to do what you think is right, keep doing it until the
good Lord tells you there's some better place for you, and then move on.
That's sort of what I've done.

While that's been my way, everybody's different. But we share the
same quest to find our own way, our own calling, how best to use our
gifts, and how to manage work inside the other things in our life. Going
to Arkansas was a great way to launch my career. I quickly got on the
front line at a very high level at a young age (I was in my early twen-
ties). But it took me half a country away from my family and friends,
isolating me for four or five years. That was a very big tradeoff and one
of the reasons I moved on. That's an example of why these are such
personal decisions.

Fortunately, you don't have to figure out what you're going to do
with the rest of your career. You just need to figure out what you are
going to do next. Then there will come a point when it is time to ask
again, "Do I keep doing this or do I do something else?" My career planning has been a series of these, "What do I do next?" decisions. There
used to be a stigma about doing different things. That's gone. More than
in the past the professional wanting to create change will move from
opportunity to opportunity. If you think about it, seeking out or creating
opportunities where you can maximize the use of your talents is an act
of leadership. We might as well be leading rather than just responding.

7
Mike Dombeck - Keep Them Busy

In government, either you keep them busy or
they will keep you busy.
– Mike Dombeck

When Mike Dombeck joined the Forest Service in 1978 as a GS-6 biological technician, he and his wife settled in the woods near the south shore of Lake Superior expecting to stay there for a regular career. But he became Director of the Bureau of Land Management and later Chief of the USDA Forest Service—responsible for 20 percent of the nation's land and supervising thousands of employees. As the only person in history to have led the nation's two largest land management agencies, responsible for nearly 500 million acres of land, Mike wanted this journey to be about redefining land stewardship as something more than producing commodities like timber, grazing, minerals, etc. Conservationists hailed him as revolutionary. Timber and mining interests reviled him as, in the words of one western senator, ". . . delusional." To Forest Service employees he represented change. Mike puts it this way, "Everybody likes trees. Some like `em vertical. Some like `em horizontal." His career has been about how to keep more of them vertical and why that is wise stewardship.

Mike grew up in the north woods of Wisconsin and was raised, he says, in ". . . probably the ideal way—tromping in the woods hunting and spending summers as a fishing guide." By the time he was a sophomore in college he knew every animal and plant within a 50-mile radius of home by its common and scientific names. Then he met George Becker, author of *The Fishes of Wisconsin* (Becker 1983), who became Mike's major professor at the University of Wisconsin-Stevens Point. Becker became a mentor when he united Mike's emotional appreciation of the out-of-doors with a scientific appreciation of the same experiences. Mike completed a master's degree under Becker researching speciation of the rainbow darter (*Etheostoma caeruleum*). He did another master's at the University of Minnesota using radio telemetry to study muskie (*Esox masquinongy)* biology, focusing on spawning habitat. Then he completed a Ph.D. at Iowa State on the early life history of muskies. The influence of one mentor, George Becker, steered Mike into a traditional fisheries management career that ultimately influenced natural resource conservation for a whole nation.

Not being a philosophical fit with the new George W. Bush administration, Mike moved back to Wisconsin in 2001. Sitting in his office at the University of Wisconsin-Steven's Point, Mike still projects the image of the Forest Service. Wearing jeans and a Forest Service belt buckle, he projects the quiet competence and courtesy I've seen in most Service employees I've met. It is effective, if not a bit disarming, when he levels an incisive critique of the Service and those who want to use it to their own ends. Mike repeatedly makes three points. First, he asks that I not report his career stories as demonstrations of unusual abilities. He makes sure I understand that his is a career punctuated with substantial luck. Second, his critique is not about 'good people' versus 'bad people.' It is about how and why the management system and agency culture behaves the way it does—even when that behavior is dysfunctional. And third, professionals should not wait for their organization to do the right thing. He tells stories of conservation managers out of sync with public opinion or unable to change because of the incentive systems and culture in which they work. His point? A conservation career inside a management agency can create change that makes a difference. We began with the question of how.

My first experience with change in natural resource management actually occurred when I was a teenager working as a fishing guide in northern Wisconsin. I watched the evolution of catch-and-release fishing for muskies; the most significant event in the history of managing that species. Interestingly, the idea did not come from the professionals. It was an idea that bubbled up from the grassroots without any fish manager or researcher saying, "Hey, you know, if we started releasing these big beautiful fish unharmed, musky fishing will improve." Peer pressure among the anglers themselves caused things to change very quickly when it dawned on the guides that putting the word 'released' beside their name on the fish camp's catch board meant more prestige. The evening camp talk over beers shifted from, "Why would you throw back a big fish like that?" to, "Why did you kill that big fish?" That was a magical moment, a change in the ethics and culture of anglers. Today, and I'm 54, muskie fishing is better in northern Wisconsin than at any time I've seen. So, early on I learned that much of resource management tends to depend on social issues that we don't typically address.

It has always been curious to me why the professionals who managed muskies lagged behind the fishermen themselves. As managers and researchers we were focused so intently on hatcheries, size limits, survival rates, spawning behavior, habitat assessments—the more technical and scientific detail—that we glossed right over some simple, basic questions about how to achieve sustainability of that species. Today, does anybody look at the positive impact of catch and release and think, "Gosh, this is really rocket science." Instead, they say, "Well, that's just common sense." But at the time it was almost as though the idea was too shallow since we couldn't apply enough statistics to it to earn a master's or a Ph.D. degree. The innovation came from outside the scientific circles. This highlights the need to focus on people and their values.

I saw this same issue in forest management where I've spent a good part of my career. We tried to address land management as a technical question ignoring the substantial management innovation that was emerging from social change. I've dealt with all of the natural resource professions and the forestry profession is the most overconfident and, perhaps, the oldest. Realize that when I say this I am not critical of any agency or the people in them. Managers do what's expected of them at the time and they have to play with the cards they've been dealt. But if

you critique, not criticize the history, foresters have been overconfident
and with the strongest utilitarian attitudes, especially about the merits
of large scale clear-cutting. A traditionally trained forester has likely
never seen a forest they can't improve, their big question is, for what
purpose?

In the early '70s the Izaak Walton League, not exactly a radical
group, brought suit against the Forest Service over large clear-cuts in
West Virginia's Monongahela National Forest. Despite losing the lawsuit the Forest Service never really changed its clear-cutting policy until the early '90s. Why was the Service so slow to change? Well, the
great increase in timber demand during and after World War II was a
major factor. Later, Congress and the Reagan administration were ordering the Forest Service to increase harvest big time. The nation's
foresters were simply doing as directed and they did it very, very well.
Harvest from the national forests went from around two billion board
feet or less prior to World War II to more than twelve billion board feet
by the time the spotted owl issue reached its peak around 1990 when
excessive cutting hit the wall. It eventually took a court injunction to
stop that unsustainable timber harvest.

When I went to work for the Forest Service, the passage of the
National Environmental Policy Act, the Clean Water Act, and the Clean
Air Act meant agencies like the Forest Service had to start taking a
multidisciplinary approach and look at the full range of natural resource
values as well as social issues. To do this the agencies needed 'ologists'
—hydrologists, fish biologists, wildlife biologists, geologists, and sociolo-
gists—sometimes to the dismay of forestry, the ruling discipline. I was
one of those ologists. We were 'combat biologists,' not really welcome
but the agency had to hire us to meet the requirements of the new laws.
Some visionary didn't say, "Hey, we've got to get broader input, there-
fore we need soil scientists, biologists, and so forth." The ologists were
thrust upon the agency by outside pressure. When a new ology issue got
in the way of timber production it was dubbed a 'timber constraint.' The
budget and the real reward system in the Forest Service still favored
increasing timber harvests, grazing, and mining—the commodity side
of the agency's mandate. It took outside forces to cause real changes
that led to the adoption of broader ecosystem thinking.

An irony in this story is that prior to World War II most foresters
were opposed to clear-cutting and even-age timber management. Then
came tremendously increased timber demand during World War II and
for the post-War home building boom. Economic models began emerg-

ing that demonstrated clear-cutting was the easy way to create a predictable timber flow through harvest rotation and even-age management on large tracts of land. Thus, nice, neat economic and timber management models emerged, after the fact, to justify the policy decision that had already been made. The problem recognized in the 1970s as controversy increased is that Mother Nature doesn't fit neat models even if they look good on paper. We now know that these models do not allow for the messiness of nature. We haven't even come close to knowing all there is to know about how nature operates. This is a hard reality to accept for a culture that is hooked on the utilitarian attitude that we can improve on nature.

One of the big challenges we have in the United States is that we're also hooked on money as the measure of all things. In our system, when all is said and done, it is the economic value that rules. That's how we make serious, long-term errors in resource management. We tend to think of land as just a factor of production in the economy. The Forest Service came to define timber management that way.

There is an inherent conflict between economic theory and biological theory. In biological theory a population increases until it reaches a set of limiting factors. Then it oscillates with a growth rate of pretty much zero. In economic theory an economy that isn't growing is a bad thing.

The social issue in this story is that the foresters, or I should say 'we' the natural resource managers, never thought to ask, "When the public sees these large clear-cuts, what do they think? How do they feel?" The country was changing fast. People were increasingly taking to the air in the 1950s and '60s, flying in and out of places like Seattle and Portland. When they looked down at the large clear-cuts they didn't like what they saw. Never mind that much of the cutting was on private or industry land. The public just assumed it was national forest. Consequently, the Forest Service took the heat. We made matters worse by never attempting to explain clear-cutting in an effective way. We just went ahead and did it thinking it was right because we had models that said so. That just did not sit well with a broader array of the public who started telling us they wanted the nation's forests managed for other purposes. Lo and behold, we found ourselves in gridlock over whether to cut at all. We're still dealing with that fallout today. Part of the problem is that we seriously undervalued ecological services beyond commodity production. In reality, the economics of Forest Service land management since World War II had been based on mining ecological services. Consequently, natural systems diminished as time went on. The concept that natural resources are mere commodities is still deeply embedded in our culture and thinking.

Water is going to be the issue of the 21st century. It will impact the way we manage land, the way we make public policy, and the way political systems operate. As things stand now, all resource management agencies, both state and federal, respond to two-, four-, or six-year- election cycles. Compare that to something like a forest. Some old growth forests are 300-400 years old. Our decision systems have a tendency, even a set of powerful incentives, to respond to the short term, all geared to election cycles. After all, the bottom line currency for a politician is the vote. Next, consider the models that focus on the economic value of natural resources. Long-term thinking and those things that we can't measure, like basic ecological services, get left out. The rational thing to do under the tenets of current economic thinking is, in fact, to liquidate anything old and slow growing, but, what if these old or slow-growing things are connected to something else we depend on, like water?

Now, consider a long-term ecological service like aquifer recharge. For example, we are depleting the Ogallala aquifer about eight times faster than it is being recharged. The Ogallala is the largest water tank in the United States stretching from South Dakota to Texas. When that aquifer is emptied, the time horizon for fixing the problem is way beyond anything we are thinking about now. For about the last 10 years I've talked about water more than any other natural resource issue as I worked to help people understand what land does for them and why good stewardship is critical. My view is that water and watershed function ought to be the federal land manager's basic performance measure. Water reflects both what is going on up stream and up slope.

Right now there is much Forest Service dialogue about analysis paralysis or the process predicament. The concern is that we have so much administrative process that managers can't get real work done. Well, we could cut through that complaint if we could increase the level of trust with our critics and by just having some basic indicators that are all encompassing and focused on long term. Abundant clean water is certainly one of these. If I were king for a day, I'd revamp the Organic Act to say protection of biodiversity and maintenance of water quality ought to be the primary purpose of federal land management. The reason? Because these are the really big issues we'll face in the next one-hundred years. If we don't start worrying about them now a 10-year push to do something when we've emptied the Ogallala aquifer isn't going to solve the problem. These issues require long-term thinking about land. Thinking about land management where economics overrides ecological concerns such as watershed function will not allow us to achieve sustainability and will ultimately lead to big, big problems.

Another challenge resource managers face is personal ethics versus organizational or political pressures. There is often pressure to satisfy a politician or to bring more money or good public relations into the organization. When setting up a timber sale the manager may say, "Well, let's move a little bit further into the riparian zone to take a couple more large, high-value, old-growth trees. It will make us look better since we'll produce more board feet. Yeah, we will sacrifice a little over the long term, but we won't notice it and it really won't stress the ecosystem that much more." The same tendency to overexploit or over-harvest happens with other natural resources. Instead we should always err on the side of maintaining ecosystem function.

With large-scale clear-cutting we failed to ask or think about what the public perceived when they looked at a big clear-cut. We failed to seriously ask or think about what other purposes, beyond timber, should guide our management. That is in sharp contrast to the fact that we can't re-create a water filtration plant to do what a forest does. But yet, when we look at land, what do we see? Those kinds of ecological values and services are not as visible as is commodity production. The foresters were staying within the traditional silvicultural mindset and utilitarian spirit that man can improve on nature. This was not willful. Nor were foresters necessarily being closed-minded. At that time they were trained that way and there were plenty of congressional and presidential pressures to reinforce this world view. Some people, like Randall O'Toole from Montana, argue that we ought to base national forest decisions on economic models. But the fact is that the national forests were never set up to be moneymakers. They were set up to conserve forests and water, not produce revenue.

Mike: What have you learned about how to create change while working in an agency?

All natural resource agency heads struggle with a lot of controversy and conflict. Partly, this is a result of our democratic form of governing. A democracy needs to be based on open public debate of issues and options. And sometimes the debate gets heated and the controversy becomes intense. We often think that controversy is bad but, actually, it's probably good. There is another system where we have no choices and no public debate, it's called a dictatorship.

When I became chief there was a lot of talk about the Forest Service having a muddled mission. The Service was known as a "can-do" agency. It was extremely good at getting from A to B. It just didn't know where B was. It didn't know how to act or what to do. As chief I was tugged one direction by the executive branch, then in another direction by congressional committees, then in a several other directions by local and national interest groups. As a result, it is pretty easy for an agency to become immobilized. It's like being in a vise with the jaws closing in on you. An example I encountered was roadless area management. We had been in gridlock with this issue for a couple of decades and it was eating our lunch.

The roadless issue exemplifies the need to dissect an issue, to figure out the real problem. If foresters proposed timber sales in roadless areas they had to deal with appeals, litigation, tree sitters, and negative public relations. But if foresters slowed road building the logging industry got upset and prompted congressional intervention. Nobody was happy. As a result, the Service's budget for its 386,000 miles of roads declined from 228 million dollars in 1985 to 95 million dollars in 1996. While I was chief, Congress came within one vote in the Senate of slashing about 80 percent of the road budget. Another year only three votes kept the House from cutting about 25 percent. The Forest Service's road budget was going downhill fast. When I would ask if maintaining roads was important, most said, "Yes." But, we were losing the budget. Why?

The road budget became a way for people who did not want us cutting old growth timber to influence decision making. Even though the bulk of the road budget went to maintain existing roads, their point of leverage was to cripple the entire road budget. So, the road system was unraveling and we were faced with an $8.4 billion taxpayer liability. An opportunity arose in a conversation I had with my boss Dan Glickman, who was Secretary of Agriculture at the time. Basically, I was complaining that all we were doing was going up to Capitol Hill and responding to a flurry of legislative proposals from various members of Congress. Idaho's Senator Craig was proposing legislation to revamp the National Forest Management Act. Congressman Bob Smith from eastern Oregon, chairman of the Agriculture Committee, and other pro-timber harvest members of Congress were proposing major changes. The Forest Service was continually playing defense and saying, "Well, we agree with the objectives, but we are opposed to the legislation because . . . da de da de da." Basically saying we didn't like the details. We were not proposing anything, only reacting rather than leading by coming up with ideas or proposals ourselves. The agency had been battered around so much in controversy it seemed like we'd lost our skill at showing initiative.

Secretary Glickman gave me a green light, saying, "Well, let's go ahead and develop some proposals ourselves and move them forward." That was the genesis of the Forest Service's *Natural Resources Agenda*. At the time, that was a turnaround for the agency. When we rolled out the *Natural Resources Agenda* it caught many in Congress totally by surprise because this was the first time in over a decade that the Service had taken a fairly aggressive leadership stance on difficult issues. Nobody expected it.

The first thing I did was to announce a moratorium on road building in roadless areas. That had the biggest impact because it decoupled the road maintenance issue from building new roads in roadless areas. Those opposed to old growth harvest or entry into roadless areas no longer had to worry about that fight. Decoupling gave us the opportunity to focus on the nation's forests having a huge road system with a significant maintenance need. The Service's road budget started going up after years of decline. That action also caught the attention and support of the White House and President Clinton.

While the main point of concern was over access to old growth, a benefit arising from this controversy was the opportunity to take a hard look at the logic of development versus no development in roadless areas. As a business issue roadless areas are roadless for some very good reasons. The cost of getting out a board foot of timber almost doubles in roadless areas. When you enter a roadless area you deal with a lot of controversy and that increases your planning and decision-making costs, not to mention costs to your credibility and public good will. And timber sale proposals in these areas have a high failure rate so the risks go up, making you and your budgets more vulnerable in the future. No private-sector business CEO would spend time and energy where the unit cost, collateral damage, and risk of failure are the highest.

Also unresolved was the question of who was ultimately responsible for the eight billion dollar maintenance liability? Was it Congress? The president? The chief? Local government? Plenty of local interests, especially in Idaho, eastern Oregon, eastern Washington, and western Montana wanted local decision control. This would have been death by a thousand cuts from many, many local jurisdictions making independent decisions with nobody looking at the big picture. Local interests wanted decision-making authority without responsibility for the ongoing maintenance of roads; simply let us make the decision and let Uncle Sam foot the bill.

Local versus national decision-making priority is a very tough issue for federal land managers. Local people feel, "Well, we live here. Do we really want people from all over the country having a say in what happens on the national forest next to my land?" It is a very big challenge to balance local and national interests. Are things biased toward local interests? Typically, yes. The problem is that local control usually means a strong bias toward resource extraction and a focus on economic gain. The simple fact is that these lands belong to all citizens and all the country's taxpayers pay the bills.

Taking the initiative allowed us to put other proposals forward like reforming the county payments issue. There was a provision passed about 1910 saying that, depending upon where you were, either 25 or 50 percent of the receipts from timber or other commodities extracted from public lands were returned to the county or township to fund community needs like schools and roads. This may have been appropriate in its time but it became yet another incentive for commodity extraction and overexploitation. The basic question was, is it good public policy to tie the funding for important social services like schools and roads to the most controversial programs of the Forest Service? Especially with the risk of court injunctions bringing timber sales to a halt. Three years in a row we proposed legislation to change how these payments were made. After three years Senator Wyden, a Democrat from Oregon and Senator Craig, a Republican from Idaho, agreed to move the legislation forward that ultimately passed and was signed into law by President Clinton

The county payments provision had become a sort of perverse incentive because, as the timber harvest declined, the counties and schools were getting less money, thereby increasing the pressure to cut even more timber from the forests. Could the timber industry have a better lobbyist than schools and school boards with our children's educations at stake? The timber industry was very much opposed to changing county payments, as were the pro-harvest members of Congress. I recall the time I was invited to speak at a meeting of the National Association of Counties. Senator Craig found out I was to talk about the county payments issue and invited himself onto the agenda just ahead of me. We sat next to each other at lunch and talked about the issue a bit and had a generally friendly conversation. When he got up to speak, basically he said, "Hey, this is another hare-brained idea from Dombeck. This dog won't hunt." Ironically, after three years of dialog, he became a co-sponsor of a bill to make that same proposal. Things can change.

The *Natural Resources Agenda* and the road building moratorium put us in a leadership position. We began defining the issues. Prior to that time we were very busy responding to proposals thrust upon us by others. Interestingly, employees complained, "We're too busy. There are too many things on our plate. We can't keep up with all this." My response was, "Are you really any busier than before? We have always been very busy but now we're working on our issues. Which would you rather spend your time on, our issues or their issues?" I was gratified to see that while we were still going to lots of congressional hearings, they became oversight hearings on our proposals versus us having to play defense to issues put forward by others. In government, either you keep them busy or they will keep you busy.

The roadless issue is an example of taking the lead on a specific tough issue. Another way to initiate change is through consensus building. To create the four elements of the *Natural Resources Agenda* we hosted several meetings between agency leaders and employees, state and private foresters, and other interests to answer the questions, "If we are conservation leaders, why are we not proposing things?" and, "What should we propose?" From these meetings we identified watershed restoration, recreation, sustainable forest ecosystem management, and roads as the top priorities for the national forests. Then we began talking about specifically what to do in each of these priorities. We were building consensus by seeking common goals, by talking, and, even more, by listening.

A good case history of failing to look for common goals is grazing in the West. We all know that grazing fees are too low, except for the industry lobbies who also know it but have a self-interest to say otherwise. And yet, think about what the National Cattlemen's Association has in common with the Wilderness Society and the Sierra Club. They have a shared interest in maintaining large tracts of undeveloped land in the West. Instead of working together on that issue they spent too much time fighting about how many cows are in the creek and what the grazing fee should be. Are both parties better off with subdivisions? So here is an example of failing to focus on what the conflicting parties have in common. Instead they're focused on disagreement.

Change in public agencies is also difficult because managers have a hard time getting rid of unnecessary work and outdated programs. In government, unlike the private sector, you can't spin off your losers. Congress and administrations keep adding responsibilities to public employees but they rarely allow agencies stop doing things. I spent three years as head of the Bureau of Land Management asking the question, "What can we stop doing?" The answer back was, "Nothing." This is because every government activity has supporters and interests who benefit from the status quo. Stopping an activity mobilizes that support even though the activity may be a loser or, worse, be causing damage (here I am thinking of the 1872 Mining Act). So a reality of government work is that there are lobbies to support everything and their ability to prompt congressional oversight means the government CEO does not get to call nearly as many of the shots as most people think. Where a private company would just get rid of a loser, refocus on the core mission, shift gears, and move forward, government agencies tend to be increasingly cumbersome as they accumulate more and more programs or responsibilities over the years. While this, by itself, is a significant problem, I haven't even touched upon the internal culture of agencies working to preserve the status quo.

We actually took this approach to heart when we attempted to put the fisheries program on the map within the Forest Service by starting the program we called *Rise to the Future*. At the time, in the late 1980s, there were 107 fisheries biologists in the Forest Service and a budget of about $5-6 million. We developed *Rise to the Future* as a program to recast, on a national scale, the Service's approach to fish management. We didn't take a technical approach trying to write guidelines for stocking rates, fish ladders, or habitat improvement. Our work was all about building program support and making sure decision makers and the public knew why our work was important. It was not, "Just give me money, let me do my research, and I will give you all kinds of great scientific information." We figured somebody had to explain to the public and politicians why our work was important. At the same time we were building strong partnerships with the fisheries community active in Washington, D.C. That was a period of tremendous unity among these groups because this gave them and us something to rally around—improved fish management throughout the whole national forest system. I haven't seen as much unity among fisheries interests since. *Rise to the Future* was initiated during the Reagan administration whose push was all about increasing timber harvest. Chief Dale Robertson couldn't publicly promote increases for the fisheries program but he was okay with us bringing new money in the side door. He recognized it as a good thing and quietly let it happen. We thought, "If we go from five to twenty million dollars that will really be tremendous." Well, within three years, it was forty million dollars. The number of fish biologists in the Forest Service doubled. All because a new purpose was conceived around a broad coalition that cared enough to make it happen.

So, trying to answer the question of how to create change is rather large and complex. A good start is to take the initiative, not wait for others. Learn something about consensus building and basic marketing. And start building a community of support for your issue. Be street smart about your approach.

Mike: Tell me about working in a conservation agency.

Well, first and foremost, the American public doesn't appreciate the breadth of professionalism in public agencies. But a reality these days is that politicians often campaign against government. That really started in the 1970s with presidential and other national candidates questioning government saying things like, ". . . they must be slackers if they are in government, otherwise they would get a real job in the private sector." In contrast is what I observed in my 25 years of working with hundreds of employees in a number of federal and state agencies. The quality and productivity of employees were impressive.

A reality of agency work is that people tend to get locked into loyalty. It is just something that happens when you are a member of any group for a lot of years. And this is not unique to government, it happens in all organizations. You start working for an organization like the Department of Fisheries or Division of Forestry, or whatever. There's a fairly widely shared reason why you and your peers took up that kind of work, you like the mission of that organization. And there is a lot of personal reward for making that choice. These are the touchy-feely aspects of our work and the mission of the organization. Everything is in sync.

After a person works for an organization for 10 or 15 years, there is often a gradual loyalty shift. It's a natural progression from loyalty to the mission to loyalty to the agency itself and its culture. Loyalty shift explains how agencies become inwardly focused. To get a sense of how this works think about families. An outsider who complains about one of the jerks in the family soon has the entire family on his back.

That case has been made for the Forest Service family, but it is not confined to the Service. There's too much in-breeding in all the agencies, even academia. I believe individuals should work for more than one organization during a career. This helps an agency because, as employees move to new organizations, they bring their networks, values, and alternative ideas with them. A geneticist would call this maintaining hybrid vigor.

A big challenge for agencies is to stay true to their mission. Take the spotted owl debate as an example. The Forest Service's mission is about watershed protection and sustainable timber harvest. Under pressure from Congress, presidents, timber companies, and local communities it was easy to ignore water and timber sustainability and just focus on short-term timber production. In the era of big timber harvests there were few meaningful incentives for achieving the Service's broader conservation mission but plenty of incentives to increase timber cutting. It also is a story of denial that kept the agency from seeing the emerging shift of public opinion. Barry Noon and others rang the spotted owl warning bell in 1972. By the late 1980s a very untraditional thing happened. Sixty-four forest supervisors, that's almost half the leadership from the national forests, wrote a letter to the chief, saying, "We can't keep up this rate of timber harvest." It took courage for the forest supervisors to send such an unprecedented letter. That letter was going against a strong culture of loyalty to the agency and to the leadership. It was also going against substantial pressure from Congress, the president, and local communities to keep cutting. Therein lies a manager's dilemma. *Esprit de corps* is a necessary element of a cohesive and productive work group but it is easy for loyalty to shift from the mission to the agency itself. There was pressure for the Forest Service to close ranks and that's largely what happened. It moved toward self-protection. Even with the warning of the 64 forest supervisors, the agency couldn't seem to change so the real change was thrust on the Forest Service from outside. This time it was the judicial system with Judge Dwyer's ruling that shut down timber harvest to protect owls.

This is not a story of bad leaders. They were responding to the pressures in their work lives and just doing what the leadership expected of them. Their behavior made sense because employees were rewarded for outputs instead of outcomes. Outputs are things like user days of recreation, board feet of timber, animal-unit months of grazing, tons of coal, and cubic meters of gas. They tend to be hard things that can be measured and have a market price easily put on them. In fact, outputs govern much of the Forest Service's budget appropriation. And timber harvest was king. Outcomes, like the condition of the land, aquifer recharge, quality of topsoil, and maintaining watershed function tend to take a back seat. Resource professionals need to be as forceful as they can in focusing on long-term outcomes instead of short-term outputs, but it is tough to do. Just look at the members of Congress who currently chair the natural resource committees. They are, basically, agents for the industries who extract resources from public lands. The dollar benefits of commodity production from the public's forests flow to a relatively few people's hands in the private sector and these interests create pressure on the Forest Service to produce outputs, like timber, grazing, and mining. But the consequences, negative outcomes in these cases, remain with the land for a very long time and the costs are long term, paid by future generations. It's a subsidy to commodity interests, we just don't call it that.

The source of change coming from outside the agency is not a new pattern. Where have our conservation leaders like the Aldo Leopolds and the Rachel Carsons come from? People outside the management structure are the ones that usually come up with new, creative ideas. Many of these innovators start out in agencies but ultimately they have problems because they do not conform to agency expectations or they 'rock the boat' too much. Just think about Rachel Carson. She started in an agency and then left. Then she was considered a rebel and troublemaker because her new ideas challenged the status quo. She made both politicians and agency leaders, even the established scientific community, uncomfortable. But she was right. Again, an example of fresh perspective coming from outside the established management system.

Another problem I've seen in natural resource agencies that holds back change is that we are not very good at marketing. We think marketing is advertising. Marketing, in the strictest business sense, is identifying a social need and fulfilling it. We need to do a lot better job at marketing because natural resources are losing market share big-time in the United States. The proportion of the federal budget allocated to natural resources has declined by 50 percent of what it was in 1962. That would kill any private-sector business. It's the natural resource managers' responsibility to help turn that around.

I used to talk with Bureau of Land Management and Forest Service leadership about the need for resource managers and scientists to talk in simple, plain English and use terms all Americans understand. Get away from speaking in scientific and agency lingo. Think about why Bill Gates is the richest man in the world. He never tries to explain the complexities of the personal computer. His genius was in taking something very complex and by using basic marketing concepts and by simplifying he made computers relevant to people's lives. Our profession needs to be effective at this kind of marketing and communication.

For example, very few people in the United States understand watershed function. The National Education and Environmental Training Foundation did a survey asking, "What is a watershed?" Only one in five Americans could even get close by guessing. As somebody who has worked for more than 25 years in one form or another of watershed management all over the United States, I never had a realtor, Chamber of Commerce, or local developer say to me, "Hey, you've got to do a better job managing the watershed because our communities and economy depend on it." Yet, look how many communities in the West are water-limited. Instead, they are busy building new pipelines, squeezing even more out of the overallocated Colorado and Sacramento Rivers, increasing the flow of the Central California canal, and taking water from one another. Almost nobody is focusing on land management as it affects water. In California, for example, 20 percent of the land is national forest but 50 percent of the runoff comes from that 20 percent of the land. Yet local governments, who should care, don't think about that connection as much as they should. I see this as a communication failure. Resource managers are failing to tell the story in ways so the American public can see and understand the implications of bad land management. The public does not understand why the work we do is important.

As chief of the Forest Service and especially as head of the BLM, I noticed that an outsider listening to our staff meetings would have no idea what our business was. We were supposed to be in the resource stewardship business but we weren't talking about it much. Our talk was all about budgets and administrative details. We rarely talked about our core mission. We rarely talked about what condition we want the land and water resources to be in. The public's resource managers need to spend a lot more time focused on stewardship values and talk more about our aspirations and needs to support these values.

Any private-sector corporation would kill to have a product line like that of the Forest Service or BLM. It is great stuff. We ought to be telling everybody who will listen about why the work we do is important and why they should join us in caring for the resources. Instead, we spend an awful lot of energy talking about the conflicts, the down sides.

One time I listed the Forest Service's recent accomplishments at a House Appropriations Committee hearing in front of Ralph Regula, a congressman from Ohio who was the subcommittee chairman. I listed a long litany of things like the fact that we issued 27,000 special-use permits a year; we maintained 144,000 miles of trails; the national forests provided drinking water for 60,000,000 Americans in 43 states; and many more accomplishments. I laid out a bunch of these positives in simple terms. I don't know if he intended for everyone to hear, but Ralph leaned over to his staffer and said, with the microphone on so everybody could hear it, "That's really impressive."

There is a connection between failure to make the case for stewardship and downturns in agency budgets and support for natural resources. We ought to be talking about how magnificent the salmon runs were at one time and what we can do to make them better. About the importance of water quality. About what nature does for our spirit. About those values that tug at people's hearts. Instead, we're spending our energy talking about all the 'administrivia' and controversy. If our office conversations lack a discussion about core values, we are missing the boat.

Mike: What did you learn about how professionals can manage their careers?

Number one is the value of focusing on the positive even when confronted with problems. I've always found it useful to think about three kinds of issues: red, green, and yellow, just like traffic lights. Red-light issues are intractable. We can fight over these until the cows come home. Then there are green-light issues, where there is complete agreement. And then there are the yellow-light issues. These are the ones where there is some level of agreement. Maybe agreement on the goal but not the methods. Spend energy on the yellow- and green-light issues. Every once in a while, when working on these, a red-light issue turns yellow. Then begin to peck away at it. Dwelling on red-light issues is an all too easy way to stay very busy and get nothing done. I try to be the kind of person who continually looks for new ways of doing things and for different challenges. Rather than putting so much energy in the red-light issues try to search out the yellow-light and green-light opportunities.

I also attribute a lot of any career successes I had to the people skills I gained as a fishing guide when I was an impressionable teenager. I had the great fortune to get to know a lot of people from almost every spectrum of society, heard a lot of different opinions, and learned to listen to the feelings people bring to their perception of politics, nature, religion, personal crises, and the like. They viewed natural resources more from an aesthetic rather than a technical point of view. It helped me appreciate the importance of connecting people with nature in a way that shows why resource conservation is so important. In resource management we talk to ourselves too much and we tend to use techno-speak when we do talk to others. I was lucky to have learned many of these communication skills from my guiding days.

Your credibility is important. My chance to work on and do research in areas that were cutting edge, on issues perceived as important, and on projects with high visibility brought me credibility as well as some measure of visibility. I was also lucky to be in the right places at the right times.

Life demands continuous learning and sometimes it can be tough. Early in my career I was very comfortable in the Midwest. I knew the scientific name of almost everything. When I moved to California I simply didn't have the technical knowledge I felt I needed or could acquire. I was forced onto a new playing field. My biological and technical knowledge was inadequate and no longer served me. This meant I needed to move out of my comfort zone. It meant I needed to quit trying to be the technical expert and learn a lot about program development and administration. I had to figure out new ways to help my programs. Ways which ultimately led to the same end point of doing good things for fish and the forest's aquatic resources. Success required that I gain a different skill set.

As we already talked about, it is important to look outside your profession for ideas and solutions that can be adapted for your situation. Innovation requires an outward focus. Innovation requires embracing the novel and reaching out to the uncertain. Preserving the status quo only requires rejecting the new and retreating to the familiar.

The professional needs to always think about how to set the stage for progress. For example, during the anticonservation and antienvironment thrust of the Reagan administration some people cried, "Ain't this awful." Others used that negative political environment as an opportunity to quietly develop long-term strategies. Then, when we went from Reagan to Bush One, who was much more environmentally friendly, the stage was set to move forward. Then came Clinton and the door was open to make lots of progress.

You can't control controversy, you've got to work with it. It helped me to realize that this is just the way the system works. So getting good at working with controversy is an important skill for today's manager. I also found that developing personal relationships is important because when you have to deliver bad news at least you will be trusted. Don't ignore or discount the critics. Have a working relationship with them. Their criticisms and questions will reveal the strengths and weakness of your ideas, often more than will spending time with supporters. You've got to have a mind-set of not taking criticism personally. People have asked me why I have a tendency to go out of my way to talk with or be nice to people that either don't like me or are opposed to a position I am taking. I always feel this is time well spent. You can have a positive working relationship based on one value while disagreeing about other values or issues. To get respect you have to give it.

In a bad political climate look for what can be done under the radar. An example is increasing the Forest Service's fisheries budget as happened with *Rise to the Future*. Even though that wasn't a thrust of Reagan, who would have killed it on the spot, or the Bush One administrations, the Forest Service chief let budget increases and the associated change quietly come in the door. Initially, he could not champion it because it wasn't administration policy, but he certainly welcomed the shift within the agency and soon became a staunch supporter.

Working under the radar of the conflict industry is particularly important. The conflict industry is the array of those folks who make their living by pitting interests against one another. As long as there is controversy, they have lots of work and good incomes. One of the errors we made implementing the road-building moratorium was that many Forest Service field staff did not know enough of the details when it was announced. Shortly after we made the announcement their phones were ringing and they didn't have enough background to provide answers. But the alternative was that if we had talked about the details in advance the conflict industry and special interests would have very quickly taken the issue away from us. It would have turned into a debate between the extremes—the preservationist groups versus the timber industry. They would have energized their members of Congress who would likely have written me a letter saying, "We don't want you working on this." That would have put me at a tremendous disadvantage. Stalemate or gridlock is easier to engineer than is change and stalemate maintains the status quo. Would I handle the roadless issue any differently today? Probably. At least some aspects of it. But there's a need to anticipate the conflict industry, otherwise you can lose your opportunity for leadership on an issue.

Mike: In your speech *The Resource Agenda for the 21st Century*, you said "we," meaning the Forest Service, have an obligation to lead. What does that mean?

There was a debate in the American Fisheries Society a few years back about whether or not the Society should lobby. They may not have used that word, but, basically, it was about the question of scientists and professionals pushing a point of view on public policy. There were two very divergent schools of thought. One, was, "We're professionals. We work with science. It is not our job to influence the public." Another group said, "No! We need to be in there with both sleeves rolled up working hard at it, providing the best information we can." I support the second school of thought. We ought to be showing leadership to help politicians understand the consequences of the various options. If we're not, who's going to do it? Decision makers ought to be getting the best, most current, accurate, science-based information. That's a role for professionals.

Part of leadership is advocacy—encouraging politicians and policy makers to take on tough issues and to do so with a sense of obligation to the mandates of the resource agencies. For example, what are we going to do about the dams on the Columbia River? Are we, as professionals, just going to look the other way until the salmon are gone? If that's a social or political decision, that's fine, but, let's not have it occur because we weren't at the table. Remember that the issues of spotted owls, clear-cutting, and roadless areas became problems because we, as professionals, didn't deal with the situation early enough. It was easier to look the other way and not take on these really tough issues. The longer you wait, the more decision space you lose. Just sitting by and letting nothing happen is, in reality, taking a stand on an issue. It supports the status quo. At a minimum we need to be communicating what we do, what we know, and why the things we do are important. If we don't fulfill that responsibility we throw the ball to the vested interests. Then, as Teddy Roosevelt said, ". . . the greed factor" moves in.

Fortunately, we're not selling plutonium. Our product line is all positive stuff. We're talking about scenic beauty, we're talking about water, we're talking about building topsoil, we're talking about the quality of the air we breathe. It pays to talk about why our work is important. Red lights will then start turning yellow. Thankfully, we now understand more than ever that "ecosystems are not only more complex than we think, they are more complex than we can think." So, management is now more accepting of the need to continually adjust our strategies and learn as we go. It's adaptive management. That's real progress over the past few decades. But further progress depends upon helping people understand and appreciate why the work we do is important—at an intellectual, social, and emotional level. A real challenge in our urbanized high-tech society is reconnecting peoples' hearts and minds to nature. Helping them understand why our quality of life is directly connected to the health of the land.

8
Phil Pister - Finding an Internal Compass

As professionals, nothing would be worse than to leave as our legacy a
boxcar loaded with reprints concerning recently extinct species.
– Phil Pister

Sitting in the Desert Fishes Council's world headquarters, a 12' x 16'
workshop in Bishop, California, now converted to an office, I am concerned
that my request for three long interviews with Phil Pister will fall flat. After all,
two hours a day for three consecutive days is a long conversation. It is hard
to imagine my questions drawing out much that is new after the first day. Not
a problem. When I ask what he learned from his career Phil's energetic mind
immediately finds voice in compelling stories about epiphany, confrontation,
and legacy as a fish biologist.

A career fishery biologist with the California Department of Fish and
Game, Phil actively ducked promotions as a career goal. Instead, his 38-

year career was a search for purpose and meaning as a natural resource manager in an environment he loves. Phil supervised research and management of a thousand waters on the eastern slope of the Sierra Nevada Mountains, stretching from the 14,000 foot crest of the mountains to the floor of Death Valley, 280 feet below sea level. Pister became deeply involved in desert fish conservation during the mid-1960s, largely motivated by near extinction of the Owens pupfish (*Cyprinodon radiosus*). His association with renowned ichthyologists Carl L. Hubbs and Robert Rush Miller and being a student of A. Starker Leopold inspired his career decision to advocate for native fish conservation.

Phil was a seminal influence in the formation of the Desert Fishes Council and served as its first chairman. In the 1960s groundwater pumping near Ash Meadows, in Nevada but adjacent to Death Valley National Park and the California border, began to impact native fish habitats. With Phil in a leadership role, concerned university and agency professionals convened a symposium to address threats to the unique desert fishes in the area. At the symposium, in November 1969, the Desert Fishes Council was born. Phil went on to a deep involvement in the preservation of Devil's Hole pupfish (*Cyprinodon diabolis*) at Ash Meadows. This effort culminated in a U.S. Supreme Court decision according standing to desert fishes and a federal requirement for their preservation under the relatively new Endangered Species Act.

At 71 when interviewed, Pister, attired in his preferred biologist's uniform (tired blue jeans, suspenders, T-shirt with pupfish logo, ball cap, and tennis shoes), is a rapid-fire talker with anecdotes, histories, and probing dissections of events to illustrate important lessons he learned during his career. Unlike most natural resource professionals, Phil has written extensively about his career, including essays that reflect on what it means to be a professional (e.g., Pister 1985, 1992a, 1992b, 1993, 1994, 1995, 1998, 1999a, 1999b). Partial to quotes, he punctuates our conversation with wisdom and wit from Aldo Leopold, Benjamin Franklin, Max Planck, and B. F. Skinner. His office wall holds a lot of career keepsakes: pictures of golden trout (*Oncorhynchus mykiss aguabonita*), Owens pupfish, A. Starker Leopold, Carl Hubbs, Albert Einstein, and the first members of the Desert Fishes Council. Also on the wall are many awards from the U.S. Bureau of Land Management (for partnership with the Desert Fishes Council), Cal-Neva Chapter of the American Fisheries Society (Conservation Achievement Award), American Motors Corporation (for exceptional conservation service), Western Division American Fisheries Society (Award of Excellence), California Trout (Golden Trout Award), the American Fisheries Society (Carl L. Sullivan—

the 'Sully'—Award), and the Society for Conservation Biology (Edward T. LaRoe III Memorial Award). When I ask Phil which is the most important he points to a home-made picture of a pupfish painted in glaring green by two young sisters. Along with their picture Sara and Jenny Cain included a personal note thanking Phil for his efforts to save the Owens pupfish from extinction. This is the award he has carefully framed and placed at the top of his career achievement wall. It is a fitting reminder of his work as an insider in the California Department of Fish and Game advocating for native fishes. We first talk about his path to becoming such an advocate.

I think the reason you and I are talking today is because, early-on in my life, I had an acquaintance with natural resources, particularly through fishing. My dad was a high school teacher in Stockton. Every summer, this was back in the '30s, we would pack up the trailer and spend the entire summer just over Tioga Pass in Yosemite. That's how I got my deep interest in mountains, lakes, and streams.

Next came college at the University of California, Berkeley. I knew I liked living things so I went into premed. Luckily, the first two years were pretty much basic, liberal arts courses. I never really intended to become a doctor, but I didn't know what else to do. My brother phoned me one day (about 1948) and told me that there was something in the general catalog that kind of fit me. It was a course being offered by [A. Starker] Leopold in Life Sciences. I talked to Dr. Leopold and, because of that conversation, immediately changed to wildlife conservation.

There's a difference between me and the average Joe coming out of college and interested in biology. Because Starker was very much a chip off the old block I was inoculated very early on with his father's Land Ethic. One day Starker brought into class a sheaf of mimeographed material for us to read. It was the first draft of *A Sand County Almanac,* before it was published. It made a huge impact on me, yet I didn't have enough experience to put it into context.

I started my career as a research biologist with the U.S. Fish and Wildlife Service then in 1953 I went to work for the State [California] as a seasonal employee. I kind of went along without any real questioning of our work. I had been inoculated with the Land Ethic philosophy but it hadn't taken hold yet. I was pretty much the old blood-and-guts type of biologist; the fish are there to catch and eat.

In 1955 I was promoted to the North California Coast and worked for three years with the Coastal Streams Anadromous Trout and Salmon Project. We were evaluating coastal fish stocks between San Francisco and the Oregon border. The main emphasis was the impact of hatchery-reared steelhead on wild runs and assessing the chinook salmon [*Oncorhynchus tshawytscha*] runs in the Trinity River before Lewiston Dam was built. Planners needed some idea of the size of the chinook runs to backfill with a fish hatchery. This was in the era when we thought hatcheries would solve our problems. I came back to Bishop in late 1957 and have been here ever since. My real interest was in mountain systems and, later, expanded to desert fishes.

A couple of things happened in the '60s. About 1964 I'd had a tough summer. Mine was a huge job trying to maintain the biological integrity of about 1,000 waters in the Eastern Sierra. It was like playing short-stop where the infield is littered with rocks. You never knew which way the ball was going to bounce. You didn't even think about catching it. You'd just try to stop the ball by jumping in front of it.

I'd walk into the office each morning not knowing if I was going to handle a drying up spring in Death Valley, a trout die-off in upper Bishop Creek, a disease problem somewhere, or some guy trying to build a hydroelectric plant and, in the process, drying up a stream. In that work environment you quickly start to feel like a fighter at the end of the 15th round. You're reeling. That's when my wife told me to take a couple of weeks off and go to the family cabin near Lake Tahoe. So I did. I took along *A Sand County Almanac* and read it again. It was like a religious experience. Leopold's paragraphs came off the pages as if illuminated. Survival in a job like mine required making an assessment of what is and is not important. Rereading *A Sand County Almanac* made me question if I had lost track of what was important in my work.

About that same time I got a phone call from Robert Rush Miller from Ann Arbor. He'd done just about all the systematics on desert fishes. He said, "When I described the Owens pupfish, we thought it was extinct. There is a chance it may still be there. If Carl Hubbs and I come up there, would you take us to Fish Slough to see if we can find it?" I told him I had to check with my boss (back then I was a little bit more compliant) who was in Los Angeles. If there is a key to anything I accomplished here in Bishop it is because I worked at the end of a 300-mile isosceles triangle. My bosses were at the far ends of the other two legs—one in Los Angeles and the other in Sacramento. That meant I could do things without the chain of command looking directly over my shoulder. I wrote to my boss saying, "I've got this request from Dr. Miller and Dr.

Hubbs to go sample Fish Slough and I've agreed to give them one day of my time. That's all." I was making the case to my boss that sometimes when academics show up they expect you to drop everything and help. On a hot July day we went to Fish Slough. I remember Dr. Hubbs yelling out "Bob, they're still here. We've still got them." At that moment I literally dropped everything that was the agency's traditional work of pleasing license holders and I never picked it up again. I went 90 degrees from the agency because of that experience and essentially stayed there for the rest of my career. Also, I was lucky to have supervisors who let me do nontraditional work without raising too much hell. My shift toward preservation work operated much like an inoculation for a virus. It takes a while for it to take hold. I'd been exposed to Leopold's ideas in college but they didn't take hold until the mid-'60s, after I'd accumulated some direct experience.

In 1967 a guy from the National Park Service in Death Valley called and told me I needed to come look at what was happening on the Nevada side of the border because it would affect California. I went down the next day. A huge development project was going in just east of Death Valley at Ash Meadows, right on top of an area with an incredible number of endemic species. A land developer was drilling wells all over that country to irrigate land that would never amount to anything. His wells were immediately outside the property corners of his lease on Bureau of Land Management land. It was his way to get control of water rights through supposed land improvement activities on BLM leases. The real agenda was never agriculture, it was to put in subdivisions using that water.

In the middle of this place was a small spring called Devils Hole. It was literally being dried up by the developer's irrigation pumps. In that country, when you put in a couple of 16-inch diameter wells, the water table falls quickly and any nearby springs are soon gone. We could actually watch the water level dropping in the spring that held the world's only population of Devils Hole pupfish. This issue eventually made it to the U.S. Supreme Court in 1972. Here I was, an employee of a California agency dedicated to providing recreation to license holders, but working more and more with federal agencies and the State of Nevada on an environmental project in Nevada! My boss wasn't happy, but I made matters worse.

Nathaniel Reed was Assistant Secretary of the Interior over fish, wildlife and parks during the Nixon administration. Reed gave a talk at an American Fisheries Society meeting in 1970 or 1972. He was trying to convince state directors to handle nontraditional fish and wildlife issues such as pupfish preservation. Reed was clear that if the state directors didn't, the federal government would have to intervene under the new Endangered Species Act. I wrote Reed a letter thanking him for his talk.

As was normal, I sent a copy of the letter to the president-elect of the Desert Fishes Council, who happened to work for the Nevada Division of Wildlife. He was on vacation when my letter arrived in Las Vegas. Apparently, their office policy was to have a secretary open and distribute mail. The secretary made a judgment that, because the guy I sent the letter to was on vacation, it was something the big boss needed to see. My letter went all the way up their chain of command to the director of Nevada Fish and Wildlife. That director then called my director and said, "Hey. Your guy is preaching something we don't want to hear—involvement of federal agencies in state affairs." I then got a call from my headquarters to see if I was going to be in Bishop the next day for a meeting. All I could think was that maybe they'd found out I was getting in too deep across the Nevada State line in Death Valley.

My bosses flew in from Sacramento and asked me to meet them at their hotel, here in Bishop. Picture this. When I walked into their hotel room, here was the director, deputy director, and the chief of operations. It was like a B movie. I sat in a straight chair in the middle of the room. There is a light bulb hanging from a cord. The chief had a copy of the letter I had written and the meeting began with him asking what I could tell them about it. I said, "Well, I wrote it." He said, "This has been highly embarrassing to all of us and to our colleagues." I asked them if there was anything wrong. "Well," he said, "not factually, but we don't like the intent of it, which is essentially saying we are not doing the job ourselves and the federal government may have to step into the affairs of a state fish and wildlife agency. We don't want the feds involved. We're not selling licenses for our guys to think like that." I had to admit that I did believe the states were not doing their jobs and had no interest in native fishes. But I'd been in the Army long enough to know you can't get off KP by fighting with the general. So I told them I was sorry if I had caused any problems and that I didn't intend it that way, but, I was deeply concerned about the future for our native fishes. I said, "If you look at the constitution of California, it doesn't say a thing about maintaining an economic perspective; at least it doesn't give it anymore emphasis than it does to the entirety of California's fish and wildlife." They hadn't ever really thought of that. I told them that I appreciated their intent and would try to be more careful in what I do. They went their way and so did I.

Mike: That sounds like you sensing a need for the agency to change its management perspective. Talk about how that happens in natural resource management.

While change is often hard in an agency, it is really important to show that one person can make a difference. I was able, by doing some of the things we did here in the eastern Sierra, to help shift the emphasis of aquatic management in the Department of Fish and Game. We went from the era of a put-and-take, catchable-trout mentality to something much broader. We did this despite pressure to be in the recreation business. Remember Leopold's point about the value of thinking 90 degrees from your agency, "Nonconformity is the highest evolutionary attainment of social animals." It is so easy to be a conformist in government. You get to work at 8:00, do what the boss wants you to do, and you get good reports. A director is not concerned about the resource but is very much concerned about what the governor's office is going to say. I guess I started my career as a regular kind of fish bio but sort of evolved to a greater concern about stewardship and then greater activism to make that happen. This period during the 1960s and '70s, when the Desert Fishes Council was formed, constituted the first major revolt against conventional fisheries management.

Conservation leadership has to originate from the lower ranks because that is where the idealism is and from that stewardship evolves. This has been one of my themes for a long time. When you think about it, your best people are those who are right out of universities. They come along with new ideas—ideas that are, too often, squelched by the agency. These new employees have yet to be hammered into the mold by the realities of biopolitics. I gave a talk at Keystone, Colorado, a few years ago at a Fish and Wildlife Service refuge managers' conference. It turned out to be a standing-ovation talk. The point I made to this group of about a thousand people was that innovation, new programs, and new thoughts within an agency are often inversely proportional to the square of the GS [General Schedule] rating and that the worst examples are found in state agencies. There were a couple of old-timers in the front row who just sat there. You could tell, they weren't buying it. After my talk one of these guys wrote a letter to the Fish and Wildlife Service director saying that I should never again be allowed to speak to Service employees. To me, that was one of the greatest compliments I'd ever received!

Sometimes constructive change is stymied because natural resource professionals are in denial about the role of values in our work, even though values determine everything we do in our waking hours. They are the internal compass that keeps us from going off course. I remember an experience with a guy from FERC [Federal Energy Regulatory Commission], who handled eastern Sierra hydroelectric development matters out of their Washington office. He came to Sacramento during the early days of enthusiasm for small hydrodevelopment and was one of FERC's big shots. We were talking about hydroelectric development and I said, "To me, this is far less a matter of electricity than it is ethics." His response was most revealing, "When you talk about ethics, you lose me." Now you can take that two ways. Either he didn't understand ethics or he felt ethical considerations were not important; that kilowatts transcended ethics. It is very clear to me that our problems in natural resource management stem far less from the lack of technology than from very poor value systems. And this pervades, of course, into agencies responsible for stewardship. Value systems drive an agency. When people ask me, "Why do you have this interest in philosophy?" my typical response is, "Did you ever think that your philosophy determines what you do or don't do?"

When I was a student at Berkeley I could not see how all my lower division courses were relevant. Why would I need to study German, math, and history to become a wildlife biologist? So I talked to Alva Davis, the Dean of Letters and Science. This older gentleman sat back in his chair and pulling on his pipe, said, "We want your education to make your life far more than your living." Today, when I talk to fish biologists, the message I'm trying to pass along is that a successful education is not just about learning how to turn a crank and make more fish to catch. We need people that are capable of making broader judgments. We're talking about the difference between education and training. Education is what survives after the training has been forgotten.

Another example of resistance to change I encountered was when the personal preferences of agency staff got in the way. My department bought a major property in northern California, near the town of Coleville, a place called Slinkard Valley. We bought the whole valley, lock, stock, and barrel, over 18 square miles of land. We bought it because the valley is great winter habitat for mule deer and an important corridor for their migration to lowlands in Nevada. The only negative thing about the place is the many rattlesnakes that live there.

This land also happened to include all of Slinkard Creek, a tributary to the West Walker River. The creek had been planted with non-native, eastern brook trout [*Salvelinus fontinalis*], although a distinctive strain of Lahontan cutthroat trout, the Walker strain [*Oncorhynchus clarkii henshawi*] was native to the stream. Department records showing brook trout stocking in Slinkard Creek go back many years to when the department often gave fish to citizens for stocking. We did have a remnant group of the native cutthroat but they were in ByDay Creek, just over the hill. But, ByDay's remnant population was vulnerable. In dry years we had to net them out of downstream holes that were drying up and move them upstream where springs provided a refuge during droughts.

Slinkard Creek was a great opportunity for native trout restoration as it had better, more stable habitat and it originally had the same strain of cutthroats. But the stocked brook trout, because they are so highly competitive, effectively wiped out the natives. You're really lucky if you own a whole watershed. You do not have to negotiate with anybody. You can just implement a program. So I proposed cutthroat restoration back into Slinkard Creek using a transplant from the remnant population in ByDay Creek, but first we had to get rid of the brook trout. When I came up with my plan, with a philosophical rationale and all the technical details, it included removing the brook trout. My boss, the regional manager, took one look and said, "No. If it ain't broke, don't fix it." I said, "Well boss, we are looking at it in different ways. You're thinking that Slinkard Creek is a good place to go fishing. I'm thinking that we are trying to preserve a native subspecies and the genes in these cutthroats are worth keeping. We owe it to them. It's a great use for department property." He said, "Nope. No way. Leave it the way it is."

I sent in my plan anyway. The response back from my boss was, "Look, you can't do that. The fishing is great there. I fish there myself." I said, "People can fish in literally thousands of other places that are just loaded with brook trout. We have higher value for Slinkard Creek." He said I would have to go through him to do a restoration. I've got a copy somewhere of the letter that I wrote to him [Figure 8.1]. I said, "We are going to do this anyway. If you don't like it, that's up to you. You can haul me in for a personnel board hearing for insubordination, but you

State of California   The Resources Agency

Memorandum

To   : Region 5   Date : August 12, 1986

From : Department of Fish and Game — Phil Pister

Subject: Slinkard Creek, Mono County: reintroduction of Lahontan cutthroat trout.

We were very disappointed to learn that permission to proceed with subject program has again been denied, especially in view of the fact that we had fully complied with the provisions of Mr. Fletcher's letter of June 3 outlining the steps to be taken prior to receiving final approval. The reasons for the recent denial were not clearly defined, but they are irrelevant. The purpose of this memorandum, is to serve notice of my intent.

The Walker River strain of the Lahontan cutthroat trout remains in great jeopardy. Unanticipated delays in implementing our recovery efforts add to this jeopardy, inasmuch as the proposed transplant population could easily be destroyed through a catastrophic event. We need badly to establish populations in other locations.

We shell continue to monitor the situation. If, in our opinion, it becomes necessary to treat Slinkard Creek in order to save the Walker River cutthroat strain, it is my plan to proceed without delay, and without further authorization.

I am fully aware of the possible consequences to me of such an action, and I assume full responsibility. One thing would be far worse, however, and that would be to lose an irreplaceable gene resource because of some ill-defined political, administrative, or personal reason. I would welcome a full discussion and public airing of all relevant facts in the disciplinary hearings which would inevitably result.

On August 18, 1969 the entire world population of the Owens pupfish lay helplessly in a rapidly drying pond north of Bishop. Three of us worked late into the night as we carried the survivors in small buckets to a spring habitat, from which began a slow and laborious recovery effort. If we had not done this, the species would now be extinct. In good conscience, I cannot allow this to happen to the Lahontan cutthroat trout.

It occurs to me that such an experience by our top administrators within the Department would do much to place the Department's operations in the proper perspective. It emphasizes the fact that our obligation to the resource transcends our obligation to ourselves.

E. P. Pister
Associate Fishery Biologist

cc: Inland Fisheries Division
     file

Figure 8.1. Letter from Phil Pister to California Department of Fish and Game administration regarding Walker strain cutthroat trout (*Oncorhynchus clarkii henshawi*) rehabilitation in Slinkard Creek, CA.

know I'll win because I'm right and you're wrong." We went ahead with the rehab on our own. He was furious but he knew I had him backed into a corner. That was as close as I came to an absolute confrontation. We did the project and now the cutthroat are doing real well. He goes fishing in other places. It was kind of like Kennedy and Kruschev during the Cuban missile crisis. Who's going to back down? I had no authority. I just went ahead and did it anyway despite the fact he was the boss. Today we exchange phone calls and Christmas cards and remain good friends.

My bumper sticker, "Question Authority," applies here because my boss's conclusion was wrong and I knew it. Furthermore, I knew that whoever heard a complaint about me couldn't help but make a judgment in my favor. This was in the mid-'80s. Things had advanced well enough in government that if I got called in for a hearing, the facts, that were strongly with me, meant more than earlier in my career. A favorite quote from Benjamin Franklin also applies here, "My rule, in which I have always found satisfaction, is, never to turn aside in public affairs through views of private interest; but go straight forward in doing what appears to me right at the time, leaving the consequences with Providence."

This incident was more a gap in basic values than in perception. My boss was a good administrator and better trained and educated than most. He just let his personal preferences get in the way. I approached the issue with essentially Leopold's philosophies directing me, "A thing is right when it tends to preserve the integrity, stability, and beauty of the biotic community" [Leopold 1949]. That's exactly what we were trying to do up there. My boss's thinking was, "Boy, these fish are fun to catch and I love to do it." Both perspectives are valid things but you have to make choices when they are in conflict.

Sometimes change is blocked because a lack of trust keeps professionals from working together, even though they have the same interests. I had a revealing experience during the early days of concern about desert fishes. We called a meeting of agency managers and university scientists in November 1969. The meeting was advertised as, "Bringing people together who share common concerns about the integrity of desert ecosystems." When I took the podium at the Death Valley National Park's interpretive center it was a real eye-opener. On the left side of the auditorium were all the university professors and their students and on the right side were the agency people. They weren't even talking to one another. They were essen-

tially there for the same reason but totally untrusting of each other.
I realized that if we could accomplish anything it would be to bring these
two sides together.

Risk of personal consequences from your agency holds many people
back from pushing for change. In the early days of desert fishes conservation my state and federal colleagues told me they were concerned but
just could not act for fear of the consequences. Agencies tend to stifle
criticism if it focuses on economic development. One solution we hit
upon was formation of the Desert Fishes Council. Under that
organization's letterhead these same people could express their concerns and ideas and get them out without reprisal. Before that they
were often shot as the messenger bearing bad news to agency execu-
tives and other power players.

Agency values are another powerful obstacle to change. It says a lot
when California refuses to change the agency name from 'Fish and Game'
to 'Fish and Wildlife.' There is still a lot of pressure, both legislatively
and from within the department, to be traditionalists. All you have to do
is look at a pie diagram of how the money is spent. You can see that the
things we should be emphasizing, like biodiversity issues, are tiny sliv-
ers of the budget pie. The big pieces still go to things like law enforcement, the deer program, and fish hatcheries. That's the way things are,
despite 30 years since the start of the environmental movement.

I once was on the Endangered Species Committee of the Western
Division of the American Fisheries Society. We had a meeting in Las
Vegas in 1974, back when we met in conjunction with the International
Association of Fish and Wildlife Agencies. A committee was talking about
getting endangered species programs going. The western states were
saying, literally without exception, that they didn't have money for this
kind of work. The feds told the committee that funds were available
under the Endangered Species Act for the states to handle much of the
work. Some guy from Montana's commission got up and said, "I would
rather have every species in the state of Montana go extinct than let the
feds into Montana." He sincerely felt this way. It's going to be a long
time before that mind-set totally dies out.

These traditionalists are not irrational. They're acting on the values they think important. It may be illogical from the standpoint of an
ecologist saying the Montana commissioner is not doing anything for
the overall biota. Leopold said it so well, "We fancy that game species
support us, forgetting all about what supports game species" [Leopold
1949]. The commissioner's political ideology was just getting in the way

of this larger purpose for fish and wildlife management. Until we can get more thinkers with ecological orientations into decision making, it's going to continue to be an uphill battle. But there is good news, the old guard is dying off or retiring!

Change is hard because decision makers and agencies respond to their environment. Take aerial fish planting as an example. During my graduate work we studied everything we could about a two acre lake in the upper part of Convict Creek. There were no fish in it. We took water samples, bottom samples, water chemistry samples, plankton samples, and everything else we could think of. After we had all this baseline data, we planted 1,700 brook trout fingerlings. They grew quite well over their first winter, reaching perhaps five or six inches. The next summer we marked 200 of these fish to follow through the years. Twenty-five years later we were still catching marked fish out of that lake; they had grown maybe an inch in that quarter century. In the process they removed virtually everything that could be thought of as a food organism, finally consuming even things like pine needles and rocks—there isn't a plankton organism left in the lake; no midge larvae; nothing. The fish were literally starving to death across decades. They only got off one spawn in all that time.

Back in the '70s I realized no one had really studied if aerial fish plants do any good. Think of it. An average plant into a high Sierra lake may be 2,000 fish every other year, maybe every three years. We've always assumed, based on the work of a student from Humboldt State College, that if you get 10 percent of those fish back as catchable you are doing pretty well. Two redds along the shoreline will produce more fish than that airplane will.

I designed a big research project on the effectiveness of aerial planting and sent it to headquarters in Sacramento for approval. After it was there for a couple of weeks, I got a call from the chief of the fisheries division. He told me that research to evaluate aerial fish planting would never get off the ground. He said, "The director doesn't want any information that might undermine keeping his private airliner"—which is exactly what it was. There are people in the legislature who know just how expensive it is to operate an airplane. The best answer a director can give to a legislator's criticism is that, ". . . we use that plane for our aerial fish planting," totally evading the fact that we're not sure if aerial plants work. All directors, if they are going to survive very long, secure friends in the legislature. These are the friends who push the budgets, etc. VIP trips, like flying the power players from Sacramento out for field trips, was part of the director's work of cultivating friends in the legislature.

The director's perquisite of a private airline was a factor, but his behavior was also an expected response to stakeholder support from both inside and outside the department. If you set up a huge fish hatchery system to provide trout for people to catch, you set up an expectation. There's going to be resistance to stopping that program. From inside it came from the established power structure; for example, the fish hatchery people who grew the fish and the pilots who planted them. It's a simple question of, "Will the entrenched programs in an agency be threatened by new information and new ideas?" Of course they will. From outside, the public, mostly through organized angling groups, made their views known. When the department started cutting back because fish planting was impacting native frogs [the mountain yellow-legged frog (*Rana muscosa*)], my local county board of supervisors wrote a strong letter of protest to the legislature opposing the change. In a community like Bishop, fishing is a bread and butter income source for sport stores, packers, motels, and the like. When they saw department planes dumping baby fish into 'their' lake, they liked it. These people sent plenty of positive feedback to the director about aerial planting. For them more planting meant more fish to catch without ever questioning if that was true. Agencies tend to reflect political pressures, which are reflections of people pressures. These push agencies into bureaucratic comfort zones. A population of fish cannot advocate but an entrenched government program has many effective, noisy, and powerful advocates.

In recent times voices from the other side appeared; people like the Sierra Club. They started asking tough questions like, "How do you know your fish planting isn't destroying something else?" That kind of dissent is healthy. It happened to me with frogs. When Roland Knapp originally said there may be a relationship between fish planting and native frog declines [Knapp and Matthews 2000], my first reaction was that this guy is nuts. I knew of lakes that had never had fish near them where the frogs had died out. Even though I think about these issues, Roland's ideas were new to me. I had to adapt to the new thinking. I had to change. His observation and judgment could not be summarily dismissed and were later proved to be at least partially correct.

Most change is a result of putting out fires, like the pupfish issue we already talked about. All of a sudden you are confronted with a problem and your job is to try, within the system as much as you can, to put out the fire. You can put in the call, but expect that the fire department is not going to show up for a long time. You have to put out the fire yourself. The real challenge is to do just that; see the problem, be able to handle it, and then wait for your bureaucracy to catch up. There is typically a decade between noticing a problem and getting official support to handle it.

That happened to Felix Smith, the U.S. Fish and Wildlife Service biologist who blew the whistle on bird poisoning at Kesterson [National Wildlife Refuge]. Felix is out doing his canoe surveys and starts seeing dead and deformed waterfowl. He reports this finding to the boss and then up the chain of command to the regional office in Portland, saying, "We've got a real problem." Felix had discovered the problem of pesticide residues from big agriculture in the central valley of California draining into Kesterson. The first response Felix got was denial. I think people knew deep down that he was right, but they didn't want to acknowledge it because of the enormous economic forces behind the issue. Felix put up with hell. He and I both got the American Motors' conservation award in the same year for essentially the same reason. We were willing to go up against the system and say, "You just can't keep ignoring the problem." It took a long time for the agency to catch up with Felix.

Dealing with entrenched economic interests is a part of our challenge. A good example is golden trout here in California. Golden trout are native in two drainages in the head waters of the Kern River. I knew, intuitively, they were different strains but I didn't have any real hard data. Later, when genetic assessment technology came on line, the fish from each drainage did test out as distinct. Up into those habitats swam brown trout from our attempts to make sport fishing better downstream. In the early days we weren't really managing rivers or groups of fish. We just planted hatchery trout, mostly introduced species, and expected fishing to be good. We had some regulations, but, basically, the native fish were managing themselves. I was first alerted to the problem when a Kernville fisherman told me, "You know, Phil, every time I go up there I catch brown trout higher up in the drainage. I'm concerned." I thanked him for the information and kind of filed it in my mind. Not too long after that one of our game wardens from Lone Pine told me his next-door neighbor caught a brown trout just about as high up in that drainage as you can get. I thanked him but this time, as I hung up the phone, it sunk in. I was overwhelmed. I could envision what it would take to keep brown trout from taking over the entire drainage and, in the process, wiping out golden trout.

We went up there the next day with a fish shocker. Out of a stream about as wide as from me to you [10 feet] we caught a 5-pound brown trout and no golden trout within 100 yards of that fish. In some areas browns outnumbered the goldens more than 100 to 1; in a few places 200 to 1. There was nothing left in the way of a healthy golden trout population.

In the way of saving golden trout was a major public relations problem—removing the browns. People liked to catch these fish and the horse-packing industry wanted them for their clients. On the other side of the coin we were helped because the golden trout is California's state fish. In the upper areas I tried to get rid of the brown trout using a chlorine fish toxicant. It did a good job of knocking down the numbers of browns, but it wasn't powerful enough to kill them all. We realized that a refuge was needed—one that prevented upstream migration after eradication of brown trout. So, in the early '70s we began to build barriers. We ended up building a series of three barriers and then worked our way downstream removing brown trout and restocking goldens. Luckily the two streams that held the goldens nearly touch, with only about 200 yards separating them at one point. We shocked-up about 6,000 golden trout from the badly impacted stream and carried them over to live cages we had placed in the other stream. Then we eradicated the brown trout by working our way downstream from the upper refuge. About a month later, after the invertebrate populations bounced back, we restocked goldens. That was the immediate crisis and solution, but brown trout was only one of the threats for golden trout.

Upland habitat degradation due to grazing was a longer-term threat. When cows and trout mix in the same stream, the cows usually win. In this case the chairman of the National Cattlemen's Association ran cattle on Forest Service property throughout the golden trout area. When we were doing our recovery work, the chairman's cowboys were constantly asking what we were doing and why. They said, "Don't get rid of the brown trout, get rid of the goldens because they're no good to eat." The chairman said, "I'm not having anybody tell me how to run my cows on my land." Never mind this was public land. We were the intruders because we were asking for changes to his cattle management.

He eventually sold his permit to a retired American Airlines captain who could fly into a little airstrip up there. His thinking was not much different—Americans need to eat and that means beef. Then the

Anheuser-Busch Corporation bought property on Owens Lake, where some big springs provided water to truck to their breweries in L.A. in case a drought interrupted their normal supply. Their purchase included the airline captain's grazing permits and they hired a local cowboy to run the cattle operation.

Golden trout restoration not only brought up the debate of brown trout versus golden trout versus cattle, it also energized the animal rights people. They jumped in saying, "What right do you guys have in killing anything off? Brown trout have as much right to live as anything else?" Luckily, I remembered reading a section from the book *Environmental Ethics*, by a good friend, Holmes Rolston. [1988] He used the golden trout situation to point out that sometimes you have to make concessions. He said, essentially, "When you deal with a native species as opposed to something that is there illegitimately and destroying the natural biology of the situation (brown trout should never have left Europe), the exotics have to go." Having this third-party opinion from a guy who was not viewed as a nut helped satisfy the animal rights people.

Finally, the native trout advocates got into the act (Trout Unlimited and California Trout). They set up meetings with the publicity people from Anheuser-Busch, essentially saying, "If you don't get the cattle off that land, we're going to raise hell. How would you like to see full-page ads in the *New York Times* on how Anheuser-Busch is destroying California's state fish?" The grazing fee paid to the Forest Service was something like $5,000 per year for a couple of thousand of acres. The beer people decided it wasn't worth it. In 2001 they agreed to not run beef up there at all.

There is a lot going on in stories like the ones I'm telling but one element is that the status quo is difficult to overcome. It's so much easier to take your head and stick it deeply into the sand and say we are going to keep going the traditional way. Another reason the status quo has power is fear of the unknown, a basic human problem. Turf is another problem. Because there are different kingdoms in an established bureaucracy you can expect resistance to protect established programs. If there is uncertainty about the future, people will use that as an excuse not to change. It's worse when a government program is popular with businesses, legislators, and users. Under these circumstance it's easy and somewhat natural to settle into a stable bureaucratic comfort zone. It wasn't until we had more groups like the Defenders of Wildlife and the Sierra Club that agencies were forced to think differently on issues like aerial fish planting and golden trout conservation.

Another blocker to change is the issue of agencies having multiple-use mandates. One of our big problems with the small hydro issue was the multiple-use philosophy and mandate of federal agencies, ". . . the greatest good for the greatest number." When an agency has energy production as one of its mandates, they can't say no to hydroplants. My Department could. One of the big advantages that I and my agency had is that we are not mandated to produce energy. Our job is to protect the fish and wildlife resource. This is a luxury compared to my counterparts in the Forest Service or the BLM. They have to look at multiple use as part of their legal mandate.

A recurring dilemma in our work is resolving the choice between immediate gain versus long-term benefit. In a way, these decisions distinguish between the politician and the statesman. The statesman will be concerned about the long-term and everything that contributes to a great nation. The politician focuses on those activities that will reelect him which means, by necessity, he has a shorter time perspective. Doing the right thing for the long term may very well work against the best interests of the short term. The reward structure is backwards. I guess what I'm saying is that anytime you perceive a significant change is needed the safer assumption is to expect significant inertia. The smart manager has a plan to manage around excuses like the ones I encountered.

Mike: You mentioned small hydrodevelopment. Tell me about that issue.

In the early 1970s there was great concern about a perceived energy shortage. New laws resulted in tremendous enthusiasm to build hydroelectric power plants on small rivers in the West. Well, the eastern Sierra's many short, steep rivers were just what developers were looking for. In the West there were hundreds of proposed projects and no methodology set up to evaluate them. Again, the environmental laws were there, but nobody was paying much attention because it was convenient and safer to ignore the laws. A breakthrough for us was realizing we could take advantage of the laws. Then the hard work started.

First, knowing the biological, recreational, and aesthetic value of these streams we believed it was wrong to put them into a pipe. This would have destroyed the best values of those streams. We knew the recreational use of these streams was intense and we knew that in another 100 years it would be vastly greater.

A turning point was when we figured out that the handful of hydro-electric projects in our area, run the way they were planning to run them, wouldn't make any real contribution to the nation's electric power needs. Along with this we relied on the corollary concept of promoting perception as the only truly creative part of recreational engineering—another Leopold canon. As people gain a greater appreciation of these natural resources they will want the streams for more than just electricity.

Next we had to define what was needed. Well, we knew we needed water in the stream beds, but how do we quantify this? Nobody had worked out the assessment methods. That's how we got going on the IFIM [Instream Flow Incremental Methodology] work—we had to. I also knew I didn't know much of anything about the engineering of these facilities so I went looking for and hired a new employee who did to work along side me.

Our biggest conceptual breakthrough was the presence of mind to reject the developers' mind-set. When the hydrodevelopers brought in their project plans their attitude was, "We have a right to the water unless you can prove damage to the resource." That meant to stop a project we had to prove it would hurt fish. We were able to turn that around by saying back, "It's your job to show us that you're not going to hurt the public's resources. You have to prove no harm." We then backed that up with the early manifestations of the IFIM process. Having that technical tool helped us keep the onus on developers.

As part of our procedure we required that developers send us their assessments showing that their projects would do no harm, including all their back-up documentation. That requirement, along with my new staff person who knew the engineering issues so they could not pull the wool over our eyes, put us in a position to critique their work, not develop a bunch of new work of our own to refute their claims. Out of the 95 applications in our area only one of the small-hydro proposals was built and it was a retrofit of an existing facility that needed fixing anyway. Actually, that was the intent of the small-hydro law in the first place; retrofit old dams, not take streams in an arid area like the Sierra East Slope and put them in pipes.

Another success factor for us was the one I mentioned before of being far away from anybody looking down my back. At the time we had a very conservative governor who was pushing development because it was part of the Republican agenda. My boss at that time was in Long Beach. He also was conservative and agreed with the pro-development agenda. He'd call me on the carpet for going ahead with our small-hydro work but he couldn't come up with a reason to stop us, other than to say we needed direction from headquarters in Sacramento. My boss also was your typical organizational person. He went strictly by the party line. And the party line was consumptive use of the water. That quickly became the unstated, but nevertheless real, agency policy. Being away from his daily oversight was an advantage as we grappled in Bishop with strategic issues like what standards we would set for developers and building the technical capacity to respond. We pretty well had these wheels in motion before the bosses got involved. This made our efforts more difficult to stop.

Another thing that helped was our willingness to question authority. That is, of course, a somewhat simplistic thing for me to say. But, when you think about it, there is good reason to do so. Be wary of the concept of the team player. I despise that concept. If I can be sure of what the team is trying to win, what the captain's goals are, I can then think about becoming a team player. But just to go into an organization and say, "I'm going to be a great team player" shows a totally unjustified trust in who the captain is and what goal he is trying to achieve. If I had been a team player we wouldn't be talking right now about what to do with Owens or Death Valley pupfish. They'd be gone!

Mike: In America, we've chosen to manage natural resources primarily using government agencies. Talk about what that is like.

The greatest problems I encountered in promoting preservation of native fishes came from my agency's entrenched belief that fish and game work was about providing recreation—an attitude that predominated after World War II. Most upper-echelon agency personnel were utilitarian thinkers. They just could not see the loss of desert and other native species as being significant. If an issue did not address sport fishing—where there was a lot of noise and confusion—it did not get attention. When I pressed them on the issue they'd simply dismiss it by denying its significance. Their question would be, "What are you messing around with these worthless little fish for? What good are they?" I had colleagues try to get under my skin by saying things like, "I'm going out to get some pupfish because they make good bass bait." You just had to ignore the barbs and become agile in responding. Leopold's A-B cleavage fits well here, "One group (A) regards the land as soil, and its function as commodity production; another group (B) regards the land as a biota, and its function as something broader" (Leopold 1949). Our agencies still retain a good share of 'A' types, but that is changing.

Today, most students coming out of school are already of the 'B' persuasion, reflecting an ecological education and not just trained to turn a crank to produce fish. It remains a bit of a shock when they run into the old guard, 'A' persuasion employees who relegate the meaning of a forest to board feet of lumber. The German philosopher and physicist Max Planck [1950] caught this essence when he said, "A new scientific truth does not triumph by convincing its opponents and making them see the light. But rather because its opponents eventually die, and a new generation grows up that is familiar with it." I think there is progress. I don't see many of the old guard anymore. Those that remain are approaching retirement. Managers today seem to be far more receptive to new ideas than when I was starting my career.

There is no easy answer to things like pupfish preservation. The Owens pupfish was one of the first listings under the Endangered Species Act. Sadly, these fish are not much better off now than back then. All one can say is that we are currently much more aware of the fragility of the resource and that there are recovery plans in place. It is going to be a constant battle. We will never be able to walk away from these fish, either legally or ethically.

Biologists now must face increasingly difficult questions, such as, "Some projects are inherently bad for the resource. Should an ethical biologist become involved?" Or, "Irrespective of the righteousness of the cause, is distortion of the truth ever permissible?" There's a paper, *Ethics and the Environmental Biologist*, that Don Erman and I wrote that looks at this question [Erman and Pister 1989]. It came from an American Fisheries Society meeting in 1988 where I opened the discussion by posing the situation, "What are a professional's obligations when working on a project that is inherently bad, like building a dam on an anadromous fish stream?" Then, as now, when I ask this question the answer from my audience is, usually, "Yes, I should be involved because the bad thing is going to happen anyway. Maybe I can make it better." I ask back, "Is distortion of the truth ever acceptable?" My answer is, No!

I remember back in the early days of working on endangered fishes, you were a voice in the wilderness. Nobody could understand what you were doing and pretty much everyone adopted this mitigate-because-you-can't-stop-progress outlook. You'd think up spurious reasons to preserve a species—like research links to human health—even though, deep down, you know you are really stretching it. As an aside, this may be true for pupfish since you can take them from almost pure water and put them in high salt concentrations and they'll just shake their heads and swim away. Their kidney structure has to be amazing and could well be useful for research. Nevertheless, you know that these over-dramatized justifications are not the right thing to do.

It was in the *Pilgrim's Progress* paper [Pister 1987] that I talked about my change of thinking. It's been interesting to stay in contact with environmental philosophers. They are a smart bunch. I found out real quick that they know a lot more about fish biology than I do about philosophy. It's been challenging to stay up with the literature, but it's been real productive. David Ehrenfeld has written a very fine paper called *The Conservation of Non-Resources* [Ehrenfeld 1976]. He uses the Houston toad as his subject. He talks about how you shouldn't come up with all these spurious reasons, no matter what. He goes into why these species should be preserved from a moral perspective. That got me motivated to think in that direction and to write the *Endangered Species Costs and Benefits* paper [Pister 1979].

So, a person coming out of university should probably want to know how their prospective boss wants them to act on their professional conscience. A person looking for the right boss needs to know more than whether or not they're getting into an agency or firm that is out to rip off the environment. It is easy to say, "Nope. I don't want anything to do with them." It is more difficult to deal with the truth-or-mitigate quagmire that you find in most management agencies.

Now it does make sense to be constructively critical; not to say that everything is going to hell, but to say, "Let's try to make it better." If I've ever done anything really worthwhile, it is defined in the minds of who you are talking to. The boss wants to know, "What are you doing to promote my goals or those of the department?" Sport anglers want to know, "What are you doing to make fishing better?" Each person you meet defines your job in a different way. I'd try to pull from each of these different definitions and put those needs into a more biologically supportable perspective that leaves something for future generations—a resource essentially undiminished from the one we have now. Those were my job expectations. I did my very best to avoid the trivial but there are realities of working in an agency. I retired right at 60 to shake off the constraints of my bureaucracy. I never intended to retire from conservation work, per se. The time was right for me to remove the bureaucratic constraints that we live under in an agency so I could do the things that I felt were most important.

I've seen people who failed to be 100 percent honest and they paid a price. If you're always honest, you don't have to worry about what you might have said before. Establish yourself as a credible person with your boss. I'm kind of giving the impression that all bosses are worthless; that's not true. There are very good, conscientious people out there who want to do a good job, and I have had some excellent bosses. It's important to support these people. In the end, though, by your own behavior and your own works will they know you. If you can show that you can do good work you will be trusted. That trust gives freedom to do lots of stuff. If the boss is thinking you are not trustworthy, you will have trouble.

A person looking for work should want to find out about the boss. Are you going to go head-to-head with their basic philosophies? Do you have a boss who might allow you to work for them and provide the chance for your thinking to be accepted? Will you have any freedom to do your own research if you want to? If I were to go to work for an outfit now, I would want to know these things.

And be really good at understanding values, conflicts, and ethics. It's always bugged me that most Doctors of Philosophy in our field probably wouldn't know a philosophy book if somebody threw it at them. I'll often say that, "Your Ph.D. is good, but, how much do you know about philosophy?" A typical answer is, "I was so busy on my dissertation I never had time to take that class." It's education versus training again.

Mike: Reflect on what we've talked about and summarize advice you have about being a constructive force for change.

Don't assume that the organization you work for will always do the right thing. There are powerful reasons why this often does not happen. Understand what being a team player means. Question authority but respect it. You can question authority—being aware of errors that your bosses might make—but also be aware of the fact that you still have a degree of loyalty to these people. Communicate honestly and accurately so you build credibility. Being credible is important because at some point your issue gets handed off to someone else, whether it's a court, a commission, or somebody higher up the chain of command. If you do not have squeaky clean credibility you are easily, sometimes actively, ignored. Think about third parties. Ask yourself, "Is there a third party that needs to be involved?" and when the answer is yes, figure out how to make that happen. But, when you run into a stone wall, you've got to have enough guts to go ahead and follow your conscience.

If there is a risk, consider going underground or using a neutral body to get otherwise suppressed information out into public view. This was and still is one of the reasons for the Desert Fishes Council. It is more difficult to shoot the messenger if the messenger is a group rather than an individual employee who can be singled out. Think about how to get people working together. The Desert Fishes Council helped get the agency people talking to the university people. It focused attention and sparked needed technical work. The council was essentially a coalition dedicated to advancing and sharing knowledge about desert fishes. It was easy for decision makers to ignore the losses and turn unique desert aquatic habitats into housing developments. The council made it impossible to hide that impact by simply ignoring it.

Recruit champions, if you can. Several times in my career it was important that I had a boss who would let me do things and then stand up for me. Another important kind of champion is the well placed leader or colleague who is not in your direct chain of command or even in your agency. In the small-hydro case we were lucky. I had a contact at FERC who was instrumental in understanding and denying the hydroelectric projects here on the East Slope. Having people willing to champion your issue gives you more options than simply staying inside your own chain of command. Speaking of 'chains of command,' when you eventually reach a supervisory position avoid referring to subordinates as 'my' assistant or 'my' statistician. You do not own these people. You simply work with them. Use 'our' rather than 'my.' It is arrogant to do otherwise and is likely to evoke ill feelings.

Create a respectful working relationship with people in your chain of command. Empower them to achieve something they want through you as opposed to just asking them to support you. It helps in two ways to have a respectful working relationship with your bosses. Obviously, they can help you through direct intervention when the going gets rough. The second way is that it makes disagreeing with them easier. You are better positioned to honestly and directly confront them since you have credibility and their respect. That's what I essentially did with cutthroat in Slinkard Creek. One of the reasons I could confront my regional manager was that we had a respectful relationship. Just be careful to not get into the trap of horse trading favors. Lead with your ethics.

Create watchdogs. Unfortunately, natural resource decisions are almost always one direction. Once a fish stock is displaced, especially by land conversion or water diversion, it is permanent. Conservation requires that you win repeated battles. Development only requires that you win once.

Get publicity for your issue. Most of the time biologists, even those in the private sector, are working on a public resource, whether it is using water as a place to dump wastes, produce hydropower, or whatever. Repressing information and tailoring professional opinions about projects is equivalent to hiding information. Preventing the public from knowing what is going on is a neglect of professional responsibility. Giving information has to be done right, obviously, or you can get yourself in a big pile of trouble. You need some public relations skills. Be wary of the boss that says information is too sensitive to release.

Never overlook the positive value of a crisis. Often, in our system, the present situation has so much power it takes the perception of a crisis to get past the denial. Sometimes an event will whack you in the face, but maybe you can seize the opportunity for change that a crisis often creates. Actively decide for yourself where your comfort zone is for doing advocacy on behalf of the resource. Don't let that decision creep up on you.

What I do at the start of my lectures is say, "What we're going to be talking about a lot today is values. If I were to hand out paper and ask each of you to write your definition of values we'd find similar definitions but they would not be the same." What this tends to show is that we all take the term values and define it based on our own experience, background, and teaching. I then try to develop an understanding by asking the audience to assume they are the parents of a family whose home is on a flood plain and that a flood is imminent. As parents they are faced with the choice of saving only one of two things—their children's favorite video game or the family Bible that has come down across generations. When I ask which to save, most audience members choose the Bible. Then we have a discussion about why. This discussion usually ends with the judgment that the video game is left behind because the family Bible has a more profound importance and is irreplaceable. I'll then show a photograph of an old Bible and a video game and say, "Now perhaps in your mind it's a little clearer what profound values are compared to transient values. Your job, as I see it, is to make those definitions and early on in your career establish what really matters and what does not." I encourage professionals to make it a career goal to spend more time working on profound values and forgetting the transient values. If you choose right in our line of work, you're never going to get wealthy, you're never going to starve to death, but you can always go to bed at night and feel good about what you've done. As professionals, nothing would be worse than to leave as our legacy a boxcar loaded with reprints concerning recently extinct species.

9
Max Bazerman - Why We Say One Thing But Do Another

It is an error to assume that everybody
uses the same thought process.
– Max Bazerman

Why do people say they want one thing, but decide to do another? Is that question relevant for natural resource professionals? Harvard professor Max Bazerman believes it is. Bazerman is a leading researcher and thinker about the difficulties humans have making decisions. His research spans a wide array of questions about why wise policies—for individuals, organizations, and governments—do not easily occur, including the topic of poor environmental decision making.

Bazerman is the Jesse Isidor Straus Professor of Business Administration at the Harvard Business School, but he gets around quite a bit. At Harvard he is formally affiliated with the Kennedy School of Government, the Psychology Department, the Institute for Quantitative Social Sciences, the Harvard University Center on the Environment, and the Program on Negotiation. In his prior position at the Kellogg School of Management (Northwestern University), Max was the founder and director of the Kellogg Environmental Research Center. And he's served on the board of a number of organizations, including the Consensus Building Institute, Sterling Gorge Natural Area Trust, Maine Coastal Habitat Foundation, The Israel Center for Negotiation and Conflict Management, and the National Council for Science and the Environment.

He is the author or co-author of over 175 research articles and book chapters, and the author, co-author, or co-editor of 15 books, including: *Judgment in Managerial Decision Making*, now in its sixth edition (Bazerman 2006). His list of consulting clients reads like a *Who's Who* of successful government and corporate organizations.

Bazerman's research focus is decision making, negotiation, creating joint gains in society, and the natural environment. His recent work has centered around themes such as barriers to effective governance, creative negotiations between environmental and economic interests, intrapersonal conflict, and judgment in managerial decision making, the first subject we talk about.

Unlike the other people you've interviewed, I'm not out there doing front-line resource work. I'm here in academia where I play the role of observer. I watch how others behave in their decision making and offer some commentary that I hope is useful. I'm basically a researcher who looks at the systematic ways our judgment fails us. Some of the things I've written about deal with the inconsistency between the preference people say they have versus the direction they actually take in their decisions.

I'm interested in the fact that people claim they want to leave their children a world in as good a condition as they received it, yet their behaviors are quite incompatible with that goal. And that can go from the biggest issues like climate change, to regional issues like the over-harvesting of fisheries, to day-to-day issues like our propensity to drive SUVs when we don't need them.

For example, think about our tepid efforts in the United States to manage climate change. The people I talk to, unless they work for an oil company, say the verdict is in. Climate change is occurring and humans are a cause of it. While they may not know the details, these people know it's a potentially devastating effect that we're leaving to future generations and it will dramatically affect their lives. Yet, the United States is doing so little policywise to address the question. Why? Then there are individuals like SUV owners. They easily talk about how much they care about the earth and their children's future but they keep driving these wasteful vehicles when they don't need them. Why?

I look at this problem of all talk and little action and ask why we do so little? The answer, at least part of the answer, comes from thinking about how the human mind works. When I look I see some common human behaviors repeated across a wide array of issues from financial decisions, to public policy decisions, to environmental decisions. There is a set of cognitive biases that seem to grab hold of the decisions and determine an outcome that is frequently not in the best long-term interest. Cognitive issues are, at least, a partial explanation for why we say one thing but do another.

In climate change an example of one bias contributing to our failure to make strong decisions is that people hold positive illusions. That means we put a positive spin on our expectation for the future. Even though the scientific data may be clear, if there is uncertainty we somehow hope that the future impact won't be as bad as it appears to us today. Another version of a positive illusion is an optimistic assumption that technology is somehow going to rescue us because technology has been important in the past. Given the time lag that exists between our actions today and bad events occurring in the future, it's very easy to have optimistic illusions about what's going to happen.

We also know that people overly discount the future. Sometimes it is with simple decisions like buying a refrigerator. People who say they care about the environment pay attention to the capital expense and don't pay attention to the yearly cost for the energy they're using. In fact, they end up paying more over the lifetime of the refrigerator and, in the process, are less environmentally friendly. They discount the future consequences of today's decision.

When we move from refrigerators to climate change, we have a similar issue of the present being weighted far more than the future. And when the future is across generations, when it's uncertain, and when it's going to hit a third party like Bangladesh before it hits us, this discounting becomes extreme. We may claim to be good people who care about the environment, but our behaviors don't reflect that talk. The consequence is that politicians and the citizens who affect the politicians are letting climate change drift as a topic. It's the environmental parallel to the huge debt the U.S. government is accumulating in Medicare, Medicaid, and Social Security, and that corporations are incurring with pension obligations they're not going to be able to meet. We're basically creating problems in the future and our mind is able to ignore that. That's the kind of analysis that I think about. How is it that the minds of even good people allow terrible events to occur in the future?

Perhaps the most amazing example of judgment problems in our natural resource decision making is fisheries. Here we see the same pattern occur over and over. I understand that 11 of the 17 largest fishery basins in the world are now commercially extinct. The way we got to this state is relatively parallel across basins. In the '60s and '70s, governments throughout the world, certainly the United States, subsidized modernization of fishing fleets. Fishers could then catch more with less effort. All of that seemed amazingly efficient if you ignore the problem that catching too many fish does not leave enough behind to make more fish for the future.

After modernization of the fishing fleets scientists started picking up the pattern that fish populations and harvests were shrinking. At that point government became convinced the scientists were right and started recommending stronger interventions. The fishing industry, in order to maintain its current harvest, quickly said that the scientists were just seeing a minor abnormality, everything was fine, there was no real need to further regulate harvest. Add to that the fact that the people who fish typically have more political influence than do scientific findings and the stage is set for no change to occur. The fishing industry responds by lobbying their politicians to keep fishing rates high, still working under an optimistic illusion and a tendency to discount the future. There may have been some compromise but, typically, by the time a harvest reduction was worked out it was too little too late. This seems to be the pattern.

A usual analysis attributes this management behavior to a dysfunctional incentive system. The core problem is lots of independent fishers in the same basin setting up the well known Tragedy of the Commons. From a long-term perspective society does not want to catch more fish than is sustainable. But each fisher has the incentive to take a bit more. After all, their small additional catch doesn't make that much of a difference. When everybody takes a bit more we end up harvesting at a level beyond sustainability. As catch declines the pressure for harvest increases even more to keep the fishers economically solvent. Over time all of the fishers end up being worse off because fish stocks decline to commercial extinction. While true enough, I think there's more going on in this dilemma that makes it difficult to resolve.

This something more is an array of judgment problems we see repeated in human decision making. In particular are cognitive biases. Three cognitive biases jump out at me from our history of fishing. One is that we have positive illusions. Many fishers, I believe honestly, assume that the problem isn't as big as the scientists are suggesting. They're thinking the problem is going to correct itself without us having to change our fishing patterns. About the worst case they allow for discussion is that it's a temporary abnormality, stating there's always some year to year fluctuation when, in fact, we're seeing the beginning of a systematic decline.

Then a second bias, discounting the future, kicks in. We tend to focus on this year more than we focus on next year, even though future generations are relying on our behavior in the present. So we discount the future because, after all, today's fishing need is a certain reality but tomorrow's problem is only a prediction; it may not occur. Denial is more frequent when there is uncertainty or there is some question about the risks. When there is risk or uncertainty, we underweight the future.

Some people think there is no distinction between risk and uncertainty. Others see risk as when we have a pretty good idea of the odds and uncertainty as when I can't even give you an idea of the probabilities. Managing both is appropriate in future thinking, but in either case, both lead to cognitive bias issues. Rather than dealing with the uncertainty and risk we largely ignore it. This is selfish behavior but people aren't thinking of it as being selfish; they're simply not bringing that decision dynamic into consideration. In so doing they discount the possibility of bad events occurring in the future as a result of our behavior today.

Curiously, we're also more willing to let bad outcomes occur by inaction. That is the omission bias. There's lots of problems out there that we wouldn't let happen if we had to explicitly act to create that situation. A classic Peter Singer story illustrates this. Singer is a very famous, very controversial, and highly visible utilitarian philosopher. He notes that if somebody was to actively kill a child we would react with horror. But if we see a child drowning in a lake and a person does nothing we're disturbed but it doesn't have the same emotional impact.

Yet the net effect is the same; the child dies and it was preventable. The first act is one of commission and the second is omission. Humans have very different responses to these different actions even though the outcome is the same.

We see a similar kind of response with organ donation, which we talk about a fair amount in *"You Can't Enlarge the Pie"* [Bazerman, et al. 2001]. Some countries have policies that say, unless you sign a card, you get buried with your organs. Other countries say that, unless you sign a card, your organs get donated. When people have to act to become organ donors they respond very differently from when they have to expressly refuse to become an organ donor. As individuals we have the same option in both cases. But the choice we set up as the default ends up being critically important in determining the final rate of organ donation. Most people don't act against the default option. Where organ donations are automatic unless you opt out, donation rates are much higher. The general issue applicable to natural resources is that it's much more difficult for people to explicitly act to protect the environment than to make decisions by default and continue damaging the environment.

Then we encounter yet another bias—the desire to maintain the status quo. We try to hold on to the world as it is. We're not willing to take a 20 percent sacrifice today that could well be sustainable and, as a result, we end up risking a 100 percent loss in the future because of delay. In order to move from the status quo people have to give up a sure loss now for a potential benefit in the future. But humans don't take sure losses well. This thinking comes from the work of Danny Kahneman and Amos Tversky, whom I cite a lot in my decision writing.

What would you do if I asked you to choose between a sure loss of $10,000 from your bank account or flipping a coin to decide whether $0 or $20,000 would disappear? In my research I find that if you actually play this game, most people opt for the risky option. That is, we don't take sure losses very instinctively. We tend to be willing to roll the dice. If we think about climate change the problem is that the costs are very real today but the benefits of controlling global warming are, in fact, quite uncertain. We don't know whether or not we're stopping Florida from going under water as sea level rises in response to global warming. The United States not aggressively acting on global warming means, in essence, we've been willing to roll the dice as our national policy.

Looking through the lens of cognitive biases we should not be surprised about the resistance we encounter to the sure loss from a 20 percent reduction in fish harvest. In the fisheries case, positive illusion, discounting the future, omission, and status quo biases ring high and we also have a political process that tends to maintain the status quo. Those are pretty stiff roadblocks to change. Rather than ending up with a 20 percent reduction we should voluntarily take today we end up with a much larger reduction in the future; often one that is forced upon us like the one we are experiencing now with the commercial extinction of fish populations in many of the world's fishing basins. We have this very typical cycle that occurs over and over again across fishing basins yet it seems like we treat each new episode as unique. Cognitive biases and the political process reign supreme and we don't intervene until it's far, far too late.

Stepping away from fisheries, a recent dramatic environmental case history is Hurricane Katrina. It seems clear there were many, many government reports suggesting New Orleans' levies wouldn't hold a storm of that category and that this size of storm had a reasonable probability of hitting us. These days storms are one of the better predicted events in nature compared to many other environmental issues that have a great deal more uncertainty associated with them.

I wrote a book with Michael Watkins called *Predictable Surprises* [Bazerman and Watkins 2004]. Katrina seems to have all the characteristics of a predictable surprise. This is a situation where people see the problem, they know it's getting worse, and yet, for a variety of cognitive, organizational, and political reasons, they don't do anything about it. Why didn't we prepare for Katrina? Well, we would have had to spend sure money up front in order to avoid only a probabilistic, uncertain loss in the future. A leader championing hurricane preparedness before Katrina would have had a big challenge convincing people, before the storm, to spend the amount of money needed.

It certainly would have been expensive to fix the levies before Katrina but nowhere near as expensive as the cost we're incurring as a result of having done nothing. But the argument at the time was about the unreasonableness of the sure cost to beef up the levies versus the low probability of such a storm coming our way. This behavior means politicians with the courage to lead us to act on climate change aren't necessarily going to be rewarded during their limited time in office. Many of our problems in natural resources management take that form. These dynamics don't compel leaders to fix problems that are probabilistic, are going to hit us after a delay, and play out in an environment of cognitive biases that hinder our judgment. Still, it's the job of visionary leaders to take action that may cost us in the short term because action today is worth it in the long term. All this means that managers have a considerable human behavior challenge. They should expect resistance to taking action. It is the way our minds work.

Mike: Tell me about natural resource management being affected by what you identify in *Judgment and Managerial Decision Making* (Bazerman 2006) as the three judgmental heuristics. I ask because as a fish manager I often encountered the situation where our technical information pointing out significant conservation problems would be countered with conflicting observations, like stories about the big school of fish just offshore that we must have somehow missed in our surveys. People were able to access evidence they wanted to hear but not able to accept information that said something different. I've also been impressed with the phenomenon of changing environmental baselines between generations. Each generation that inherits a more degraded environment tends to accept that inheritance without much questioning. Having accepted that reduced baseline as normal, it's difficult for these people to envision restoring something they've never experienced. Again in my experience, I found it difficult to convince decision makers and stakeholders about long-term conservation problems. Even though there was compelling information of a population decline that had occurred over the course of a decade or more, the expected immediate change from the previous year was not all that large. This seemed to lead people to focus more on the immediate history and underappreciate the magnitude of change that may have taken decades to reveal itself. When I read about judgment heuristics in your book they seemed to fit my experiences. Tell me about these.

I wrote about them but I credit Kahneman and Tversky with that work, like their article in *Science* [Tversky and Kahneman 1974]. There are three heuristics I wrote about in the book you cited: availability, representativeness, and anchoring and adjustment.

Availability focuses on the fact that we often pay attention to vivid and concrete information and ignore the less distinct. This is a problem when we talk about issues like climate change, overfishing, and the government giving away our timber to private industry at shockingly low prices. Each of these is a story about not acting when the information was analytically persuasive but not vivid. Instead, we often wait until there are rather graphic images on TV. Trouble is, by the time you get these compelling images on TV it's often too late. So we see this recurring theme for environmental issues because they develop over time. We need to act far in advance of bad outcomes but humans seem to be particularly lousy at dealing with decision making unless vivid, dramatic, and inescapable information is in front of us.

Your experience with people citing the existence of a school of fish you missed in your surveys seems to be a good illustration of the representativeness heuristic. Representativeness operates by humans sorting through the available information to find evidence that confirms their stereotype of the 'right' answer. It's certainly easy to imagine that occurring in many fisheries situations such as you describe. People have a bias to find confirming evidence ahead of believing information that says their thinking is wrong. Its not much more complex than that.

I think your experience with changing baselines and small year-to-year fishery declines fits the anchoring and adjustment heuristic quite well. Imagine a story where you actually get the fishers to acknowledge there's a problem or you get loggers to see that the current cutting program is not sustainable. The next question is, how big does the harvest adjustment need to be? Humans start at the current level of harvest and adjust from there. But, as Kahneman and Tversky point out, that tends to lead to insufficient adjustment. Instead of dropping harvest by the 40 percent that is needed for a sustainable population we drop down to, say, only 15 percent, anchored to the previous year's experience. The problem is that this level is not sustainable. Three years later, when somebody creates a discussion again, dropping by 40 pecent won't work; it's too late because we've further reduced the base population. So humans tend to anchor adjustments to their recent personal experiences, not a more abstract estimate of what it would take to solve the problem.

A parallel example from the corporate world is the Sarbanes-Oxley legislation having to do with reducing corporate corruption. The problem with Sarbanes-Oxley is that it's a variety of very annoying, small changes based on the status quo rather than referencing changes against a true estimate of needed reform to solve corruption problems with American corporations. We too often start with what we have and figure out what adjustments we are willing to make from there, not what is needed. Anchoring is just a bias managers should expect to encounter.

Mike: I recall work you've done on forestry issues that illustrate that we sometimes miss opportunities for environmental gains when private interests and government managers believe that what is good for one is bad for the other. Tell me about the experiences you've had that illustrate this issue.

A good example is Ben Cone, Jr. His story is about the problems we can get into if we let a fixed-pie bias control decision making. When Mr. Cone inherited the family's forest land in North Carolina all the evidence says his family had been doing sustainable forestry for many years. Then the red-cockaded woodpecker [*Picoides borealis*] was found on part of his land. As a species protected under the Endangered Species Act the government, in a normal regulatory form, said, "Thou shalt not pull down timber from that portion of your land." Mr. Cone's response was, "Well, if the government can act this way, I better start harvesting the rest of my land before the government can get to me." And that meant clear-cutting, which was a practice his family had never used in the past.

Mr. Cone's situation is a an example of the fixed-pie bias—the landowner assuming that what was good for the environment was bad for him and the government assuming the opposite. Ben ended up pursuing a course of action that was worse for both. It would have been better to first say, how can we come up with a plan that, while it might lead to incidental take of woodpeckers, is a better plan overall for the species and for the economic interest of the landowner than if the landowner acts within the law and starts clear-cutting? A more hopeful approach is to create decision-making environments where government officials and landowners have the knowledge and the skills to go about creating joint solutions that make both parties better off. That is a better dynamic than the government trying to create heavy-handed regulation and landowners looking to maximize profit by ignoring government's interest in environmental protection.

In the Pacific Northwest where you live there was a forestry and fish story involving Plum Creek Timber Company and the federal government dealing with salmon listings under the Endangered Species Act. During the Clinton administration, Bruce Babbitt, as Secretary of the Interior, was very involved in developing something called habitat conservation plans. These plans were really a response to frustrations that occurred over the ESA. As I'm sure you know, the Endangered Species Act provides that, when a species is listed, even private landowners are prohibited from engaging in activities that result in harming or killing that species.

The problem with the Act, from the perspective of a private land-owner like Plum Creek, is that sometimes they incur enormous costs in order to provide fairly minimal environmental benefits for the listed species. That soon leads to all kinds of newspaper stories about how silly the ESA is. Never mind the fact that most regulation isn't custom-tai-lored with a specific landowner in mind; it can't be; it's too expensive to identify a specific regulation for a specific landowner in a specific con-text. When landowners don't appropriately protect the environment the government ends up intervening in ways that private interests often find unacceptable. Lack of government intervention, however, leads to unacceptable loss of the public's interest in environmental protection.

Habitat conservation plans provided an opportunity for a private landowner to submit a proposal to the government to exempt them from the letter of the law in the Endangered Species Act. In exchange their proposal was to provide broader, overall benefits on their land to make the listed species better off than if we went only by the law. The objec-tive was to create a solution that is a better aggregate environmental plan for the species and a better aggregate economic plan for the private landowner.

Habitat conservation plans attack the assumption that what one side gains the other side loses—the fixed-pie bias. In many ways habitat conservation plans are an ideal model for what negotiation researchers talk about as creating more value by coming up with wise tradeoffs. And wise tradeoffs are one way to overcome a fixed-pie bias. If we can find wise trades there can be a mutually beneficial solution that is quite different than either side's position on an issue.

As a negotiation professor as much as a decision researcher, I thought that habitat conservation plans were a wonderful instrument. In retro-spect, for forest and fish issues in the Pacific Northwest they were a wonderful instrument in theory that needed a lot of improvements in implementation. The problem was that we were switching to a system where private landowners have an enormous financial interest to de-velop a habitat conservation plan that was profitable to them. Unfortu-nately, the government side was typically underfunded and under-trained. When Plum Creek saw they had an endangered species on their land, they assigned a manager the job of managing the habitat conser-vation plan process and they created a $2 million budget to do it. Trouble was, he ended up negotiating with government officials who knew what a habitat conservation plan was supposed to deliver but did not have the institutional support or the training to pull it off. So despite having created a process for logical negotiation we certainly didn't implement it as well as we could have.

This outcome was repeated under the Clinton administration's Environmental Protection Agency on something called Project XL. That process told corporations with pollution issues, "If there are some consequences of EPA regulation causing enormous economic harm, come to us with a plan that will make both the environment and your economics better off. If you do you can obtain some regulatory relief." Once again, the process ended up with corporations, who had tremendous self-interest to create a Project XL proposal, working with government individuals who were undertrained and without sufficient resources to handle their side of the negotiation. Government officials ended up claiming that the private interests were abusing the process. The private corporations claimed that the government had a bunch of bureaucrats who weren't flexible enough implementing these same processes. Again, we created a promising negotiation framework without creating the appropriate support to go along with it.

My overall assessment is that habitat conservation plans and Project XL were both good processes with real promise to deal with fixed-pie biases, but they didn't have great implementation. When the George W. Bush administration came to power any notion of cooperating with environmental interests basically disappeared. So rather than fixing a good process that could have been a great process, the Bush administration basically wiped it out. He weakened environmental regulation across the board and thereby weakened the incentive for corporations to negotiate.

Mike: Talk about how a natural resource professional can be effective working in an environment where there are decision-making difficulties like the ones we've talked about.

Let me start conceptually and then we can aim for some applications. In our book, *"You Can't Enlarge the Pie"* [Bazerman, et al. 2001], we put the title in quotes to emphasize the myths that people bring to environmental and other government policy decisions. In this case the myth is that you can't find mutual gain when, in fact, you often can.

A problem hindering our ability to resolve a number of decision-making biases is the way our mind works. Imagine you have one job and you get another job offer. Most of the time there are some things about the new job that are better and some things that are worse. A purely logical human mind would simply weigh the gains versus losses of the new job and see how they balance out. But what we know is that—and this idea comes from the work of Kahneman and Tversky—losses loom larger than gains. This means that when you have to give up on some dimensions to gain on other dimensions, we weight the losses more. Your personal balance sheet needs to show a gain that is far greater than the losses in order to make the new job attractive enough to take. If there is anything close to an even split between gains and losses, expect inaction. People just do not handle the risk of loss well in their decision making.

The problem is that overweighing losses prejudices us toward inaction. The need for an overwhelming case for action rather than just a logical case for action is a barrier to change in all kinds of environmental issues. If you think about a major issue, like climate change, a fundamental problem is the very real, very significant short-term costs. Now, the people who know a lot more about this than me, like the excellent climatologists working on the issue, would argue that the long-term benefits of stopping climate change dwarf the costs of taking action today. But the costs are in the here and now and loom large compared to distant gains. Using this insight from a cognitive perspective helps us understand why people aren't making wiser, long-term decisions. That means the first thing you can do to manage things differently is recognize the need to consciously manage cognitive biases.

If you don't manage cognitive biases there is a pretty good chance they will manage you. Some researchers talk about a distinction between System 1 and System 2 thought as a way to manage around cognitive problems. System 1 thinking is your normal intuition when you're in the midst of a decision. System 2 thinking is stopping and analyzing a decision in more careful, systematic way. This System 2 analysis might be complex, like doing some kind of mathematical analytics or it might be just taking a sheet of paper and listing the costs versus the benefits of action and inaction. However complex, System 2 thinking is about creating some kind of deliberate process. What we know is that most of our actions in professional life are in a System 1 mode; that is, we're using our intuition to make relatively snap judgments. Trouble is, that's also where we see the greatest amount of bias. Danny Kahneman argues that most of us have an insider and an outsider. The insider is the person in the middle of the decision, using System 1 processes. The outsider is the person able to observe how this insider is going about making the decision and being more deliberate because they are distant enough from the pressures of the moment.

For example, when I ask corporate teams working on a new project, "How long will this project take?" They may answer, "Six weeks." If I then ask, "Okay, for past projects that were estimated to take six weeks, how long, on average, did they actually take?" It is very routine for these same people to tell me, "Well, maybe 10 to 15." There is a bias to think we can get things done more quickly than we actually can. Another common example, one that has taken on the status of folklore, is a family remodeling their house. We know from experiences all around us that, more often than not, the process takes longer than expected and it costs more than expected. But each of us, when we're in the midst of that decision making, think our project is somehow different. That's the insider using System 1 thinking and responding to positive illusions.

The goal in System 2 thinking is to get yourself out of the moment, where people are emotionally connected to their decision, and get them into an outsider mode. As an outsider looking in at their decision they are more likely to bring a more objective lens to the analysis. As youngsters most of us are taught to count to 10 before taking action. That is a simple model of trying to get into outsider, System 2 thinking. For other issues it may mean talking to a friend whom you view as an objective advisor. In natural resource management it may mean hiring an expert analyst or setting up a review team to think about your problem with greater expertise than you and with a more distant, third-party perspective. The whole idea is, don't just go with your gut. This is not a very popular notion. People like going with their gut and we have popular, mostly dysfunctional, myths promoting that point of view. The recent book *Blink* [Gladwell 2005] is on the best seller's list and highlights the brilliance of your first intuition. Unfortunately, that book is very, very selective in its review of the literature. There is plenty of evidence that our first intuition has far more bad judgment than good. What's needed is to bring thoughtful analysis to our problems. And we can do that by bringing in an outsider's perspective capable of thinking through a decision in a more systematic way.

What might happen if we could take the same fishers who want to go fishing today and have them think about a fishing story like theirs but one where they are not involved? Or have them look at five different case studies, such as the current story in the southeast with its shark population? Doing things like that can put these people into System 2 thinking. That can increase the chance they will see and accept an undesirable pattern that may not affect them tomorrow but will have devastating consequences over the long term. But the challenge is, of course, how do you get people to analyze problems without the immediate emotion of issues like fishers needing to feed their family today, which is, obviously, a very salient motivation. To the extent everyone recognizes that System 1 and System 2 thoughts are generating different answers you can start analyzing how to reconcile the two and pushing decision making more into the outsider's perspective.

Shifting from System 1 to System 2 thinking, I would argue, affects all the cognitive biases that humans are prone to. Any way of slowing down and thinking more analytically is likely to improve our odds of avoiding bias. Often this is not rocket science. It is simple things like designing a process that avoids making a decision in the heat of the moment; creating a process to analyze decision options with some sort of rigor; bringing in outsiders who don't have a stake in the current decision; and having a group discussion that forces multiple, even competing explanations. Constructing processes that take the heat out of the decision causes us to look at things more carefully.

For example, many assume that in natural resource management market forces operating unfettered by regulation will sort things out appropriately. But that just isn't right in lots of natural resource issues. That's how we managed 11 of the 17 major fishery basins to commercial extinction. Any time we have a management story like the Tragedy of the Commons and the human psychological impediments to wise decisions that we've just discussed, the free hand of the market and its belief that prices will solve the problem is shockingly naive, optimistic, and misplaced. Now, I'm a fan of markets and incentives, but a religious belief that the market fixes all problems is not a solution in the real world. We want to use the market when the market is operating right, not when this approach has the poor track record it does with issues like fisheries.

Mike: This focus on economic markets is one of the themes the other people I've interviewed talk about. Embedded in our management models, whether biological yield models or economic models, is an assumption that utilitarian use is a higher and better allocation of the natural resources. Have you thought about what we're buying into when we choose to use some sort of conceptual framework like microeconomic and biological yield modeling to help us make decisions? An example earlier in this book is the manager of public lands on the Front Range of the Rocky Mountains who had a choice between allowing oil and gas extraction or preserving the natural setting because of amenity and legacy values. How does one approach a question like that if the models available tend to focus our decision making towards commodity utilization of resources?

I think these other people you've interviewed are correct, but I'm not sure that means we don't want to use these modeling approaches. When I accept the fact that we're going to use natural resources and not leave them alone, I ask, is it better to overharvest or would I rather the resource continue to be harvested in the future? My answer is that sustainability wins. For me, any reasonable decision has to start with what we are trying to achieve. If we misspecify what we're trying to achieve, then, undoubtedly, the tools we choose aren't going to give us a different answer. So the criticism that our management models have values imbedded in them is right but we need to be careful when we decide not to use a tool. If you don't use such tools you end up sub-optimizing part of the decision.

That still is not an answer to your question about incorporating nonmarket values into decisions. I don't know if I have a good answer for dealing with nonmarket values in your oil and gas example, but I'll offer a couple of general thoughts. The broad problem that I see in your question, and I'm not thinking of any specific situation, is that we don't have a fair competition between the value of the land for extraction values versus the array of amenity values available and how they accrue for the next couple hundred years as a legacy to future generations. Compare that to an oil company who is a monolithic actor able to capture immediate, concrete, and substantial economic value from mineral extraction. When a state government is under financial pressures, mineral extraction can end up looking very attractive. The same dynamic is true when you have somebody who wants to develop land versus preserving open space. In these situations the ability of corporations to harness immediate value from natural resources that are very salient in a specific community often wins out over the long-term interests of 300 million Americans dispersed across the entire nation or the unborn who don't have an ability to put together their preferences into a unified voice. As a result, those corporate interests end up being weighed more and the soft interests aren't able to bid up the price to its true value because we don't have any mechanism to put those dispersed or distant interests together.

It's the job of government to identify the long-term benefits to society as a whole and either regulate or act as a bidder in competition with development interests. We rarely do that and it's very, very difficult. A more immediate problem, usually involving corporate interests, is use of lobbying to create corporate welfare. The American public subsidizes a variety of extraction activities, whether we're talking about nonrenewable resources like oil and gas or renewable resources like timber. In other words, we're not getting a fair playing field because of the ability of extraction interests to more effectively lobby the system.

Mike: Another issue described by the narrators in this book is managing the triangulation between their ideals that drew them into their profession, the obligation they feel to their family, and the sense of responsibility they have to the people they work with or work for. I'm wondering if there aren't some cognitive issues associated with this internal tension?

One very vivid, recent example was among police officers in New Orleans during Katrina. Some left duty without authorization to take care of their families as the storm was striking and the flood danger was rising. I, like most people, think these police officers neglected their duty because they agreed to serve the public even in this kind of situation. On the other hand, I've heard experts in crisis management say that it was really a problem of incompetence by city officials who, as part of the disaster management system, could not tell critical disaster personnel the status of their families. Knowing there is going to be this internal conflict for key personnel the disaster manager must make sure key people know their families are safe. Otherwise, managers should expect employees to feel conflicted between responsibility to family versus responsibility to employer. Undoubtedly, we think it's a positive virtue to look after your family but we also think it a virtue to show responsibility to others. Sometimes these two virtues can be in conflict.

For people doing natural resource work there is a personal and a societal perspective worth maintaining. On the personal side there's a reason why people get involved in environmental jobs to begin with and they're good reasons. Too often motives drift. One of my good friends and a good example is Billy Shore. He is head of an organization called Share Our Strength, a group dedicated to ending childhood hunger in America and abroad. He wrote *Revolution of the Heart* [Shore 1995] about citizens taking responsibility for their communities versus just looking to governments or economic markets for solutions. Billy left

politics to get into that work when he was Chief of Staff for Senator Bob
Kerrey. One day he reviewed Kerrey's list of activities and realized it
was all things like fund raising. There was nothing to do with why
Kerrey—who I think is a great public official—got into government.
Billy Shore decided to change back to work that was more directly related to his values. It's important to keep your eye on why you got into
your profession and to think about how you want to be remembered in
the future. What contribution do you want to make? There will always
be short-term pressures to sway from that personal commitment. What
we really want to do is maximize long-term benefits through our long-
term decision making. Doing that effectively requires thinking more
broadly, thinking about the decision-making processes of other people,
and, with that more realistic understanding, figuring out how to move
forward in the most productive way possible over the long haul.

From a societal perspective it's very helpful and very necessary to
better understand how people make decisions. It is an error to assume
that everybody uses the same thought process. What we've learned about
cognitive biases and other problems humans have in making decisions
helps us diagnose how we can make better decisions in this multiplayer,
very complex environment that exists today. It's our obligation to leave
the world in a better place than we found it. Hopefully, deeper understanding of human decision-making behaviors is one way to help us do a
better job in the future.

Broadly speaking, the goal of natural resource managers is to make
wise or rational decisions from a long-term perspective. What we end up
doing all too often is suboptimizing in a wide variety of ways. The cognitive biases and some of the other things that we've talked about, like
decision heuristics, all limit our rationality. Working to get around these
decision-making problems is, to me, productive conservation work.

Lessons Learned

There seem to be few fields of research where the means are so
largely of the brain, but the ends so largely of the heart.
—Aldo Leopold (p236, 1936)

Each time we face our fear, we gain strength, courage, and
confidence in the doing.
—Anonymous

It's a great satisfaction knowing that for a brief point in time
you made a difference.
—Irene Natividad

Look upon the narrators' stories as raw material useful for informing career choices. In this final chapter I combine their stories as a way to look for such insight by considering three questions. First, what are the keystone issues behind career events encountered by natural resource professionals; i.e., what things determine outcomes even if they operate unseen, behind the scenes? Second, what personal attributes seemed to help people in the narrators' stories grapple with these keystone issues; i.e., what does personal career development look like? And third, what premises underlie a natural resource career of meaning and purpose; i.e., what makes the narrators useful role models?

Keystone Career Issues

The narrators encountered nine keystone issues. While often operating behind the scenes, these were powerful forces shaping outcomes. Learning to recognize when these keystones are the real issues in play makes it easier to diagnose what is going on in a professional's work environment and, thereby, devise effective responses.

Keystone 1: Incentive Systems and Goal Displacement.

Lesson Learned: The unofficial rules rule. Incentive systems appeared in all the narrators' stories and were more powerful than the official mission of their management institutions. These incentives guided, even compelled, some professionals and agencies to take actions that hurt their conservation mission. Although I label this as a keystone issue, it has a blanket effect exerting influence over all the other keystone issues.

Good-old-boy networks for deciding promotion opportunities, particularly those in the Forest Service and Park Service, are examples. Promotion was linked to one's ability to deliver goods, e.g., timber, grazing, minerals, recreation. More conservation-minded use of these natural resources was not similarly rewarded. Promotion was linked to being in sync with the core values that unofficially defined the agency culture, such as being a member of the Forest Service family. And promotion was linked to the ability to protect the agency from criticism, especially criticism that escalated up the political ladder to such levels as members of Congress. Another example of incentives driving behavior is the threat that Utah State University would lose a new building for the College of Natural Resources because a faculty member spoke out against the politically powerful sagebrush rebellion. The clearest example in the narrators' experiences is the incentive system created by county payments in the Forest Service. Counties were unambiguously positioned to advocate for short-term commodity extraction from the nation's forests at the expense of long-term stewardship because schools, roads, and other basic community infrastructure became dependent on these payments. This incentive system was increasingly dysfunctional as timber supplies declined, causing county payment revenues to decline, which caused local interests to demand ever-increasing extractions. The Forest Service was rewarded for letting the informal goal of supporting local communities displace the statutory mission of sustainable management of timber, water, and other environmental goods and services from the nation's forests.

It is tempting to interpret these case histories as good-manager versus bad-manager events. That is too simplistic. Often, the mangers who allowed natural resource damage were behaving entirely rationally. They simply responded to the real incentives in their work environment, even if these operated behind the scenes. Agency employees know these unwritten rules and respond to the true reward system by adopting substitute goals. This is the organizational behavior of goal displacement (Scott 1987).

The notion of rational behavior resulting in irrational outcomes for a conservation mission admits a difficult reality. Agencies responsible for conserving natural resources are, themselves, part of the conservation problem. It is overly generous to assume that an agency with a stewardship mission will do the right thing. The narrators' experiences show that perverse incentives are often strong enough to carry an agency far afield from its conservation mission.

Keystone 2: Social Need and Mission Drift.

Lesson Learned: Management agencies are part of their community and, as such, act as defenders of the status quo more than as a voice of dissent or a wellspring of innovation. While goal displacement is about incentives driving behavior, mission drift arises from the values of the managers being in sync with a substitute mission. Managers who have drifted actively support the substitute mission which tends to reflect the worldview of the community where management takes place. In the narrators' experiences, management innovation routinely originated from forces outside the agency and the agency's frequent behavior was to defend the status quo.

During Phil Pister's career the California Department of Fish and Game damaged native cutthroat trout, golden trout, and mountain yellow-legged frogs by indiscriminately stocking non-native fish to support recreational fishing. It was easy for agency employees to follow this policy as they mirrored the same values held by the constituents perceived as their customers—recreational anglers—who wanted fish stocking. Another example is Phil's work to preserve desert pupfish. Phil received barbs from colleagues, such as, "I'm going out to get some pupfish because they make good bass bait." While said in jest, in reality such comments reflected underlying philosophical alignment of these agency personnel with mainstream customers.

Of course, part of these case histories is a claim of ignorance of adverse consequences—a logic of honest mistakes in an environment of scientific uncertainly. But that is not a complete explanation. Other than Phil's lone voice the question of adverse consequences was never examined until outside forces compelled the California Department of Fish and Game to do so. Until then most agency personnel were solidly behind indiscriminate stocking or were willing to look the other way as the agency's management, or lack thereof, harmed native species. When Phil, as an agency insider, tried to introduce an alternative worldview there was substantial denial by the agency and he was even labeled as a troublemaker. The agency's mission had uncritically drifted from conserving native species to meeting customer demand for recreation.

Mike Dombeck and Gloria Flora encountered mission drift in Forest Service employees who held the post-World War II ethic of providing timber to build homes for Americans. These Forest Service managers rose to that challenge, and their mission simply drifted from sustainable management of forests and water to producing the timber needed for home building. In the Park Service Roger Contor encountered uncritical acceptance of fire suppression as the agency mission instead of preserving ecosystem processes. Agency employees agreed with these value choices and found it easy and satisfying to support the alternative missions. If a community appreciates one aspect of an agency's mission more than another, expect to encounter an agency mainstream that mirrors these more popular values (Kaufman 1960).

Although the narrators encountered substantial mission drift in their agencies it is not correct to describe agency employees as a kind of monolith of values, all committed to defending the status quo. The narrators told stories about the increasing number of employees who are voices of creative dissent, as were the narrators. These internal voices of conscience are present, just frequently ignored by the mainstream agency culture. Examples cited by the narrators are Don Oman's attempt to fix damaging cattle grazing practices on Forest Service land and Felix Smith's attempt to introduce the difficult news to the U.S. Fish and Wildlife Service that pesticide residues from powerful California agricultural interests were poisoning waterfowl in Kesterson National Wildlife Refuge.

This comfortable fit of employee values with mainstream values in the work environment is changing. One explanation for the impression that natural resource agencies are experiencing increasing conflict (Wondolleck and Yaffee 2000) is that community values are changing. Historically, there has been general agreement that natural resource agencies have a utilitarian purpose, usually concerned with producing commodities or providing recreation. This consensus is breaking down and a new agreement for the purpose of natural resource management has yet to emerge as generally accepted. In the meantime more preservationist values are emerging and clashing with the old utilitarian values that are still widely held.

From this perspective the intense conflict Gloria Flora found in the Jarbidge issue was inevitable. A broader national interest in sustainability and the touchstone issue of protecting bull trout via the Endangered Species Act came into conflict with the local value system in Nevada committed to extracting commodities from federal lands and an entrenched ideology of local control of decision making. The expression of this collision was the anger, threats, and violence leveled at Gloria and other on-site Forest Service employees. Agency employees represented a flint of new national values striking the stone of old local values. Value systems that collide produce sparks and the people caught in the middle, like Forest Service employees, can get burned. One of the most distasteful lessons learned from the Jarbidge case history is the real possibility that agencies are capable of withdrawing support for employees working in these intensely conflicted environments. Gloria Flora asked for but did not receive legal support in the Jarbidge issue, despite the extreme and menacing behavior of local community members and the obstructionist activities of county officials. When she looked over her shoulder expecting to see support from her employer, none was found.

Keystone 3: Substituting Models for Value Choice.

Lesson Learned: Managers are often willing to delegate tough value choices to a theoretical model without acknowledging that the assumptions embedded in that model are value based and predetermine management outcome. Economic and biological yield models as a basis for natural resource decision making appeared as examples in the narrators' stories. Max Bazerman points out that models are useful after specifying what kind of decision is needed, not as a substitute for defining the needed decision.

The commodity economics of clear-cutting led to devaluing other forest uses such as recreation, amenity, and legacy values. It certainly trumped real but un-marketable ecological services like producing clean water from the nation's forests. As Mike Dombeck, says, "We tend to think of land as just a factor of production in the economy. . . . Part of the problem is that we seriously undervalued ecological services beyond commodity production. In reality, the economics of Forest Service land management since World War II had been based on mining ecological services." A reason for the misfit of model to true management need, according to Max Bazerman is, ". . . we don't have a fair competition between the value of the land for extraction values versus the array of amenity values available and how they accrue for the next couple hundred years as a legacy to future generations." The acceptance that the decision-making model for forest management was about commodity production made it easy for Forest Service managers to define the new 'ology' issues as timber constraints and not worthy management objectives in their own right. The model simply did not include these alternative worldviews. Gloria Flora's most impressive achievement in her decision to ban oil and gas leasing in the Rocky Mountain Front Range was the insight to reject commodity values as all that mattered and admit into her decision making nonmonetary amenity and legacy values as legitimate.

Yield models conditioned the teaching and policy prescriptions coming from professors at Utah State University. They could easily put a monetary value on converting the West's range lands to livestock grazing areas and, in so doing, turn a blind eye to nonmarket values of these same lands. As Bern Shanks observed, "A lot of my academic colleagues were, through their technical discipline, really advocates for the traditional use of resources—maximum sustained yield in forestry, the idea that we should improve rangeland to grow more cows—that sort of thing. They cloaked their arguments in science but really, they had a very traditional, utilitarian worldview." Choosing a model to inform management decisions carries with it a caution. Values are embedded in this choice. Uncritical acceptance is, in reality, adopting a set of values posing as science.

Keystone 4: Human Psychology is a Trump Card.

Lesson Learned: Conservation progress is impeded by human psychological shortcomings that repeatedly arise in difficult decision-making environments. The role of cognitive issues impeding conservation decisions is underappreciated by natural resource managers. Of considerable importance for front-line managers is human behaviors that cause people to focus on immediate decision-making costs and ignore much more significant consequences in the distant or obscure future. Max Bazerman observed that this asymmetry is with us on world-scale environmental issues of our times, like climate change. But it is easy to see this behavior in the other narrators' stories such as Mike Dombeck's concern about depleting the Ogallala Aquifer. Current mining of this water is ignoring the extremely large monetary and social costs that will fall on future generations when that well runs dry.

While present on the big issues, cognitive issues are also relevant in the more typical, smaller-scale, place-oriented, day-to-day work of the natural resource professional. Tom Peterson experienced the pragmatic realities of human psychology impeding progress with his involvement in deer and wildlife area management in Arkansas. His analysis was that stakeholder reluctance to embrace change was well described by the business concepts of a conceptual sales cycle and decision making for high-involvement goods. His agency initially misstepped by ignoring these psychological needs. Max Bazerman described the example of landowner Ben Cone's decision to shift from sustainable to nonsustainable forestry on his private land in response to concerns about recolonizing red cockaded woodpeckers. On the private-manager side Mr. Cone chose to capture current timber values to avoid potential negative consequences if woodpeckers were found on other parts of his land. On the public-manager side agency employees, working in a rigid management system and with a regulatory mind-set, did not show a sophisticated ability to manage tradeoffs. Both sides ended up with a loss— long-term economic loss of timber value and long-term woodpecker habitat loss.

The judgment heuristics of availability, representativeness, and anchoring and adjustment and all the cognitive biases operating under these (e.g., positive illusions, discounting the future, power of the status quo) are important controllers of decisions. These shortcomings of human decision-making behavior are important in determining a manager's ability to achieve sustainability. Yet, the natural resource research and management communities do not seem to be focusing on improving human decision-making behavior as a conservation opportunity. Of special concern is erosion of what successive generations perceive as normal environmental conditions. This example of the anchoring and adjustment heuristic is contributing to human decisions to allow incremental environmental degradation across generations. Why is this happening? How can we change it?

The current path of human dimension research is focused more on understanding human tastes and preferences for natural resource experiences. This focus is heading that discipline into a cul-de-sac of irrelevance. A more interesting question, as Max Bazerman poses for his research is, why do people claim they want to leave their children a better world but behave quite incompatibly with that objective? More fruitful than studying tastes and preferences would be research on how cognitive issues impede sustainability decisions and how these obstacles to sustainability can be overcome.

Keystone 5: A Bias for Passive Decision Making.

Lesson Learned: A passive manager, one that goes along to get along, is common. Andrea Mead Lawrence encountered this phenomenon as a consumer when she asked the California Department of Fish and Game to intervene and stop the illegal cutting of willows in the wetland meadow near her mountain home. The first response came from an inexperienced biologist who understood what was wrong, but was too timid to enforce the regulations. This passive response was, in effect, making a decision to sanction the illegal cutting. As a sophisticated consumer Andrea reacted to this professional lapse with further activism to involve a different Department employee. This second employee, who had greater self-assurance and experience managing this kind of conflict, intervened with sufficient assertiveness to stop the illegal activity. Bern Shanks encountered passive advocacy at the University of Utah where fellow professors chose not to speak out about the sagebrush rebellion nor speak up in support of their alumni. In so doing they were tacitly endorsing the beliefs and behavior of the sagebrush rebels. Max Bazerman summarized the results of behavior research showing that humans do not handle sure losses very well. Potential losses loom larger than gains and, more often than not, people retreat to passive decision making—usually a failure to move from the status quo. When Bazerman looks at the problem of all talk and little environmental protection, he sees an array of human judgment problems that routinely get in the way, such as the omission bias where humans are more willing to let bad outcomes occur by inaction. And Tom Peterson and his colleague in the Environmental Protection Agency sharing spotted owl duties encountered substantial pressure to conform and not oppose administration policy to allow an exemption from the Endangered Species Act. In response they had to hone their skills at saying no to people with considerable positional power.

The consequences of passive decision making are substantial. How well present management is working is rarely questioned and leadership is implicitly handed to others. That, in turn, usually means that pro-extraction and pro-development interests are placed ahead of the public's conservation interests. As Mike Dombeck said, "In government, either you keep them busy or they will keep you busy." The natural resource manager that does not make active decisions is doomed to react to the initiative of others. The narrators were clear. A nondecision is still a decision.

"... If you're financially vulnerable, you can suddenly find there is pressure to accept things that your value system would suggest you not accept. That's a big source of inner conflict for many resource managers I've met. That dynamic changes people's willingness to take a risk. And this is not about government employees being more risk averse than private sector employees. The same conflicting incentives exist for them as well." (Flora)

"When subject to criticism from all sides, to being battered and bashed about, a normal response is to crawl inside yourself. You become more passive." (Lawrence)

"'Don't rock the boat' is often a very successful career strategy, at least for conventional trappings like promotions." (Contor)

"Just sitting by and letting nothing happen is, in reality, taking a stand on an issue. It supports the status quo." (Dombeck)

Keystone 6: The Burden of Proof.

Lesson Learned: When the going gets tough, expect others to place the burden on you to prove that conservation actions are justified. When that happens the natural resource manager is at a substantial disadvantage because the other party's position is assumed correct until proven otherwise. The disadvantage increases when it is difficult to disprove the assumption, when the decision rules are not firm, and when scientific uncertainty increases. When the burden of proof is difficult, expect to hear an argument something like, "I get to do what I want because you can't prove that I'll do any harm." When the decision rules are not firm, expect to hear an argument something like, "You are required to let me do what I want because there is no regulation against it." And when scientific uncertainty increases, expect to hear an argument something like, "There is insufficient scientific information to justify you stopping me from doing what I want to do." One of the first fights over natural resource conservation is about who carries the burden of proof. Expect to see substantial energy and resources spent to place this burden on the conservation-minded manager.

A key reason Phil Pister effectively countered the pressure for small hydroelectric power development in the Eastern Sierra Nevada Mountains was his handling of the burden of proof. Developers walked into his office with an attitude that, "If you can't prove you need the water, we get it." Understanding the risk, Phil successfully reversed the burden of proof putting it back on the developers with an attitude that, "You can't have the water unless you prove no harm."

Gloria Flora encountered Forest Service employees who accepted, without question, that they always had the burden of proof. Before announcing her decision to ban oil and gas leasing along the Rocky Mountain Front Range she carried her decision up the chain of command. At successive links, "[a]s I explained my decision my colleagues would say, 'You can't do that. You've got to give them something.' It just did not occur to them that we could say no." There was an unwritten assumption that development was okay unless the Forest Service could prove otherwise. She describes this mind set with a parable, "If you think about it, it's like somebody walking into my house, taking my possessions, and then saying 'Okay. If you give me your TV system, I'll give back your stereo system.'" Gloria just rejected that mind set.

Keystone 7: Expect to See Logic Traps.

Lesson Learned: Often, the debates a manager encounters contain simple logic flaws. One is an *illusion of choice*. I recall a vivid example when a colleague was being cross-examined in court for his decision to curtail fishing in a year of low fish abundance. The plaintiff's attorney, using undisputed data showing the existence of economic hardship for his clients, made the case that because of low fish abundance there was an economic need to increase fishing opportunity. This attorney, whom I will call Mr. Smith, then asked my colleague to justify to the court his decision to do economic harm to his clients. My colleague turned to the judge and answered, "When Mr. Smith comes to the council representing his clients in a year of high resource abundance he says, 'You must let us go fishing because there is a surplus that will otherwise go to waste.' Now, in a year of low abundance, Mr. Smith is saying, 'You must let us go fishing because there are not enough fish.' If those two arguments prevail, I must ask back, 'Will there ever be a time when it is appropriate to reduce harvest?' Such logic requires us to allow fishing when stocks are abundant and also when stocks are in trouble. Surely, a management system should stand for something more—something like appropriate use when there is abundance and appropriate conservation when there is scarcity." My colleague revealed an illusion of choice when, in fact, all of Mr. Smith's choices led to the same conclusion—harvest. A comparable example in the narrators' careers is the county payments issue in the Forest Service. An abundance of trees was used by local communities as justification to increase harvest and a scarcity of trees was also used as a justification to increase harvest. Managers who examine the logic behind the reasoning they encounter can often find a way out of traps like these.

When Roger Contor and his National Park Service colleagues uncritically accepted the definition of fire in a national park as a good vs. evil choice they were reacting to the logic of a *false dichotomy*. As Roger discovered, fire management was a ". . . more complex question of land management"— one that has multiple choices. Roger questioned the logic that there was only an either/or choice. Gloria Flora, in puzzling out the basis for her decision to ban oil and gas leasing on the Rocky Mountain Front Range, had presence of mind to challenge the logic that *all evaluation metrics must be equal*. Gloria also did not respond to the logic of *sunk costs* being a justification for allowing oil and gas leasing. She shocked some of her Forest Service colleagues when she challenged the accepted logic that ". . . all the time and money we spent to study the proposal meant we had to do something." She did not accept that past investment in pre-project evaluation was an appropriate rationale to justify making a pro-development decision.

In my own career I repeatedly encountered *two-wrongs-make-a-right* thinking as justification for overfishing (Fraidenburg and Lincoln 1985). I spent the majority of my career working in highly competitive, mixed-stock fisheries where independent jurisdictions managed the same fish stocks. In that setting it was common to encounter an intransigent party who rejected conservation-based harvest reductions. That position was then accessible to and frequently used by other parties to justify their own continued overfishing. It was seductive for these managers to use the logic that, "If you get to go fishing, I get to go fishing," despite their collective impact on the fish stocks. These managers accepted the logic that two wrongs make a right instead of two wrongs making a bigger wrong.

Keystone 8: Loyalty Conflicts.

Lesson Learned: The most difficult issues for a professional to resolve are internal loyalty conflicts. Each narrator experienced these. The most demanding situation encountered by the narrators was a triangulation between loyalty to their personal conservation ethic, loyalty to their organization and co-workers, and loyalty to their family. To get a sense of why this dynamic is difficult, imagine a thought experiment. You are called to a meeting with the big boss. He/she directs you to delete material from a report you wrote that is critical of a pending agency decision. You know that the boss's request will lead to a small amount of resource damage. You agree with your boss that omitting the critical material will help the agency get funding from the legislature. You know that funding is important to preserve the long-term ability of the agency to deliver conservation programs. You also understand that the jobs of co-workers, your friends, depend on this funding. Failing to modify your report could define you as not a team player and affect your promotion prospects. Your children are in the middle of expensive college educations. And you chose conservation work because of your personal commitment to natural resource stewardship. How will you approach this request to change your report and in so doing sanction resource damage? Professionals, like the organizations they work for, tend to be mediocre performers if they have unresolved internal value conflicts (Clarke and McCool 1985).

Loyalty conflict is part of what Phil Pister means when telling about his bosses and colleagues pressing him to ignore the impending demise of desert pupfish or allowing native cutthroat trout in Slinkard Creek to be displaced with popular non-native trout. This is what Mike Dombeck means when he says, "After a person works for an organization for 10 or 15 years there is often a gradual loyalty shift. It's a natural progression from loyalty to the mission to loyalty to the agency itself and its culture." This is what Gloria Flora means when she observes, "We took a human core value and gave it to an agency and, thereby, gave the agency the power and rights of a family. Conferring those rights meant loyalty to the agency was and is highly prized, just as is loyalty to one's own family." This is what Max Bazerman means when he described the trouble New Orleans's police officers had during Hurricane Katrina managing their divided loyalty between public duty and duty to their families. And it is what Tom Peterson means when he describes the radically different ways three of his employers handled bad news. In one, the law firm, loyalty to the mission meant embracing the reality of bad news and taking action. In the other two organizations, the nonprofit and the bank, it meant squelching bad news in loyalty to the interests and desires of individuals in the organization.

The narrators encountered loyalty conflicts and so will you. They reached points in their careers where they negotiated with themselves about the risks they were willing to take when presented with internal value conflicts. Indeed, these were necessary dilemmas to resolve. The successful professionals in the narrators' stories resolved the choice between working for someone else at a job, which meant doing what others wanted them to do versus working for themselves at a life's work, which meant fulfilling their own aspirations through their paid employment. The narrators did not hand that decision off to their employers. Each narrator, in his or her own way, made conscious choices, understanding the ideals important to them, the responsibility they had to the people around them, and the realities of the limited support they could expect from their work environment.

On paper resolving this dilemma seems easy—just choose the value you hold more dearly. When loyalties are far apart in our personal hierarchy, the choice is relatively easy. Things get tricky when loyalties are close together in importance and someone pressures you to swap their importance. When this happens there is a temptation to use tradeoff analysis to address this conflict. The hope is that compliance today will buy future opportunity, usually in the form of acquiring positional power either through direct promotion or by being judged a team player who will be given important assignments. The underlying assumption is that compromise today will give you new power in the future when you will then be in a position to do the right thing. The risk is incremental erosion of independence or the loss of your internal compass. Roger Contor observed this phenomenon in the Park Service, "I worked for one Director of the Park Service who compromised with so many people to become Director that when he got into that position of real power, he was totally impotent. He couldn't say or do anything without fear of alienating someone to whom he owed a favor."

The narrators and the people they respected as role models were not loose cannons totally out of sync with their agencies. They could work with the dualism that although their agencies might be part of the problem, improving them was also an important conservation opportunity in its own right. The employers in our stories all changed significantly during the narrators' careers and these positive changes came, in part, from the narrators' efforts. Mike Dombeck is a good case history of a person with a deep commitment to the Forest Service family who also could recognize that the family's behavior needed changing. His is a career of service to both direct, hands-on conservation work and work to improve conservation by improving the conservator.

A common factor helping the narrators resolve loyalty conflicts was reflection about and ordering of the values at stake in an issue. Gloria Flora experienced this in her decision to ban oil and gas leasing on the Rocky Mountain Front Range. Should she act in support of the Forest Service family and allow leasing? Should she act on her own commitment to the agency mission? Or should she act on a sense of responsibility to her own family by protecting her job security? Resolution emerged with time and reflection to sort out her own hierarchy of values and how these intersected with the impending decision. "The anguish before I made the decision was intense until I sat down on a river bank and had a long talk with myself about me and my future. It became abundantly clear that this decision wasn't about me." The narrators' ability to get clear on the hierarchy of their internal values helped clarify decision dilemmas.

Keystone 9: The Professional Is Always Advocating.

Lesson Learned: The debate over science versus advocacy confuses the separate issues of neutrality of the professional versus absence of bias in their work. From the time Gifford Pinchot popularized the idea of professional management as scientific knowledge dispassionately applied by technical experts, it has become a core value (Hays 1980). So much so that the use of science-based management is an accepted requirement for a quality natural resource program. Although the narrators saw applied science as a positive and truly important contributor to the advances they've seen in natural resource management, they did not describe it as value neutral. At present there is a lively debate in the natural resource professions about advocacy. If you want to raise the hackles of those attending a professional conference, sponsor such a discussion. Expect two camps to immediately stake out terrain.

Camp One - Neutralists. These folks will say something like, "Professional management is pure. There is an obligation to distance the professional from decision-making outcomes. True science-based management focuses only on what is and should not be concerned with what ought to be. That is the domain of policy makers. Yes, professionals should inform policy decisions, but only about the impacts of alternative choices. The professional should not prescribe any particular outcome. Doing so is an act of commission and as such is a subversion of duty." Neutralists say, "Advocacy? Never. If you do, you taint the science."

Camp Two - Advocates. These folks say something like, "Natural resource professions are part of the human experience. As such, it is not possible to escape the 'ought' question. The values embedded in our management and economic models establish an advocacy stance from the outset. Besides, our management institutions all have missions. These missions prescribe a responsibility for employee activism to achieve that mission. The peer review process is adequate for ensuring credible (i.e., unbiased) technical input to decision making. Yes, a professional's work must be objective, honest, fully reported, and conveyed with measures of precision. But professionals have the obligation to speak and even to criticize decisions that compromise their mission. There is an obligation to go beyond just providing data. The professional ought to make affirmative recommendations to achieve the mission. Professionals need only disclose when they are acting in the technical evaluation mode and when they are shifting to the normative mode and advocating for a specific policy." Advocates say, "Advocacy? Yes. If you don't, remaining silent is an act of omission and as such is a dereliction of duty."

The narrators tend to reside in Camp Two. They believe that the existence of a stewardship mission implies an obligation to advance that mission. The narrators also believe in the values of objectivity, truth, completeness, open-mindedness, etc., as professional obligations in providing inputs to decision making. But they do not accept these as a justification for inaction nor do they accept that decision-making models, themselves, are value neutral. Besides, they maintain, you cannot escape advocacy. As Bern Shanks said, ". . . professionals are advocates, even when they remain silent."

The bad news—there is no consensus. The good news—you get to decide for yourself. The role of professional as advocate is a challenging question that is in flux. It remains for the next generation of professionals to resolve.

Expect these keystone issues to appear in a natural resource career. How you respond depends on how they operate. Three tend to operate at the systems level, four tend to operate within specific issues, and two tend to operate at a personal level.

At the systems level *incentive systems, mission drift, and substitution of models for value choice* tend to capture decision-making outcomes from the outset. When you first encounter a management issue, these forces are usually in motion. Countering them requires strategies to change these systemic pressures. More and better data is unlikely to push these keystones in a different direction. What's needed are interventions such as coalition building, creating advocacy for a return to a conservation mission, or inviting a diversity of people to participate in decision making as a way to challenge misplaced values that are embedded in management models.

At the level of issue-to-issue work *human psychological impediments to decision making, passive decision making, burden of proof, and logic traps* have significant tactical influences on the outcome of specific issues. Again, more and better data in these situations has less of a chance to redirect management than does interventions like forcing active decision making, using System 2 decision-making processes, putting the burden of proof back on the exploiters, etc.

At a personal level *loyalty conflicts and advocacy* operate deep inside each of us. Expect mediocre performance when these remain unresolved. Resolving loyalty and advocacy questions is about resolving your aspiration for a life's work. It is the difference between a career as something to do (e.g., be a fish biologist) versus a career to do something (e.g., preserve native fishes).

Showing intelligent courage in a natural resource career requires examining these keystones from the personal to the issue to the systems level. Ignoring these is like sailing a ship through dangerous waters while refusing look at part of the navigation chart. Decoding when one or more of these keystones are the behind-the-scenes forces driving decisions increases your ability to select the right intervention strategy. Managing a natural resource career is less about a monolithic application of science or a one-size-fits-all success checklist and more about managing these multiple variables that are constantly moving in a dynamic environment.

Career Success Attributes

What are the personal characteristics and skills that allowed the narrators and the people they admired to effectively manage the keystone issues? Taken together these qualities serve as a model for improving personal effectiveness. Besides staying current in their disciplines, two career development themes emerge from the narrators. First is study and reflection on the values behind career choice. This deep exploration of, "Why do I want this work?" is an important internal dialog about motivation, personal mission, ethics, social commitment, etc.—the topic of intrinsic rewards. The narrators worked hard getting clear about why they wanted to work with natural resources and used mid-career pauses to reflect, reassess, and redirect their careers. The second career development theme is exploration of "What operational skills are needed to support my career choice?" These are the tools needed for effectiveness in a work environment and include skills like communication, conflict resolution, and program management. These are the topics of traditional management training. The narrators were willing to learn an array of skills far outside their chosen discipline to be effective inside their work environment. Beyond these broad themes the narrators observed or demonstrated 12 specific career success attributes.

Work with an underlying sense of purpose. The narrators consciously built work lives of service to a personal mission; they did not just work to

earn a living. The narrators talked with considerable affection about colleagues who were inspiring because they had such motivation. It was this
make-a-difference attitude that animated the careers of positive role models.

Gloria Flora was inspired by simply watching the behavior of Forest
Service colleague Don Oman as he worked to align grazing on public land
with sustainability principles. Mike Dombeck recognized the importance of a
professional's personal commitment to natural resources when he observed,
"There's a fairly widely shared reason why you and your peers took up that
kind of work, you like the mission of that organization. And there is a lot of
personal reward for making that choice." This is the difference between career as avocation versus career as just vocation.

Career purpose was not instantly clear from the first day on the job. As
the narrators' careers unfolded they paused to reflect on career meaning.
They used work experiences, good and bad, to define and refine their chosen career purpose. Phil Pister went on a mid-career, personal retreat where
reflecting on his job and re-reading *A Sand County Almanac* oriented the
remainder of his career choices, especially his interest in preserving native
fishes. Among the results—desert pupfish are still part of desert ecosystems in the West. Bern Shanks leaving the National Park Service and returning to college to study natural resource policy led to a professorship.
Among the results—the first credible critique of the sagebrush rebellion that
was riding roughshod across public lands. Roger Contor spring-boarded his
mandatory training experience in Berkeley and the opportunity presented by
a new park. Among the results—his chance to break out of management
orthodoxy to embrace a new mission for preserving wilderness experiences
and try innovations like let-it-burn fire management in the National Park Service. These mid-career reflections allowed the narrators to clarify their personal sense of mission and that translated directly into positive conservation achievements.

Be a boundary crosser. Andrea Mead Lawrence introduced us to the
notion of achieving mastery through boundary crossing in describing her
path to becoming an Olympic champion, ". . . you end up feeling that your
journey into risk is to explore boundaries and free yourself to extend, not just
win." Fear of failure or criticism were the most common blocks to boundary
crossing encountered by the narrators. They saw risk as the price to pay for
opportunity. The consequence of failing to cross boundaries was to extin-
guish exploration and experimentation, which necessarily entails risk. As
boundary crossers the narrators used each career experience as an exten-

sion opportunity. They learned from each experience, no matter what the outcome, and applied that learning forward to their next opportunity. Mike Dombeck's experience of moving from expert on Midwest forestry and fish issues to neophyte about west coast salmon issues meant he would not succeed in his new job unless he crossed a boundary to become good at program development. He kept crossing new boundaries until, eventually, he became Chief of the Forest Service. Tom Peterson purposely acquired a diverse education and work experiences in private, public, and nonprofit sectors as a strategy to give him multiple career choices across employment boundaries. He is now positioned as a leading authority on climate change management by states.

Preserve the ability to act. There were career tough spots in the narrators' experiences. Understandably, their instinct was self-preservation, especially when there was risk to their families. In spite of these normal feelings they did not become passive. Instead, they continued to act by empowering themselves in a variety of ways. They brought their families into the personal side of decision making as Gloria Flora did with her husband on the Jarbidge issue. They supported themselves with needed expertise as Phil Pister did by hiring a new employee with engineering experience to help him deal with small hydro development in the Eastern Sierras. They built coalitions of support as Roger Contor did in gaining acceptance for the first let-it-burn fire in a National Park. They found ways to end-run immobile, even resistant bureaucracies as Phil Pister did by founding the Desert Fishes Council to give voice to government employees and academics otherwise silenced by their employers. They did this by looking for ways past personal boundaries as Andrea Mead Lawrence did with her resolve to ski through the visual barrier in her race at Lake Placid. They took the time to sort out their own priorities as Gloria Flora did when she spent time alone on a river bank contemplating the fate of oil and gas leasing on the Rocky Mountain Front Range. They used exit as a strategy as Tom Peterson did when he frequently changed jobs to continually move toward opportunities where he thought change would be more willingly accepted and to maximize the use of his talents. They were careful about the compromises they made to attain positional power. They avoided the seduction of compromise to attain positional power that ultimately left them powerless. And they were not immobilized by cognitive biases and the other judgment problems that Max Bazeman noted as routine in human decision making. In these ways the narrators were careful to preserve their ability to act.

Agitate but be patient. Successful professionals in the narrators' stories were good at asking, "Is the status quo working?" They were impatient with comfort and security as justification for inaction. Early in their careers they figured out that managers are pressured to give an illusion of moving on conservation when they're actually expected to be passive and let others decide the fate of natural resources. They were impatient about these acts of omission and made a range of choices about how tactfully to agitate for change. Mike Dombeck chose to take on the roadless issue instead of letting agency inaction implicitly hand off that decision to others. He was assertive but polite at each step of the process. Bern Shanks's speaking out against the sagebrush rebellion was characterized by blunt rhetoric designed to attack the intellectual premises of the rebels' argument and purposely attract media attention. He was forceful and outspoken. Phil Pister was agreeable about seeking approval from his chain of command to rehabilitate native trout in Slinkard Creek, but he was ultimately willing to ignore their direction when they turned a blind eye to this need.

At the same time they were patient contributors to the long-term improvement of their organizations. They felt that efforts to change their employers was time well spent. They routinely involved themselves in the activities of incremental bureaucratic improvement, like joining task forces, strategic planning sessions, employee development programs, etc. In the end, though, they agitated for change using different methods at different times for different issues and were willing to explore options both inside and outside their chain of command.

Have a sense of history. The narrators could reach back to the roots of conservation work and draw analogies and advice about today's management challenges. Bern Shanks routinely drew upon the experiences of previous conservationists such as George Perkins Marsh to inspire his present beliefs, values, and his methods for taking action. Phil Pister frequently reached into the writings of Aldo Leopold to analyze the management challenges that came his way. Mike Dombeck and Gloria Flora knew the history of the Forest Service down pat and analyzed how that history affected current management behavior. The narrators used history for perspective and as one source of input for unraveling confusing contemporary management questions.

Be persistent, optimistic, and realistic. The narrators, when asked to share nuggets of wisdom they had learned the hard way, told stories highlighting persistence, optimism, and realism. Bern Shanks remained optimistic about turning the stampede of the sagebrush rebels and their hired guns but understood the magnitude of the task. In an ironic twist of the sagebrush rebels' own metaphor, Bern stood as the lone defender of the intellectual argument for public lands, outnumbered by the rebels who were riding roughshod over the law. Phil Pister notes the optimistic progress with desert fish preservation but knows the modern truism that we now live in an age where we can never turn our backs on active management. Mike Dombeck talks of the ebbs and floods of changing political administrations but notes the ability for progress even during dark days—as when the Reagan administration's anti-environment stance generated growing support for environmental causes. The narrators looked at career success as an ongoing process. Roger Contor did this when he took to heart Brock Evans's advice that ". . . conservation activism is constant pressure endlessly applied."

Rebound resiliently using tough times as learning. Bennis and Thomas (2002) believe that all leaders share one common experience; all have ". . . undergone at least one intense, transformational experience," which they call a crucible. That was the experience of the narrators. They used their crucibles as opportunities for personal growth. All narrators experienced hard knocks in their careers. When I asked them to talk about these difficult moments they responded with a version of, "I learned a lot from that experience that helped me later in my career."

They sustained an attitude of career-as-learning instead of retreating to cynicism or passivity as a response to the difficult moments in their careers. They emerged from the difficult experiences with an attitude of curiosity about what they learned that could help in the future. When the narrators encountered difficult events in their careers they used these crucible experiences as opportunities to expand personal boundaries—to "extend" as Andrea Mead Lawrence would say. A natural resource career, like river rafting, is interesting because of the unexpected events. A career without challenges is like rafting an irrigation canal.

Volunteer not victim outlook. Our narrators recognized that choosing to put yourself into controversial situations can generate criticism, even retaliation. They did not deny that reality but simultaneously saw these as way points along a journey encompassing multiple conservation opportunities in a long career. Although the narrators encountered crucibles, they viewed their careers as an opportunity they willingly pursued. Working in their chosen field was an important source of satisfaction. Extrinsic rewards like pay, status, promotions, commendations, etc., were important, but they saw the work itself as being the larger reward—one they volunteered to pursue for its own intrinsic value. None of the narrators or the people they admired retreated to a victim mentality when describing the hard times. The most extreme example encountered is Gloria Flora's experience in the Jarbidge issue. Despite the venom and threats levied at her she emerged with a continued energy for, in her words, ". . . [t]he idea of being able to work with large landscapes and to effect change to help communities and help people enjoy and appreciate the natural world. My God, what a calling. What service." The narrators saw the hard knocks as the normal dues for access to professions of meaning and purpose.

Make clear loyalty decisions early. The narrators deeply valued natural resource stewardship yet they also had a keen awareness of how this value can be easily set aside by the people they worked with and worked for. The loyalty conflicts they encountered involved commitment to their work versus their social contracts with family, friends, co-workers, employers, etc. These internal conflicts pitted good versus good and, for that reason, were difficult to resolve. Although the narrators took different paths in resolving these, there were some common elements, beginning with the attributes we've just discussed. They clarified their own internal value hierarchy. They decided for themselves what values guided their careers instead of assuming their employers had satisfactorily worked this out. They interpreted the instinct to be passive as a warning signal and chose to be active. They understood what it means to advocate, becoming comfortable with the reality that any action or inaction is an advocacy stance. They weighed the probability of changing an underachieving employer against the probability of finding a new employer able to deliver more satisfying job opportunities.

Beyond these strategies the narrators sometimes responded by trying to move unresponsive employers, as Tom Peterson did in using the Bradley County Courthouse and the Lost Creek Wildlife Area controversies to steer the Arkansas Game and Fish Commission toward the need to work with stakeholders prior to decision making. At other times the narrators responded by moving among people involved, as Andrea Mead Lawrence did when she kept looking for an employee with the ability to do the right thing in protecting an at-risk mountain meadow. The narrators moved the people around them to act in place of their agencies, as Phil Pister did when he formed the Desert Fishes Council to do an end-run around indifferent agencies. And the narrators sometimes moved themselves, as Tom Peterson and Bern Shanks did to find more progressive work environments.

Being clear about loyalty allowed the narrators to separate the question of "Should I take action" from "How will I take action?" The narrators tended to settle the loyalty question early in their careers. That resolve became a lodestone to guide their personal behavior in spite of how their agencies and colleagues were behaving.

Be simultaneously independent and interdependent. Although the narrators had an independent mind set about where to place their loyalty, they were willing team players when the circumstances were right. They possessed an array of interpersonal skills needed to work effectively with others, including working with people who might disagree with them. And they liked the organizations they worked for, especially as models of the conservation ideals personified by their missions. But they were not unthinking members of the team. They were firm in insisting upon congruence of the team's goal with the conservation purpose of their agency. As Phil Pister said, ". . . just to go into an organization and say, 'I'm going to be a great team player' shows a totally unjustified trust in who the captain is and what goal he is trying to achieve." The narrators were willing team players but only after validating that the team was pursuing the right goal. In the final analysis, however, they were willing to say no to their agency when asked to make a decision that they thought was not right and they developed the skills needed to say no in a way that would stick. Tom Peterson described Rob Wolcott's successful approach to managing this difficult task in a way that worked while doing the least amount of collateral damage.

Be an expert and novice simultaneously. Some professionals come out of their university training and won't budge outside the discipline of their degree. They make the decision that after college their task is to apply the minutiae of their discipline. This creates a risk for a mismatch between skill set and need. The narrators emerged from their college educations with a different mind set. They viewed themselves as works in progress. They had wide-ranging curiosity. They benchmarked continuous self-improvement against what they saw happening in their profession and in the larger, changing social system around them. They chose not to limit themselves to a self-imposed, ever-narrowing job description of more detail about species biology, harvest management, recreation management, landscape architecture, etc. At the same time they recognized the importance of applying deep technical expertise in decision making.

The narrators attended to their professional growth by doing three things beyond their formal educations. They maintained a commitment to continuous learning. They constantly looked ahead to learn skills perceived as important for success in their next job. And they willingly pursued knowledge and work experience outside their academic discipline that could advance their conservation interests. For example, Mike Dombeck responded to the shock of moving from the Midwest, where he was a recognized expert about forests and fish, to San Francisco and salmon management where he knew very little. He advanced his conservation interests by learning the new skill of program development instead of retreating to his old tool kit of technical/ scientific expertise.

The narrators did not get stuck in a single career path that precluded their options for conservation achievement. For example, Bern Shanks knew that his interest in natural resource policy meant leaving the Park Service and heading back to college for graduate work. He advanced his conservation interests by shifting from hands-on land management to working on broad policy. The narrators were also clear about their limitations. The narrators' response was to focus simultaneously on their strengths while compensating for their weaknesses. For example, Phil Pister knew a lot about fish biology but little about the engineering of small hydroelectric development so he hired a new employee with these skills. And Tom Peterson prepared himself for a multiple-option career as a conscious career management strategy. This was his way to simultaneously manage job insecurity and find work environments where he could maximize the use of his talents.

Never surrender to others the responsibility of defining a better future. The narrators took their stewardship ethic seriously. Early in their careers they learned the fallacy of assuming their employers would do the right thing. The narrators became voices of conscience inside their organizations. Some narrators were overt. Phil Pister was an unabashed native fish advocate who forced native cutthroat and golden trout conservation on a resistant conservation agency. It would have been less risky to accede to the agency culture that saw itself as a recreation provider using non-native trout. Some narrators were less overt. Roger Contor was careful about timing his courageous act and building support among potential critics of the first let-it-burn fire in a National Park. It would have been easier and more career enhancing to go along with the community expectation and agency culture that viewed the Park Service as a fire suppression agency. Mike Dombeck worked at the largest scale when he faced the challenge of realigning the Forest Service to its mission. His complaint to the Secretary of Agriculture that, "We were not proposing anything, only reacting rather than leading by coming up with ideas or proposals ourselves" led to major advances on roadless area management, timber sustainability, and water issues in the nation's forests. It would have been easier and more career advancing to remain passive. For Mike, not surrendering to others the responsibility to define the conservation agenda was rewarding, "I was gratified to see that while we were still going to lots of congressional hearings, they became oversight hearings on our proposals versus us having to play defense to issues put forward by others."

These career attributes form a model for career development. These include an array of attributes that are the tools of the trade and ways to create a good bit of independence as a natural resource professional. However, for most professionals the motivation behind acquiring these tools and for achieving independence is a desire to make positive contributions to natural resource stewardship. What career premises create the right foundation for such a career of personal commitment?

Premises for a Career of Meaning and Purpose

Each narrator created a career as a life's work meant to achieve something. They did this by using premises that animated their careers with both a vision about the desired outcome and a willingness to take action. Choosing a desired outcome has no impact without action. Action without choosing a desired outcome has little chance of creating something useful. Both are needed in a career of meaning and purpose. The narrators did this by building their careers on several premises.

Guiding Premise One. Work that was true to their beliefs became both a method and an outcome for the narrators' careers. This authenticity, in the sense of being congruent with values, was clear in the interviews and, I suspect, to the people they worked with. But their journey was not a fixed course set at the outset and never altered. Their values were thoughtfully arrived at and then examined, refined, and refocused over time.

Guiding Premise Two. The narrators' journeys included taking full responsibility for themselves and for the task of creating a better future. They talked a lot about how a career journey ends when there is no accountability to yourself. And the narrators accepted that when you have choices and fail to make one, that is still making a choice. They consciously put the long-range risks and costs of comfortable inaction in competition with the short-term risks and costs of taking action.

Guiding Premise Three. The narrators, despite plenty of frustrations, talked about how they experienced in themselves and the communities around them times of rapid, positive change—from resistence to acceptance, from defensiveness to openness, and from ignorance to understanding. One element of their success was knowing when there was a readiness for such awakenings and knowing how to transform these moments into opportunities for progress. The narrators were good change masters.

Guiding Premise Four. The narrators committed to key values widely respected in our society like honesty, responsibility, sincerity, equality, etc. This commitment became an authentic form of power that I suspect others found difficult to control.

Guiding Premise Five. Maintaining positive attitudes about their work gave the narrators an inner harmony. They did not wait for other people to deliver positive feedback about self-worth. They broke out of a world of scarce positive feedback. By conferring these rewards on themselves they worked in the more abundant world of consistent internal rewards.

Guiding Premise Six. Satisfaction in a life's work depends on being able to acknowledge when things are out of your control yet not let these become immobilizing. The narrators made peace with the gap between their aspirations and the realities of their work environment. While acknowledging this gap they avoided the temptation to stop trying by viewing themselves as innovators. They saw themselves as searchers with a responsibility to define these gaps and then do something about them. They did not descend into pessimism nor did they relinquish themselves to blind optimism. They recognized pessimism as a surrender to hopelessness and blind optimism as a form of denial. Both positions are failures to look at reality and ensure ineffectiveness and a self-fulfilling prophecy of resource loss. But simply defining the problem leaves unresolved the uneasy negotiation between hopes versus realities in a work environment. This negotiation is difficult because it requires simultaneously resolving two opposing questions, "What needs to change in a work environment?" and "What will the work environment let me do?" By constantly making creative contributions the narrators developed a certain peace of mind when facing this gap.

Precisely what is the gap that natural resource professionals must close if future stewardship is to be more successful? It is nothing short of acknowledging that old assumptions behind a natural resource career no longer hold true and then defining a new purpose for the natural resource professions. The old assumption of resource abundance as the starting place for management is dead. More adaptive is assuming a base condition of scarcity. The old assumption that there is broad agreement about why we manage natural resources has broken down in a world of rapidly accelerating human impacts. More adaptive is assuming fragmenting worldviews about the purpose for management and increasing competition. The old assumption that we need more and better technical input has not worked. More adaptive is assuming that technical input is now only one of a number of justifications deployed to capture decision-making control. And the old assumption of the professional as solely a technical expert is no longer adaptive. More adaptive is assuming that technical excellence is a necessary but insufficient condition for stewardship. We do not need increased proficiency with a dysfunctional model. We need a new model of the natural resource professional.

The contemporary management challenge demands a substantial burst of creativity about natural resource careers to arrive at something totally new. This new professionalism requires shifting to a leadership role that can simultaneously envision the radical changes needed to preserve natural resources, guide others through the arduous transformation that is required, and help communities overcome the discomfort that accompanies such dramatic change. Especially needed are professionals with the ability to act as interpreters of how humans can live in peace with the world's natural resources—professionals who move people by ideas and ideals that transcend our time and any single culture. Playing at a smaller scale does not address the contemporary need. To succeed in this remarkable future the model of a professional will need to change from technical expert to expert in community transformation. Saying yes to this new calling does not mean knowing how to handle each moment of the journey. It certainly does not mean knowing the precise route or how the journey will turn out. It is about defining for yourself what intelligent courage means and then discovering ways for that commitment to find expression through a life's work to change the way communities relate to natural resources.

The first step is willingness to engage in the creative act of shaping a new model of natural resource professionalism. Creating your own career as a learning project is a solid next step. Going through this transformation requires mid-career pauses to consider: What are the lessons I've learned so far? Is my current course the one I have chosen or is it is one that others are compelling me to follow? Is my purpose still the one I wish to follow or does it need to change? Is my behavior congruent with that purpose? And what do I most need to do next? The major achievement letting the narrators navigate to successful careers was finding their internal compass and then making that sense of purpose inseparable from a willingness to engage. They coupled vision and action with an explicit desire to make their careers count for something of enduring value to posterity as well as the present.

This book started by exploring the notion of mastery. The narrators' stories affirm that achieving personal mastery is not an invitation-only event reserved for those with exceptional abilities. It is an inner journey where the important milestones are your own, not those imposed by others. This means that mastery of a natural resource career is available to anyone willing to begin the journey and stay on it. The journey can begin with the more prosaic, such as acquiring new skills. It achieves significance when these skills of the mind are combined with ideals of the heart to choose a direction for the journey. It achieves the quality of art when the traveler gets good at taking action—committing ideals to the canvas.

None of us invents this journey alone. We are heirs to the learning and wisdom of people who have asked the same questions before us, "Why have I chosen this work?" and "What does it take to make a difference?" The narrators' stories help answer these questions, provide a guide for the journey, and offer an array of street smarts learned from practical experience. View this book as a set of field notes from experiments formed by the careers of eight remarkable people who care about natural resources and have thought deeply about what it takes to create careers of purpose, meaning, and satisfying conservation accomplishment. From their lessons learned emerges a beginning hypothesis of intelligent courage in natural resource work. Your career is the next experiment.

Literature Cited

Bazerman, M. 2006. Judgment in managerial decision making. Sixth edition. John Wiley & Sons, New York. 241p.

Bazerman, M., J. Baron, & K. Shonk. 2001. "You can't enlarge the pie": Six barriers to effective government. Basic Books, Cambridge, MA. 262p.

Bazerman, M. & M. Watkins. 2004. Predictable surprises: The disasters you should have seen coming, and how to prevent them. Harvard Business School Press, Boston. 317p.

Becker, G. C. 1983. Fishes of Wisconsin. University of Wisconsin Press, Madison, 1,052 p.

Bennis, W. & R. Thomas, 2002. Geeks & geezers: How era, values, and defining moments shape leaders. Harvard Business School Press, Boston, 224p.

Carson, R. 1962. Silent spring. Houghton Mifflin, Riverside Press, Boston. 368p.

Clarke, J. N. & D. McCool. 1985. Staking out the terrain: Power differentials among natural resource management agencies. SUNY Series in Environmental Public Policy, State University of New York Press, Albany, 189p.

Columbia World of Quotations. 1996. New York: Columbia University Press. www.bartleby.com/88/. Accessed October 16, 2006.

Ehrenfeld, D. W. 1976. The conservation of non-resources. American Scientist 64(4):648-656.

Erman, D. C.& E. P. Pister. 1989. Ethics and the environmental biologist. Fisheries 14(2):4–7.

Fraidenburg, M. E. & R. H. Lincoln. 1985. Wild chinook salmon: An international conservation challenge. North American Journal of Fisheries Management 5: 311–329.

Gladwell, M. 2005. Blink: The power of thinking without thinking. Little Brown, New York. 277p.

Hart, E. 2001. The God squad and the case of the Northern spotted owl. Video recording produced, directed, and photographed by Emily Hart. Bullfrog Films, P.O. Box 149, Oley, PA, USA.

Hays, S. P. 1980. Conservation and the gospel of efficiency: The progressive conservation movement 1890-1920. Atheneum, New York.

Kaufman, H. 1960. The forest ranger: A study in administrative behavior. Resources for the Future, Inc., Johns Hopkins University Press, Baltimore, 259p.

Knapp, R. A. & K. R. Matthews. 2000. Nonnative fish introductions and the decline of the mountain yellow-legged frog (*Rana muscosa*) from within protected areas. Conservation Biology 14:1–2.

Lawrence, A. M. & S. Burnaby. 1980. A practice of mountains. Seaview Books, New York. 213p.

Leopold, A. 1936. In: S. L. Flader, & J. B. Callicott. 1991. The River of the Mother of God and other essays by Aldo Leopold. University of Wisconsin Press, Madison.

Leopold, A. 1949. A Sand County almanac and sketches from here and there. Oxford University Press, New York, 266p.

Leopold, A. S., S. A. Cain, D. M. Cottam, I. N. Gabrielson, & T. L. Kimball. 1963. Wildlife management in the national parks. Transactions of the North American Wildlife Natural Resources Conference, 28:28–45.

Lichatowich, J. 1999. Salmon without rivers: A history of the Pacific salmon crisis. Island Press, Washington, D.C. 303p.

Marsh, G.P. 1885. The earth as modified by human action: A last revision of man and nature. C. Scribner's Sons, New York.

Oxford English Dictionary. 2nd ed. 1989. OED Omline. Oxford University Press. 4 Apr. 2000(http://0-dictionary.oed.com,cals evergreen.edu/cgi/entry/oo303097).

Pister, E. P. 1979. Endangered species: Costs and benefits. Environmental Ethics 1(4):341–352.

Pister, E. P. 1985. Desert pupfishes: Reflections on reality, desirability, and conscience. Environmental Biology of Fishes 12(1):3-12.

Pister, E. P. 1987. A pilgrim's progress from group A to group B. In Companion to a Sand County Almanac, 221–232, J. Baird Callicott, ed. University of Wisconsin Press, Madison.

Pister, E. P. 1992a. Ethical considerations in conservation of biodiversity. Transactions of the 57th North American Wildlife and Natural Resources Conference, pp. 355-364. Wildlife Management Institute, Washington, D.C.

Pister, E. P. 1992b. Ethics of eastern Sierra water development. In The History of Water: Eastern Sierra Nevada, Owens Valley, White-Inyo Mountains. Clarence A. Hall, Jr., Victoria Doyle-Jones, & Barbara Widawski, eds., pp. 294–302. White Mountain Research Station, University of California, Los Angeles.

Pister, E. P. 1993. Species in a Bucket. Natural History 102(1):14–18. American Museum of Natural History, New York.

Pister, E. P. 1994. The importance of value systems in management: Considerations in desert fish management. In Principles of Conservation Biology by Gary K. Meffe & C. Ronald Carroll, pp. 340–341. Sinauer Associates, Inc., Sunderland, MA.

Pister, E. P. 1995. The rights of species and ecosystems. Fisheries 20(4): 28–29.

Pister, E. P. 1998. The A/B dichotomy and the future. Wildlife Society Bulletin 1998, 26(4). Special issue in commemoration of Aldo Leopold.

Pister, E. P. 1999a. Professional obligations in conservation of fishes. In Environmental Biology of Fishes 55:13–20 as a symposium: Behavioral Ecology and Fish Conservation, Gene Helfman, ed. University of New Mexico, Albuquerque, 1996.

Pister, E. P. 1999b. Throwing your weight around. In The Essential Aldo Leopold: Quotations and Commentaries, ed. by Curt Meine & Richard Knight. University of Wisconsin Press, Madison.

Planck, M. 1950. Scientific autobiography, and other papers; with a memorial address on Max Planck by Max von Laue. Translated from German by Frank Gaynor. Williams and Norgate, London, 192p.

Rolston, H. 1988. Environmental Ethics: Duties to and values in the natural world. Temple University Press, Philadelphia. 374p.

Scott, W. R. 1987. Organizations: Rational, natural, and open systems. Prentice Hall, Englewood Cliffs, NJ. 377p.

Shanks, B. 1984. This land is your land: The struggle to save America's public lands. Sierra Club Books, San Francisco. 310p.

Shore, Bill. 1995. Revolution of the Heart: A new strategy for creating wealth and meaningful change. Riverhead Books. New York. 167p.

Tversky, A. & D. Kahneman. 1974. Judgement under uncertainty: Heuristics and biases. Science, 185, 1124–1131.

Wilkinson, T. 1998. Science under siege: The politicians' war on nature and truth. Johnson Books, Boulder, Co. 364p.

Wondolleck, J. M. & S. L. Yaffee. 2000. Making collaboration work: Lessons from innovations in natural resource management. Island Press, Washington, D.C.

Index